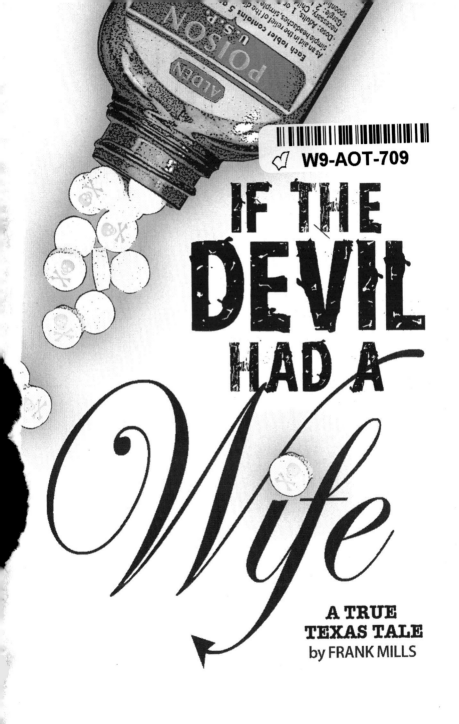

For Becky and Homer Stark

*If wealth was measured not by dollars,
but the love of family and friends,
they were the richest people in town.*

ACKNOWLEDGMENTS

Once upon a time. Happily ever after. Such are the classic promises of fairy tales. Yet in Texas we find a twist to the familiar storyline.

There is still the battle of Good vs. Evil, a beautiful maiden, a wealthy suitor, a kingdom of riches and the wicked witch, but any similarity with Cinderella or Snow White ends there. With the help of her life partner and an attorney (always necessary in these modern times), Nelda Stark executes a devious plan that elevates fraud, theft, and grand larceny to a new high. A massive coverup reaches into the Texas Attorney General's Office, stealing from both the family and the federal government.

It is a story about how those with power and wealth feel they are above the law, yet also — and perhaps more importantly — alerts each of us to the growing role of the legal profession in condoning criminal activities and becoming part of the problem. As you turn the pages of *If the Devil Had A Wife*, you will unravel a tale based on documentation and narratives of true events and characters who may have been slightly modified in order to concisely tell the story. Some names and occupations have been changed to protect the innocent or allow others a bit of breathing room.

Without the contributions of many individuals, the book would not be possible. Stories whispered behind closed doors or long left untold, documents that did not see daylight until recent years and individuals who shared information because it was "the right thing to do" are the true authors of this Texas fairy tale.

In addition to family members, special thanks to the following who provided stories, photographs or factual information that brought the story to life. Whatever the extent of information they provided – the type of pajamas, recollections of a 1911 wedding, or detailed explanations of company operations – each contribution was most appreciated: Roy Alba; Dr. John Bailey; Leona Batchan; Jane Gracy Bedichek; Anne Boykin; John S. Brown, Jr.; Anna Jean Cathey; Pete Caler; Tracy Corley; John and Runie Creswell; Homer DeLarue; John Dorman; Woody Dorman, Jr.; Dr. George Eastman; Jesse B. Gunstream; Jim Henderson; Betty Hill; Adolph Hyrhorchuk; Dr. Frank Hubert; Earl Kelly; Tom Kelly; Charles Kinney; Sam Kittrell; Mabel Wingate Lawrence; Jeff MacDonald; John McDonald; Larry Murray; Clay Newberry; James Pruter; Clemmie Rosenthal; Georgia Singletary; R. C. Slocum; W. H. Stark (son of Judge V. H. Stark); Danny Thomas; Mary Murray Weber; Julia Wells; Jerry Wise; Roland Wolfford; plus others who remain anonymous for obvious reasons.

Of special help were members of the Bengal Guards; Dr. Howard C. Williams; Stephen F. Austin University's Forestry Institute; The Center for American History at the University of Texas; Dr. Jan Todd and Dr. Terry Todd, co-directors of the H. J. Lutcher Stark Center for Physical Culture and Sports; Orange Public Library; Texas Woman's University Library; DeQuincy News; Cameron Pilot; and numerous courthouses in the parishes of Louisiana and counties of Texas.

Reviewing and editing the content was no easy task. As with any undertaking that involves emotions and family ties, it was important to solicit multiple viewpoints in shaping the final product. Lending their time and editing talents were Sherrie Addington, Anne Boykin, John and Markeeta Brown, Patti Jett, R. C. Slocum and seven members of the Stark family.

We also appreciate Mark Beal for developing the video trailer and Shawn Parsons for overseeing development of the book's website.

And how do you adequately thank a graphic artist like Holly Forbes *(Forbes and Butler Visual Communications)* who created such an amazing cover? Her design perfectly captures the tone and message one expects as you begin to turn the pages of *If the Devil Had a Wife.* She also added her artistic touch to the photo layout featured within the pages of the book.

For additional information, visit the following sites: ifthedevilhadawife.com; starkfiles.com; hcwilliams.com; or bengalguards.com.

I. **HENRY JACOB LUTCHER** *m. Jan. 23, 1858* **FRANCES ANN ROBINSON**
(b. Nov. 4, 1836; d. Oct. 2, 1912)   (b. Oct. 17, 1840; d. Oct. 21, 1924)

  A. **Miriam Melissa Lutcher** *m. Dec. 22, 1881* **William Henry Stark**
    (b. Jan. 23, 1859; d. Nov. 27, 1936)   (b. Mar. 19, 1851; d. Oct. 8, 1936)

    1. **Frances Ann Lutcher Stark**
      (b. Nov. 29, 1882; d. July 2, 1884)
    2. **Henry Jacob Lutcher Stark**   *m. Apr. 5, 1911*   **Nita Hill**
      (b. Dec. 8, 1887; d. Sept. 2, 1965)   (b. Dec. 5, 1890; d. Oct. 11, 1939)
      a. Frances Lutcher Stark
        (b. Dec. 2, 1912; died in infancy)
      b. Henry Stark
        (b. June 9, 1916; died in infancy)
      c. Homer Barksdale Hill Stark   *m. Jan. 22, 1942*   Becky Havens
        (b. Apr. 26, 1923; d. Mar. 11, 2008)   (b. Aug. 8, 1922; d. Dec. 13, 2006)
      d. William Henry Stark II   *m. June 27, 1942*   Ida Marie Dickens
        (b. Apr. 26, 1923; d. Sept. 25, 1979)   (b. May 3, 1923; d. Nov. 19, 2008)

             m. Apr. 6, 1941   **Ruby Belle Childers**
      (Siblings)   (b. Aug. 25, 1902; d. July 12, 1942)
             m. Dec. 16, 1943   **Nelda Childers**
                      (b. Feb. 9, 1909; d. Dec. 13, 1999)

  B. **Carrie Luna Lutcher** *m. Nov. 28, 1888*   **Edgar William Brown, MD**
    (b. Sept. 14, 1861; d. Oct. 3, 1941)   (b. Nov. 22, 1859; d. June 16, 1917)

    1. **Fannie Lutcher Brown**   *m. Oct. 13, 1918*   **Rucie A. Moore**
      (b. Sept. 14, 1890; d. Oct. 12, 1918)   (b. Apr. 25, 1890; d. July 14, 1967)
      a. Brownie Babette Moore   *m. May 7, 1931*   Frank Williams
        (b. Aug. 20, 1911; d. 1984)

    2. **Edgar William Brown, Jr.** *m. Jul 23, 1915*   **Gladys May Slade**
      (b. Feb. 10, 1894; d. Jan. 8, 1976)   (b. Oct. 18, 1896; d. Sept. 17, 1959)

      a. Edgar William Brown III   *m. Jan. 3, 1940*   Elizabeth McCorquedale
        (b. Sept. 26, 1918; d. 1988)   (b. June 26, 1918; d. 1983)
      b. John Shillard Brown   *m. Mar. 31, 1942*   Betty Sue Bullock
        (b. Jan. 10, 1921; d. July 21, 2009)   (b. Dec. 11, 1922; d. 1988)
      c. Lutcher Slade Brown   *m. Dec. 6, 1942*   Jane Robbins
        (b. Nov. 3, 1922; d. 1990)   (b. Mar. 15, 1922)
      d. Charles E. Brown   *m. Dec. 3, 1946*   Frances Eastin
        (b. Aug. 6, 1926; d. 1984)   (b. Nov. 25, 1925)

             m . Nov. 20, 1960   **Elizabeth Smith Hustmyre**

    3. **Henry Lutcher Brown**   *m. Apr. 19, 1917*   **Emily Wells**
      (b. July 6, 1896; d. Dec. 7, 1970)   (b. 1896; d. May 12, 1985)

      a. Joan Brown   *m. Aug. 14, 1944*   George Scrimshaw
        (b. June. 7, 1922)
      b. Fredrick Lutcher Brown   *m. June 27, 1942*   Olive McCullin
        (b. Jan. 19, 1926; d. 1975)
      c. Carolyn Wells Brown   *m. Nov. 25, 1942*   William Negley

LUTCHER – ROBINSON FAMILY

CHAPTER 1

*"The truth is a fragile thing, but a lie,
well told, can live forever."*

— *Mark Twain*

The 1964 green Chrysler traveled west on Highway 87 — drawing second looks as it sped past an occasional car on the road to Galveston. There wasn't much traffic at four on a warm August morning, but the driver had more on his mind than the Texas speed limit.

The trip from Orange usually took a little less than two hours, depending on the ferry. Tonight should find Homer Stark back at John Sealy Hospital in less than 75 minutes, a record for the family station wagon.

As he drove the deserted beach road, there was little time to reflect on the sheer beauty of the full moon reflected in the Gulf of Mexico waters or to appreciate the sound of waves hitting the sandy shores. Instead he spent every moment replaying events of the summer.

High Island, Crystal Beach, Rollover Pass, Gilchrist. The small beach communities became reflections in the rear view mirror as he returned to Galveston after a quick trip home to see Wynne Pearce, the family doctor who had known Homer all his life.

It began earlier that summer when his dad was taken to Galveston for a checkup, certainly not unusual for a 77-year old man. But that was 61 days ago and something was terribly wrong. Homer recalled the letter from Shell, a servant in his dad's home for more than 35 years, warning him that "something bad was going on in that house." But when Homer went to check the following day, he learned of his dad's sudden departure for John Sealy, the premier teaching hospital in Texas and the flagship of the University of Texas Medical Branch on Galveston Island.

Everything appeared routine at first. For almost a month, Lutcher Stark – considered by many the richest man in Texas – was listed as an outpatient and spent most of his time at the Jack Tar Hotel when he wasn't having a conference with his doctors or undergoing tests at the hospital. It appeared so normal, in fact, that his twin sons, Homer and Bill, would occasionally bring their children over to visit and include an afternoon at the beach or the hotel pool.

Lutcher Stark certainly seemed fine. It was not unusual for him to enjoy an extended stay at the hotel when he came for checkups. Summers were usually spent at his Colorado ranch, but age and distance had diminished those trips. Plus Nelda, Lutcher's third wife, never liked the altitude and always had an excuse to cut those trips short. The ranch manager joked "she was always ready to leave before she got here." Rumor around Orange was she liked to keep a close eye on Lutcher's money. That, and her friend, Eunice Benckenstein – a constant presence in and out of town – was always with them.

As the days became weeks, then months, Lutcher seemed to be getting worse instead of improving despite state of the art medical treatment. Dr. Raymond Gregory, Chief of Internal Medicine, and Dr. Edgar Poth, Chief of General Surgery, led the prestigious team that cared for the multi-millionaire.

A visit with his dad two days earlier left Homer with far more questions than answers. What started as a routine conversation in Suite 409 evaporated as Lutcher tried to tell Homer "the most important thing I'll ever tell you." But the ever-present Eunice simply positioned herself near father and son, fixing her beady eyes on Lutcher, somehow influencing what he wanted to say.

"Come back in the morning, Homer," said Lutcher. "That bitch isn't going to let us talk alone."

Homer agreed to spend the night at the hotel, then return the next day. The old man said his goodbyes and the two joked about "Miss B" – an inside joke between Lutcher and his two sons. Although Eunice was often called "Miss B" (a shortened version of Benckenstein, her late husband's name), only Homer and Bill knew the "B" stood for bitch when Lutcher used it.

Homer stepped into the hallway and came face to face with James Chatman, the private nurse he had grown to know and like during his visits to Galveston. The young black man, slightly built and clean shaven, was one of four hired to keep a watchful eye on the elder Stark.

"Won't do you any good, Mr. Homer," Chatman said, referring to the conversation he'd just overheard. "He won't know you tomorrow."

"What are you talking about?"

"Just telling you he won't know you the next time you see him. Miss Nelda's taking care of that with those pills she gives him."

Homer returned less than 12 hours later – and just as Chatman predicted, Lutcher didn't recognize his son and appeared to be in a trance as he lay motionless in his hospital bed. Nelda and Eunice said he was on a new medication to diminish the pain, but Homer had heard enough.

When Chatman arrived for the 3 p.m. shift, Homer was waiting at the service entrance and patiently listened as the male nurse filled him in on the pills being administered by his stepmother. They were in an unmarked prescription bottle, sitting innocently in the medicine cabinet over the bathroom sink. All Homer wanted was one to take with him, one to have analyzed and determine the truth behind the extended hospital stay.

At precisely 4:45 p.m., Nelda and Eunice took their customary break, returning to the hotel for dinner before making a final check on Lutcher later that evening. Homer watched from the fifth floor waiting room as they left the front entrance, then took one flight of stairs down to his dad's room. Chatman was waiting with the pill.

Rush hour traffic and large crowds of summer tourists made the line for the ferry back to the mainland seem to extend forever. Under different circumstances, Homer would have not thought twice about the delay. But even seagulls circling the dock, then the ferry, did not strike a pleasant chord with him. All thoughts were focused on the pill, and, even more importantly, Nelda and Eunice.

The trip home was filled with questions regarding his father. Adopted when he was only three months old, Homer always felt indebted to his parents – Lutcher and his first wife, Nita – for providing such an ideal life and considered himself fortunate to have been chosen as their son.

Other than a quick stop for gas and coffee, there were no diversions on the trip home. No attempt to try his luck fishing, walk along the dunes, or simply appreciate the Gulf waters he loved. His focus was twofold: find his brother Bill and then Dr. Pearce, the family doctor.

Within minutes of passing the Orange city limit sign, Homer was in his driveway and wasted no time getting inside to call his brother. It didn't surprise him to learn Bill was at Sunset Grove Country Club, playing an "emergency nine" as they called it. Bill was a scratch golfer with all the tools that came with that skill. Homer enjoyed the game as well, but was more likely to be found hunting or fishing.

One of only two courses in Texas developed by Donald Ross, the internationally known Scottish golf course architect, Sunset Grove provided a glorious emerald of a course for any golfer with its tight tree-lined fairways, difficult water features, and greens guarded by a maze of bunkers. At Lutcher's invitation, Byron Nelson opened play when the course was finally completed in 1927 and W. H. Stark, Lutcher's father and an avid – but average – golfer, had a private course to pursue the game.

"The Herd" – a nickname for the group of golfers who played together regularly at Sunset Grove – was just coming up the 18th fairway. Bill was lining up his specialty, a wedge shot from the wooden bridge that spanned the lake on the final hole, and bets were being placed as each foursome tried to position themselves for one last wager. But Homer brought the game to an abrupt halt as he pulled his golf cart directly in front of his brother, firmly telling him to get in. It was a moment that left Bill speechless, for Homer rarely reacted so forcefully and was not in the mood to discuss options.

Leaving his clubs, cart and money behind, Bill joined his brother as they took a direct route to the station wagon parked illegally by the pro shop. As they drove to Dr. Pearce's home, Homer updated Bill on events of the last 24 hours and each was anxious to discover exactly what kind of medication Nelda was giving their father.

It was a five-minute drive. Nothing was far from anything in Orange, but the good doctor was nowhere to be found. He was always making house calls, so it was anyone's guess as to his whereabouts. Or when he would eventually arrive home. Neighbors said his wife was playing bridge at the Orange Woman's Club, but no man in his right mind would voluntarily interrupt the weekly bridge club gathering.

So they waited. Sat in the car and rehashed events of the summer, ending with concerns about their father's health. Not so much his physical problems, but the possibility extra medication provided by Nelda had been in the picture for much longer than the Summer of '65. Conversations went from one extreme to the other as each recalled situations that would have raised a red flag in normal circumstances, but were always excused, explained away or diminished by Lutcher or Nelda.

The sound of Dr. Pearce's four-cylinder Ford announced his arrival as he drove to the garage behind the impressive two-story home. As the doctor opened the car door, Homer and Bill were already there to greet him.

"What in the world are you boys doing here?" said Dr. Pearce, obviously surprised to see two of his favorite people waiting in the dark. "I mean, it's always good to see you but it seems a bit late for an office visit."

Sixty seconds later he had all the answers and more to his question as Homer presented the rather innocuous looking white pill taken from the medicine cabinet at John Sealy.

It wasn't difficult at all. Almost too easy as the doctor handled the pill and took one careful look. You could tell by his expression that the news was certainly not positive. He calmly placed it on the kitchen counter, then walked over to remove a bottle of Jack Daniels and some glasses – one for each of those present—from the cabinet.

"Phenobarbital."

It was the only thing the doctor said and neither Homer or Bill clearly understood what it meant.

"What we have here is phenobarbital – a mind altering drug commonly known as the epileptic's drug of choice. One used to control seizures," the doctor continued.

Homer and Bill were stunned. Why would she want to control his mind? Why would she give their father a drug when he had never suffered from epilepsy, never had a seizure? Poison they suspected, but a mind control drug?

Almost as if reading their thoughts, Dr. Pearce offered a drink to each and motioned for them to be seated.

"It's not poison in the usual sense, but an extremely strong psychotic drug to control one's mind – sometimes giving the illusion an individual is 'here today, gone tomorrow'," he explained. "Come to think of it, probably explains why Mrs. Murray thought Lutcher had 'bats in the belfry' after he married Nelda. And while it's certainly not something your dad should be taking, there isn't much more you can do than simply get rid of it. Considering the length of time he's been in Galveston, I'm guessing he doesn't have much time left anyway if Nelda has her way."

Hours later on the road to Galveston, Homer realized he and Bill said very little during their visit with Dr. Pearce. Harming their dad was something so foreign to either of them that they couldn't imagine Nelda trying something like that.

For once, there was no line of cars waiting for the ferry. It was only 5:20, so chances were there were never long lines at this time of the morning. Only one other car – actually a pickup truck with fishing gear and coolers in the back – was making the ferry trip. It was a chance for Homer to enjoy the moment, so he made his way to the second floor of the ferry and immediately recalled how much he loved the water. River, creek, bay, bayou, gulf or ocean. He had always been partial to water and, in fact, made his living operating the Sabine Yacht Basin in Orange. Glancing around at the pre-dawn sky and listening to the ferry breaking through the calm waters of Galveston Bay, he almost felt normal. Even the seagulls respected the silence.

The jolt of the ferry docking brought him back to the present as he quickly made his way to the car and onto the island. It was only a few blocks to Harborside Drive and the hospital parking lot. With any luck at all, Nelda's care of Lutcher should come to a halt. After 21 years of her efforts to distance Homer and Bill from Lutcher, they finally would have their father back.

Slender and just shy of the six foot mark, Homer was walking tall as he made his way to the hospital's fourth floor with hopes of confiscating the phenobarbital threatening his dad's health and clarity of thought. He exited the elevator, but quickly realized there was a problem as Chatman met him in the small vending area near 409. As planned, Chatman came straight to the hospital when he received Homer's call, but the pills were gone when he arrived.

"She flushed them down the toilet, Mr. Homer," Chatman said. "Everyone at the nurse's station was talking about it when I got here first thing this morning. Miss Nelda noticed a pill was missing – she'd been counting them – and threw a fit before getting rid of all of them. A nurse told me she hid behind the couch when Dr. Gregory came looking for her after he heard what she'd been doing. Can you believe she was actually counting them?"

Homer found a chair and sat down. Any chance of proving Nelda was abusing his dad had disappeared. The only option now was to call Bill and begin taking turns, 12 hour shifts, night and day, to make certain one of them was always at the hospital so she could do nothing else to harm Lutcher.

Two weeks later, both Bill and Homer were at John Sealy as their dad seemed to be slipping away. They waited outside his room as doctors and nurses went in and out of 409 for what seemed an eternity. At 1:20 p.m. on September 2, they looked up to see Nelda coming toward them.

"Boys, there will be no autopsy."

Homer and Bill exchanged glances, then Homer asked, "Are you telling us our father is dead?"

"Yes. And there will be no autopsy."

The following morning, Lutcher Stark was buried. Less than 20 hours had passed since his death in a hospital two hours away, but the town's most prominent citizen would be laid to rest in almost record time. The only exception had been his second wife, Ruby – Nelda's sister – who died from what locals called "a mysterious illness" while in Nelda's care. She was buried at 6:30 p.m., 11 hours following her death at home and little more than a year after her marriage to Lutcher.

Except for countless floral offerings throughout the First Presbyterian Church and lining the downstairs foyer, services were simple and understated for a man some called the "King of Texas" during the years when he wielded more clout than anyone else in the State.

A gift from the Lutcher family, the church reflected the classic style of elegant Greek Revival architecture. The first air-cooled public building west of the Mississippi, it was a glorious tribute to the family's religious faith – from the native Texas pink granite mined from the same quarry that supplied stone for the Capitol building in Austin, to leaded stained glass windows purchased by Mrs. Lutcher at the 1893 Chicago World's Fair gracing the foyer. She commissioned 28 other windows from J&R Lamb Studios of New York that would be displayed not only along each side of the sanctuary, but overhead in a unique circular dome that measured 36 feet in diameter and was the only opalescent glass dome in the United States.

Rare ribbon mahogany pews and trim were exquisite, and carved Italian marble stairs rising from the ground level foyer were generously gilded in 24K gold. Fine murals, beautiful bronze and brass fixtures, the exquisite mosaic inlay on the mahogany altar, and an impressive 2,435-pipe Cassavant organ. Even today no one knew the cost of the magnificent structure. After paying each bill, Mrs. Lutcher destroyed all receipts and refused to think of it as anything but a gift to the town.

Rev. Ben Gillespie paid tribute to Lutcher and recalled his many contributions to the community in general and to children specifically. As "Amazing Grace" echoed throughout the church, Homer took a moment to check out the mourners gathered to pay respects to his father, in his mind the finest man who had walked the Earth. It was an impressive gathering, with former governors, University of Texas regents, and a sprinkling of successful businessmen throughout the crowd despite the short notice. But he was somewhat surprised to see Nelda, the bereaved widow, and Eunice almost smiling as they exchanged glances.

Following the Lord's Prayer and a closing prayer from the pulpit, the Stark family and Eunice left for the graveside service at the family mausoleum in Evergreen cemetery. There Lutcher would be laid to rest next to his beloved grandparents, parents and Nita, the love of his life who died in 1939 after 28 years of marriage.

It was a short service and few lingered as the Texas temperature and humidity sent the heat index past the 100 degree mark. But Homer stayed to share a final moment with his father, pausing before starting down the pathway to rejoin his wife and children as they neared the family station wagon.

Then he heard that distinctive laugh, Nelda's laugh, an unmistakable sound in such a solemn setting. He glanced that direction and saw her bidding farewell to three of his father's doctors and a nurse, each now the proud owner of a brand new Thunderbird – two white ones, another in red, and the fourth in baby blue. Gifts from Nelda's dealership.

If the devil had a wife, thought Homer, surely she would be it.

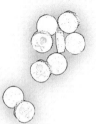

CHAPTER 2

"No one of whatever era has wielded more actual power than H. J. Lutcher Stark in the 1920s."
— **Richard Pennington in "For Texas I Will"**

A sleepy little town deep in the southeast corner of Texas, Orange was unique in many respects. Strategically located between the Neches River and the banks of the Sabine, the official boundary of the Lone Star State and Louisiana, it was perfectly poised to take advantage of the waterways that were its greatest natural resource.

With a deep water port, complemented by the Intracoastal Canal connection and access to the nearby Gulf of Mexico, it was not unusual that ships from around the world came to Orange. Venezuela, Cuba, Puerto Rico, Germany, Panama, Mexico, and Brazil – these countries and others paid regular visits to the Texas port. Shipbuilding and trade would become driving economic factors in the growth of the town.

Add miles of virgin pine and cypress forests lining either side of the Sabine southward to Orange, and you had the makings of a multimillion dollar lumber industry. Long leaf pine stands – often referred to as the Pine Curtain – were so thick daylight could not penetrate the deepest part of the holdings. And Louisiana's cypress swamplands offered yet another profitable option.

Such was the source of the Stark family wealth, a fortune based on extensive land patents purchased in the 1870's by H. J. and Frances Ann Lutcher, the family patriarchs who moved from Pennsylvania to invest in forests that covered hundreds of thousands of acres in both states, almost one fourth of Louisiana and a big chunk of East Texas.

Daily business operations of the Lutcher & Moore Lumber Company were the domain of W. H. Stark, who married Miriam, one of the Lutchers' two daughters, and Dr. Edgar Brown, husband of the second daughter, Carrie. With a background in the lumber industry, W. H. was the perfect choice to take over when Mr. Lutcher died in 1912 as Dr. Brown provided additional oversight to the extensive family holdings. Together, they supervised property in both states and expanded the business to include banking, oil, trapping, sulphur, gas and other leases to take full advantage of the natural resources of the land.

By the 1930s, Orange earned a reputation for having more millionaires per capita on Green Avenue than the main street of any comparable town in America. Impressive homes of different styles lined both sides of the avenue, most of them built by those who owned or did business with Lutcher & Moore. The Falwell house featuring Spanish architecture, the Brown home with its colonial accents, the Queen Anne-style of the W. H. Stark home, the Moore residence with a European flair, or the Ochiltree's Victorian-inspired mansion.

Yet tucked away on Pine Street, a block north of Green Avenue, was the home of Lutcher Stark, only child of W. H. and

Miriam. Modest by comparison, it was comfortable, spacious and reflected the wishes of Nita Hill Stark, Lutcher's wife.

They met in Austin when Lutcher, the first student to have a car on campus, was attending the University of Texas. Sheltered throughout his early years, it was said that Lutcher "skipped childhood" and discovered a new world when he arrived on campus. The story goes he was walking by a house on Whitis Avenue, just a block from the school, when he noticed a beautiful young woman on the upstairs veranda, brushing her just-washed hair in the sun.

"That's the woman I'm going to marry," Lutcher told a friend. Less than 24 hours later, he managed an introduction and they were engaged within the year. It was a perfect match in all respects. Lutcher was spoiled, but Nita grounded him. He had a temper, she had a sense of humor. He enjoyed power, she preferred poise and patience.

Wedding plans for the two popular young people were the talk of Austin for months as parties in the state capital focused on the upcoming nuptials. One of the engagement presents Nita received from Lutcher – a Hupmobile roadster straight from Detroit – created a stir when it was delivered during a bridal shower at the Hill residence.

Trains brought guests from throughout Texas and points across the nation, while telegrams from friends and family scattered across the United States arrived days before vows were exchanged at University Methodist Church. With Easter lilies adorning the candlelit sanctuary accented in green and white, Nita and Lutcher were married in a magnificent ceremony that included William S. Wasmund, the Longhorn head football coach, as best man. A nice touch for a UT wedding.

A three-month honeymoon followed the reception as they departed Austin by train for St. Louis, then traveled to Chicago, Indianapolis, Detroit and New York before returning to Texas via New Orleans.

The only child of Dr. Homer Hill, a prominent Austin physician who volunteered as the football team doctor from the first game in 1893 until his death 30 years later, Nita was elected Varsity Queen in 1909 – the equivalent of Sweetheart of the University in later years. She shared a love of sports with Lutcher and was quick to respond to sportswriters when she felt the Longhorns were unkindly described. It was not unusual for her to send neatly typed letters with specific examples of why Lloyd Gregory, a Houston Chronicle sportswriter and family friend, should be ashamed of comments made regarding the Longhorns. Nor was it unusual for Lutcher to add a handwritten postscript that he agreed completely with his wife.

Nita held a special place in her heart for the hill country that surrounded the state capital and enjoyed frequent visits to Austin as Lutcher served on the University's Board of Regents. Appointed in 1919 when he was 32, he was not only the youngest person ever named to the powerful Board, but served as Chairman longer than anyone else before or since.*

The *Saturday Evening Post* referred to him as the "Angel of the Longhorns" in a lengthy article detailing his tenure as both student and University Regent. From early days when he bought burnt orange blankets with "Longhorns" appliqued across the back, then draped them across the football players as they sat along the bench – a move designed to force the name change from "Varsity" and "Steers," to his generosity in furnishing the Longhorn band with new uniforms and instruments, to chairing the successful Memorial Stadium construction drive in the midst of tough economic times, Lutcher Stark was a mover and a shaker.

And he did it his way, not only contributing funding for the projects but making certain it was done according to his standards. Even before plans were announced for a concrete stadium to replace the wooden bleachers of Clark Field, he traveled to California and filmed construction of the Rose Bowl in Pasadena to use two years later when work began in Austin on a similar horseshoe-shaped facility to be built in two stages: the first, with the east and west stands in place for the opening in 1924; the second, the addition of the north side in 1926 to complete the horseshoe.

As they spent more time in Austin attending Regents meetings and state functions, Nita and Lutcher bought a home site near the campus, a 16-acre property with views of the campus from one direction and the bluebonnet-covered hills on the opposite side. Meanwhile, they could be found at the legendary Driskill Hotel on Sixth Street, a short distance from the university and a convenient location for Nita to host luncheons and other social functions.

When Lutcher's weight exceeded 200 pounds, more than his 5'7" frame should carry, he identified Alan Calvert, the top man in the field of physical training, and traveled to Philadelphia to learn the benefits of weight training for general fitness as well as for athletes. Four months later, he returned to Texas with a firm belief in a training program that would transform sports for the remainder of the century. He joined with Theo Bellmont, UT's new athletic director, and would pack his weights in the trunk of his car whenever he visited the Austin campus.** There the two could be seen working out on the grounds near Old Main with their weights neatly stacked nearby.

Austin provided a backdrop for a unique tapestry of events in those early years, a campus quite different from the one that would change forever when Santa Rita No.1 blew a gusher in West Texas, the first of 11 in 1923. It was a stunning transformation. Wooden shacks remaining from World War I dominated the campus before the oil boom, some in such poor shape that umbrellas were used both inside and outside the flimsy structures. Only an occasional brick building like Old Main interrupted the rather ugly landscape of the Texas campus. Suddenly the prevailing attitude in Texas that higher education was a waste of time took a back seat as the campus filled its coffers with black gold.

Petrodollars, as Lutcher Stark called them, transformed the Forty Acres that were home to the Longhorn faithful. The injection of money, lots of money, funded magnificent buildings and impressive showplaces where temporary structures stood only months before.

Yet the smoke-filled rooms where Regents crafted selections for Governor of Texas, battled with faculty members, and imposed decisions on the University president took a back seat in the 1930s when football moved to center stage in the person of legendary coach D. X. Bible.

Lutcher Stark, a financial godfather accustomed to getting his way, desperately wanted the best coach money could buy to return his Longhorns to prominence. In an unprecedented move, he not only offered Bible a 10-year contract, but a salary four times the Governor's paycheck and twice that of the University president. And he wrote the check to cover it.

Soon afterwards, Lutcher again made the headlines as he and Nita donated a $5 million collection of art and antiques to their alma mater. It was a substantial gift by any measure, one recognized by a joint resolution from the Texas Legislature as they expressed appreciation to the couple.

"It's the right thing to do," said Lutcher, surprisingly modest during the ceremony. "My mother put this collection together and we promised her it would go to the University in order to share it with as many Texans as possible."

Dressed in his traditional dark suit, white dress shirt and an elegant silk tie selected by his wife, Lutcher Stark cut an impressive figure despite his average size. As Governor Pat Neff made the formal presentation in the legislative chambers, however, it was Nita who would steal the spotlight with her understated manner and exquisite style. A blue French serge suit seemed glamorous as she added perfectly matched shoes, a black meline hat with white ostrich quill, and pearls to complete the outfit.

To all who knew them, Lutcher was totally smitten with Nita from the first day he saw her. Two daughters, stillborn earlier in their marriage, left husband and wife with an obvious appreciation for each other and endeared them to any causes related to children.

Described as "the nicest lady you ever met," Nita insisted on giving their twin sons, Homer and Bill, more of a normal life than children of wealth usually led. They enrolled in public schools, attended Sunday school every week, played with the neighborhood kids and were popular with classmates. While each was active in football, basketball and tennis, they also found time to master a musical instrument: Bill, the piano, and

Homer, the trumpet. When she and Lutcher traveled, whether to Austin, New York or Chicago, Nita made certain Mademoiselle, the nanny hired by the Starks, kept a tight rein on the boys.

Each Christmas, Nita planned a party in Orange and welcomed all at the impressive two-story traditional clubhouse at Sunset Grove Country Club. It was a festive evening reflecting no divisions of class or wealth. Children of servants, often wearing dresses and suits provided by Nita, mingled with those of civic leaders. It was a celebration of community with food, drink and holiday music as ingredients to a successful event. Spectacular decorations, fireworks and small gifts for each child made it the most anticipated party of the year.

While Lutcher divided his time between the UT Board of Regents and service to the Rotary Club, Nita earned a place in the heart of Orange as she worked with charitable groups and was always behind the scenes to accomplish the impossible. The hospital, the church, the soup kitchen. Wherever she was needed, Nita made a point to use her position in a way that benefited the community.

She was a treasure to the people of Orange, and indeed, Texas. Through her efforts, she increased support of a Pi Beta Phi-sponsored settlement home for the poor in Gatlinburg, Tennessee, was honored by the American Red Cross for aid given to wounded soldiers in World War I, and received an award from the Orange school district for her tireless work as a school trustee. Baylor University bestowed an honorary degree of doctor of law in recognition of her contributions on behalf of young women.

Lutcher and Nita were known for their generous gifts to public education, not only to their alma mater in Austin, but to the Orange schools. While annual contributions to scholarship funds and declamation contests were made by the couple, they long supported the local high school boys band with instruments and uniforms, plus instruction that included special summer camps led by Col. George Hurt, director of the Longhorn band. Yet it was the Bengal Guards, an all girls drum and bugle corps the Starks added in the mid-1930s, that put Orange on the national map.

Not only dollars flowed from the Starks, but Nita and Lutcher invested their time and took an active interest in the Guards. While Nita was content to view practices from the stands and sketch a Longhorn design to adorn new western-style uniforms for the group, Lutcher had an elevated platform constructed to improve his vantage point as he critiqued every move.

The finest instruments, best uniforms and special equipment buses completed the picture as the Starks spent more than $300,000 – approximately $4,000,000 today – on the high school band and drum and bugle corps.

In less than a year from its inception, the Guards were drawing crowds wherever they appeared, including more than 80,000 spectators when they twice were the featured attraction at the Chicagoland Music Festival at Soldier Field. Arriving by private train provided by their benefactor in 1939, the girls learned the 15-minute routine they had mastered would be limited to only 12. A quick phone call from Lutcher and $3,000 later, arrangements were made to keep the performance as originally planned.

A bespectacled middle-aged man, Lutcher Stark stood in the press box, nervously anticipating their performance and chain-smoking his Lucky Strikes, as he personally introduced

"America's own Bengal Guards." From the moment "his girls" stepped on the field, marching 86 abreast at a 190 cadence – compared to infantry drills at 120, the show was nothing short of spectacular.

It was a flawless performance as the girls moved from "God Bless America," "The Eyes of Texas," "Home on the Range," "The Aggie War Hymn," "Ja Da," and "The Man Who Comes Around" without missing a note or step. Formations moved seamlessly as they performed stars, figure eights, telescopes, and their signature company front featuring the entire group marching in a straight line down the field and ending with the "swinging gate" – a move that Bengal Guard members said required the girls at the end "to come damn close to running in order to keep up."

The crowd, the media, the entire city were taken with his drum and bugle corps. Telegrams and phone calls flooded the Stevens Hotel where the entire sixth floor was reserved for the teenagers from Orange. While other marching units competed in Chicago, the Bengal Guards were the featured attraction. To compete would have been no contest.

The Bengal Guards were most assuredly in a class by themselves. They would add the Sugar Bowl in New Orleans, inaugurations of the Governor of Texas, a special routine for First Lady Eleanor Roosevelt, and a feature article in *Life* magazine to the many appearances and requests they received. All the while polishing their precision marching in the new stadium at Orange High School and their musical talents in the band hall that doubled as a gymnasium.

"And it's not just any gymnasium, it's decorated quite nicely," Nita told her friends in Austin. She was absolutely right, for original art of Frederic Remington, Charles Russell and Herbert Dunton was among those selected to hang from the walls of the school gym. "High, of course," Nita explained. "We wouldn't want the basketballs to hit them."

Indeed, it was a charmed life as they spent summers at the Roslyn Ranch in northern Colorado with their sons, friends and other family members. The postcard-perfect location in North Park, adjacent to Routt National Forest, was the scene of gracious living and outdoor adventures as fishing, hunting and exploring were highlights of each trip. Tennis courts, pool tables, ping pong, croquet and horseshoes added to the activity list, with bridge and poker games a frequent diversion. Reading any of the numerous volumes displayed in the main lodge was a favorite choice of many of the guests, who seemed to delight in the mysteries and biographies dominating the selections.

Set at the base of Parkview Mountain, elevation 12,296 ft., eight guest cabins and the main lodge were outfitted comfortably and placed conveniently around the tennis courts and a lake added to the property in the 1930s. With massive stone fireplaces rising two stories on either end of the living area, the main lodge was the favorite gathering place at the end of each day as seating areas were grouped throughout the spacious room. The guest book reflected diverse friendships as politicians, teachers, bankers, employees, businessmen and high school students left comments such as the Chicago banker who asked "Could the home of the Starks be where Southern hospitality originated?" Helen Carr, the principal for whom the junior high in Orange was named, described it as "a fairyland," while another guest commented that "once in a million years a place like this happens."

But in August 1939, Nita became ill at the Colorado ranch and was transported to Orange by private train. Even when her health failed, she insisted on seeing the Longhorns play and was carried into the stands to see them one last time.*** By late September, she lapsed in and out of consciousness with only morphine to ease the pain ravaging her body.

Somehow it gave Nita's sons little comfort when Nelda Childers arrived each day at the family home. The mellow tones of Homer's trumpet fell silent each evening as he watched from his second floor window when the boyish-looking hospital administrator parked her beige coupe on 10th street and marched toward the house with her black medical bag.

When Nita closed her eyes forever on a Wednesday evening in October at the age of 49, the entire town shut down as her spirit and gracious manner were mourned.

Flags flew at half-mast on the University of Texas campus, and few students were unaware of the reason. Schools in Orange were cancelled for the remainder of the week. Friday night's high school football game with Nederland was postponed. Retail merchants and city offices closed their doors in her memory. Four blocks of Green Avenue near the Lutcher Memorial Church were closed during the service as police officers from Orange, Port Arthur and the Texas Highway Patrol helped direct traffic. Uniformed members of the Bengal Guards and Lutch Stark's Boys Band took turns serving 30-minute shifts as honor guards at the Stark home, then stood in formation at the Lutcher Memorial Presbyterian Church for services and again at Evergreen cemetery.

For Lutcher and his 16-year-old sons, life would never be the same. No amount of money could bring her back.

*Appointed to the Board of Regents when he was 32, Lutcher Stark served 24 years, 11 of them as Chairman. (May 1919 - January 1931, and January 1933 - February 1945; Chairman from May 24, 1921 - January 20, 1930, and March 30, 1935 to February 27, 1937)

**The two men included Roy McLean in the workout sessions and in 1919 McLean introduced the first modern, heavy weight-training classes taught in the United States. The history of sports and physical activity at UT will be displayed in the H. J. Lutcher Stark Center for Physical Culture and Sports, opening in 2010 at the University of Texas at Austin.

***Houston sports columnist Lloyd Gregory suggested Texas dedicate its game with Oklahoma in her memory and stated, "She always sat just beneath the press box in Memorial Stadium. And I shall look in vain for a woman, small in stature, but big in spirit, who never stopped cheering for her Longhorns...no matter what the score."

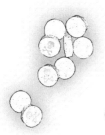

CHAPTER 3

*"Those two queers have made
my life a living hell."*
— *H. J. Lutcher Stark (June 1963)*

L ife changed quickly in Orange as rumblings of World War II were producing government contracts in the ship-building industry, and Orange was positioned to take advantage of the economic boom.

Population jumped 700% during the war years as 60,000 people took over a town with only the infrastructure for much smaller numbers. Riverside – an overnight development of temporary housing for the endless stream of laborers – spread over low-lying property along the Sabine that was walking distance to the shipyards and Navy base.

In the wake of Pearl Harbor, many of the town's young men enlisted to fight for their country. Homer and Bill, now freshmen in college, were no exception. Homer chose the Navy; Bill, the Marines. Neither considered using their father's influence to avoid military service, a path Lutcher had chosen in World War I when his grandmother sent a letter claiming he was essential to running the family business.

Each married before shipping out, Homer to Becky Havens, the drum major and twirler who led the Bengal Guards and later the UT band, and Bill to Ida Marie Dickens, a Colorado native he met during summers at Roslyn Ranch. Lutcher followed suit with a wedding of his own, marrying Ruby Childers, a secretary in the Stark offices for more than 20 years. Although she had never missed a day of work, less than a year later Ruby died in Nelda's care and both Homer and Bill were saddened when they heard the news.

During the three plus years his sons were stationed in the Pacific, Lutcher Stark married Nelda, Ruby's sister, over the objections of both Homer and Bill. While Ruby was sweet, kind and totally adored their father, Nelda was cold, distant and not known for good deeds. At least three families had children ages 5 to 14 die – two on the hospital steps, another in his father's arms – when Nelda refused them admission to the Lutcher Hospital when they couldn't afford the $25 fee. The only time Homer ever heard his parents argue was when Nita insisted on firing Nelda as hospital administrator after she learned of the death of the first child. He seemed to recall his father eventually agreed, but Nelda was soon back in charge.

Who was Lutcher Stark? Almost 20 years after he died, Homer's children felt they knew little more than they had when their grandfather was alive. The man who seemed bigger than life when they were children remained a mystery to each of them.

Rachel, Ramona, Rebel and Jake. Three girls and a boy born to Homer and Becky Stark. None of them still lived in Orange, but came often to see their parents and perhaps pay a visit to Nelda. Their step-grandmother, never known as a "kid person," actually seemed nicer to them once they were adults.

But regardless of how often they saw her, they always asked Homer and Becky the same questions:

"Why would Granddaddy marry her?"

"What in the world was he thinking?"

"Why would one of the most powerful and richest men in Texas change his entire lifestyle for Nelda?"

There were no real answers, only theories that came forward.

The most prominent centered on the premise that Nelda and Eunice were lesbians, and Lutcher may not have known it when he married her. Logic would suggest he was too embarrassed and would rather stay married than admit he had made such a tragic mistake, especially considering the strong attitudes about homosexuality that prevailed in the 1940s.

Homer smiled when this theory surfaced, for he clearly recalled when Rachel, 16 years old at the time, returned from a trip with Lutcher, Nelda and Eunice. His father invited her to travel with them to Denton and visit the TWU campus during graduation weekend. Nelda was on the Board of Regents and Lutcher was receiving an award – one Rachel learned was for air conditioning the Main Auditorium. Her grandfather laughed at the thought of being recognized for simply wanting to stay cool.

They always traveled to Denton with two station wagons, a trip of six to seven hours depending on traffic and stops. Leona, a longtime family servant, rode in one with the luggage; Lutcher, Nelda and Eunice traveled in the other. When Lutcher indicated Rachel would ride with them rather than

Leona, Nelda and Eunice became so irritated that they moved to the second car. With her grandfather to herself, Rachel loved every minute and the trip would long remain her favorite memory of the older man she seldom saw even though they lived in the same town.

While a tour of the campus and graduation were impressive, the most unforgettable moment occurred at the Holiday Inn swimming pool. Lutcher came out, pulled up a chair near the water's edge, and held Rachel's attention for at least 30 minutes as the teenager hung on the side of the pool, listening to every word of advice or fond recollection he offered. From the value of education to the influence of his grandmother, Frances Ann or "Mamoose" to Lutcher, a fear of fire, or his fascination with the number 13, he had a story for every topic.

As they were talking, Eunice opened the door of her motel room, calling his name several times, each louder than the other. After the fourth or fifth attempt, Rachel thought her grandfather simply didn't hear Eunice.

"Granddaddy," she said, "Miss Eunice is calling you."

"I hear her," Lutcher coldly declared, glancing in the direction of Eunice before adding, "Those two queers have made my life a living hell."

Rachel's grasp of the edge of the pool gave way and she slipped beneath the water's surface, totally taken by surprise. She reappeared, choking and gasping for breath, trying to understand what she had just heard. Lutcher extended his hand and helped her up the ladder.

Thus began the stories of Nelda and Eunice, ones that remained dormant for years but were now surfacing. Becky was the greatest source of information as she recalled stories of

Coach Williams when he briefly dated Eunice, but told Becky he couldn't compete when he saw Eunice slipping out to meet Nelda in her beige coupe only minutes after a date with him. Warnings that Lutcher gave to female employees to stay away from Nelda and Eunice – "they liked threesomes." Parties at Big Lake, quarrels between Nelda and Eunice over "other women," and closely guarded secrets of their lifestyle were among tales handed down by servants in the Stark household.

A second theory centered on Nelda's nursing background. Lutcher was 56 when he married Nelda, 34, and both employees and friends thought he might be looking for someone to take care of him as he grew older. She always kept a small black medical bag with her in the car, at the office or at home.

With the sole exception of the Denton trip, Homer estimated his dad spent no more than four or five hours total with his children, an average of 15 to 20 minutes each year. An amazing statistic given that they lived less than five minutes apart from their grandfather and the years spanned 70 birthdays, 19 Christmas holidays and Easter church services, plus the typical school programs, Little League baseball games, spelling bees and class plays.

Lutcher and Nelda never entered Homer and Becky's home, never invited them to dinner, never attended a softball or baseball game of one of their grandchildren. They never babysat, shared a holiday or attended a school open house. But every once in a while, Lutcher would call Homer and ask him to bring the children out to Shangri La, a 252-acre private retreat he developed over the years in three distinct parts: a botanical garden, the natural environment along the bayou, and pastures for his Longhorns and a few sheep. There the grandchildren would delight in looking for pirate treasure supposedly buried by Jean Lafitte years ago. They were too young to realize each always found the same amount of money in the sawdust and the coins were freshly minted. It was a game for Lutcher, one he thoroughly enjoyed as he quizzed each on how much they had found, then just happened to drop a quarter, a dime or a nickel nearby.

Homer recalled his dad showing up unexpectedly before Rachel's first birthday party, coming around the side gate to the back yard where tables were being set up, to deliver a delicate pink and white dress, then leaving as quickly as he came. "Roaring Rose," Lutcher's nickname for her since he heard her loud cries when she was born, was embroidered across the pinafore. Sixteen years later, he wanted to attend her high school graduation and Homer came by to pick up his dad after Nelda refused to drive him. An interesting sight: the richest man in town wearing bedroom slippers with a coat and tie, sitting in the high school stadium he built 25 years earlier, watching his oldest granddaughter receive her diploma. Tears silently went down the old man's cheeks, perhaps indicative of all the years and moments he had missed.

Becky's explanation for his behavior dated back to a letter from Nelda that surfaced in 1943 when Lutcher and Becky drove to Bremerton, Washington to meet Homer when the U.S.S. Richmond came in for repairs. As they took the ferry across Puget Sound, Lutcher meticulously tore a letter and envelope in pieces, letting them drift in the wind and eventually scatter in the waters below.

"Pop, what is it?" asked Becky.

"Nelda won't marry me," he replied. "Not unless I give up my sons, my friends, my way of life. It was right there in that letter. An ultimatum. That isn't going to happen, so we can just consider that chapter of my life closed."

He never mentioned Nelda's name for the rest of the trip, choosing to focus on Homer's shore leave, then a drive home by way of the Colorado ranch. The winding mountain roads that provided the only access to Roslyn also allowed Lutcher the opportunity to drive like the proverbial bat-out-of-hell, honking the air horn as he approached hairpin turns, warning anyone coming toward him to get out of the way. Becky spent most of the trip with her eyes closed.

When they returned to Orange two weeks later, Nelda resurfaced. Three months later, she married Lutcher in a small ceremony attended only by her parents and half a dozen friends and servants. No one seemed happy as even tears shed by the mother of the bride did not appear to be those of joy. Rev. Edward Drake, minister at the Presbyterian Church for decades, hardly believed it himself as he pronounced them man and wife in the Thursday afternoon ceremony. The newlyweds moved into the plain, one-story home Nelda shared with her parents, a small Craftsman-style three bedroom with little more than 1500 square feet – definitely understated for a man with such wealth. For her wedding night, Nelda selected red, white and blue sateen pajamas – an interesting choice for a bride. It would prove to be an equally strange relationship, and one that severed all ties with the past Lutcher had so enjoyed.

In 1990, when depositions were scheduled in a lawsuit filed after the family suspected Nita's estate was not distributed to her sons according to her will, Becky told the same story about the Bremerton ferry letter.

"But you don't have any proof that letter existed," said Robert Christopher, lead attorney for Knox and Henderson, a prominent Houston firm representing the Stark Foundation.

"I saw it. Mr. Stark read part of it to me, then tore it into pieces and tossed it over the railing," replied Becky.

"Why should we believe you, Mrs. Stark? You could be making this whole thing up."

"I don't lie, Mr. Christopher. Everything she said in that letter came true. Why else would he give up his sons, his friends?"

Becky's deposition of several hours abruptly ended as the question she posed went unanswered. Now it was Ramona's turn with the attorneys. Hers would prove far shorter, for lawyers for Nelda and the Stark Foundation seemed to have trouble even coming up with questions once they established her name, address, and date of birth.

Several times they asked about Nelda, her relationship with the grandchildren, how she treated them. In each instance, Ramona gave short, abbreviated answers. She gave them nothing to pursue.

"Tell us, if you could describe your grandmother in one word, what would it be?" asked Lawrence Watson, another of the Knox and Henderson attorneys, fishing for any clues as to how much Ramona knew. Immediately the other lawyers sat up straight around the large, oval conference table, one – Clyde McKee – jerked awake when the man to his right elbowed him.

What would Ramona say? Lesbian, evil, ruthless, murderer? The possibilities were intriguing. No one was certain what word she would select.

"Well, I guess if I had to use just one word, it would be…," Ramona paused to think, prolonging the answer for effect, "it would be mysterious."

"Mysterious?" asked Mr. Watson, obviously taken by surprise. "Mysterious in what way?"

"Well, if I knew that, she wouldn't be mysterious, would she?"

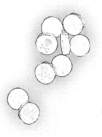

CHAPTER 4

"They begin with making falsehood appear like truth, and end with making truth itself appear like falsehood."

— M. Shenstone

Seven months later, Jamestown presented another mystery. The town's name alone elicited an instant connection with history as Rachel recalled lessons of England's first colony in Virginia. She always loved studying the colonial days and was fascinated with the fact her father's birthplace was in such an historic setting.

Although she had never been to Virginia, soon she would have the opportunity to explore the Jamestown settlement and visit Richmond, the state capital, and hopefully the source of information on the adoption that placed her father and uncle in Texas.

Houston's Intercontinental Airport was especially busy during Spring break. The flight was behind schedule, but she was too excited to care. Once in Richmond, she would be met by Dan Thomas, a friend who recently moved from Texas. Then it was on to Jamestown and a taste of the past to help her better understand the present.

Flight 982 was boarding and she would find her seat near the back of the 737, on the aisle as requested. Flying was not her preferred method of travel, but a car trip would take too much of her vacation time. She placed a carry-on bag in the overhead compartment, then sat down and automatically buckled her seat belt – a habit of always following instructions. Too nervous to say much to the couple to her left, Rachel concentrated on what she hoped to find. Possibly an entire new family, although she knew better than to approach anyone directly. One could never be too certain of reactions after so many years.

The captain's voice came over the intercom, thanking everyone for choosing American and providing details of the flight – arrival time, wind speed, flying altitude, weather, and so on. She wondered if it was really the captain speaking. Such a soothing voice that it might be prerecorded. Real or not, it was effective and soon took her mind off the fact something so large and heavy could actually fly through the air.

Midway through the flight, she put aside her magazines and reached for a worn briefcase she carried with her at all times. In it were the faded blue birth certificate and adoption papers – incomplete as they were – that she found in her father's files. Although it puzzled her that the birth certificate was not issued until 1942, 19 years after Homer's birth, and the attachment was missing from the adoption papers, they were the only clues she had to help with the search. There it was:

Birthplace: Jamestown, Virginia
Date of Birth: April 26, 1923

No indication Homer was adopted, but that fact was often omitted in the early 20th century. Her father had known from his earliest memory that he and his twin brother were adopted. No secrets there.

Throughout their lives, neither Homer nor Bill had shown any interest in locating their birth parents, and Rachel did not intend to upset anyone by looking. She was simply curious and wanted to know more about her father's biological family. Just the chance to walk through Jamestown and picture the past would be enough to make the trip a success.

Neatly placed in a bright red file folder within the briefcase were other notes she made during the last five years. Although the lawsuit regarding Nita's estate had ended, Rachel was intrigued by the hundreds of thousands of documents produced during the litigation. Lawyers had patiently explained that Nita simply didn't have very much when she died, so Homer and Bill – her only heirs – had not been shortchanged when the estate was distributed. One of these days she wanted to take time to go through the documents, but for now she was content to review the index that had been compiled and copied– all 176 pages of single-spaced topics.

Making notes as she read through it, Rachel didn't notice the time. She started to ask the flight attendant for a soft drink as the captain's voice came back on the speaker. Same tone, same cadence, same temperature. Maybe it was a recording after all, but they would soon be landing and she was anxious to see Virginia.

Dan was waiting at the gate when she stepped through the doorway. Always the perfect gentleman, he gave her a quick kiss hello and took her bag, then patiently listened as she provided more details than he cared to know about the plane ride. She had a habit of asking lots of questions, often answering them herself without providing any opportunity for feedback.

She was that way when excited about anything from a new puppy to his golf game.

One thing was certain. She had a vivid imagination and definite ideas about what she would find in Jamestown. Dan was also a history buff and equally anxious to see that side of Virginia.

From the airport, it was less than an hour's drive to Williamsburg and a chance to take in the charm of its colonial sites before continuing to Jamestown the next morning. Restaurants, gift shops, specialty stores, tourist attractions. Each had a quaint appeal that reflected a more relaxed pace than that found in the urban sprawl of Dallas or Houston.

There was something about taking two hours for dinner and not trying to be somewhere faster. A waiter, probably a college student from nearby William and Mary, seemed the absolute picture of Southern hospitality from his gracious manners to his impeccable attention to detail. Far from the fast-paced conversation at the airport, Rachel now limited her conversation to attentive listening as Dan brought her up to date on his new job and home.

Monday morning dawned, and it was spectacular. Cool breezes announced a perfect beginning to the day as they stopped for a quick breakfast and were on their way, taking Route 31 for the quick ten-minute trip to Jamestown.

The countryside was ablaze with color, including every shade of red, gold, and green you could imagine. Tall pine trees and assorted hardwoods framing the road, plus the location of Jamestown on the banks of the James River, reminded Rachel of Orange. That along with the humidity and low-lying area near the river – again reminiscent of her hometown.

The entrance to Jamestown was marked by the standard National Park signage, identifying it as government property. Once inside, the road forked; to the right was historic Jamestown, to the left a driving tour of the adjoining property.

They turned left and slowly took the curves and turns that were fashioned like a maze through the wooded area. Occasionally, a historic marker would draw their attention and both would exit the car for a closer look. Sensing her rather subdued mood, Dan asked if she was sad.

"Sad? Not exactly. More like confused."

"What do you mean confused? I thought you might be feeling a little sad thinking about your dad."

"No. I'm just puzzled that there's nothing here. No houses, just a few markers for homes that were torn down long ago. Where was he born?"

"Got me," said Dan, glancing around at the deserted forest. "Let's go back to the main entrance for the walking tour. Maybe the settlement is on that side of the park."

Circling back to the main road, they followed the signs to the parking lot in front of the one and only building. A combination theater, gift shop and restrooms. No signs of anything like they expected, not even one building that resembled anything they saw in Williamsburg. An old church, a wooden structure that housed the Jamestown Rediscovery Project, and some statues. An introduction to Jamestown was shown in the theater, telling the story of the colony from the beginning – May 14, 1607. The importance of the deep water channel, the impact of the Algonquian Indians, Pocahontas and her marriage to John Rolfe, and a myriad of details on how they lived, survived, fought and died.

It was the walking tour that provided even more information as the guide traced the timeline for Jamestown to when it was acquired by the National Park Service in 1924 as part of Colonial National Historic Park. He pointed out the location of battles, where Confederate soldiers built an earth fort, ancient burial grounds, and discoveries made by archeologists as they researched the area in preparation for the Jamestown 2007 celebration marking 400 years since its founding. The story of Pocahontas; the role of tobacco, disease, fire and weather in the ups and downs of the settlement; and the eventual relocation of the state capital from Jamestown to Williamsburg, then Richmond.

A lot of information, but not exactly what Rachel wanted to hear. She waited patiently as others on the tour asked questions of the guide. Finally she and Dan were the only ones remaining.

"Exactly what was the area like years ago – when the Park Service acquired the property?" she asked.

"Pretty much like it is now," replied the guide.

"Are you certain? I mean, were there other buildings – houses, stores, a hospital?"

"No, ma'm. No one's lived here since the mid-1850s when the last family left the area."

She was confused and tried to believe she simply wasn't asking the right questions.

"Here's my problem," she said. "My dad's birth certificate says he was born in Jamestown in 1923 and you're telling me there was no town then. Is that correct?"

"Yes, ma'm."

Giving it one more try, she asked "What if his mother was hiking in the woods and went into labor? What if he was actually born here, just not in a hospital or home?"

"Still impossible" came the reply. "Even if that happened, the birth would be recorded in Williamsburg, the county seat. There haven't been any recorded births in Jamestown since the 1600s."

Dan went to her aid, realizing she was almost speechless and had simply run out of scenarios to explain the birth certificate. He thanked the guide and they went inside to the gift shop. There Rachel purchased a history of Jamestown and several other souvenirs before walking back to the car, turning to take one more look at the landscape.

As they returned to Williamsburg, she could almost hear wheels turning in her head as she tried to put the puzzle together.

"Does this seem strange to you?" she asked Dan.

"Kind of, but there's got to be a logical answer. We just haven't thought of it yet."

The remainder of the afternoon was spent revisiting Williamsburg with plans to check on the adoption records in Richmond the next day. Then they were leaving to visit Dan's sister and her husband, the commander of Andrews Air Force Base outside of Washington, D.C.

Sometime between selecting a tiny outfit for her grandson and Virginia wine for her parents, curiosity finally overcame logic as Rachel decided to make a phone call to the Richmond Courthouse, home to all birth certificates in Virginia. She wanted to make sure they would have access to the records, even though the state's internet site stated records of adoptions that long ago only could be obtained in certain circumstances.

She was nervous dialing the number, even more so as it rang.

"Good afternoon, Bureau of Statistics and Records," came the standard greeting from an operator who certainly sounded friendly and perhaps helpful.

"Yes. I wanted to see if I could obtain a birth certificate for my father," said Rachel.

"And his name," was the quick response.

"He was born Frank Mills in 1923, but…"

Rachel never got the chance to finish the sentence, explaining her father had been adopted by a Texas family.

"Yes, we have it right here. Did you want to pick it up or should we mail it to you?"

Taken by surprise at this turn of events, Rachel confirmed they were talking about the same Frank Mills, a twin with a brother named William Mills, born April 26, 1923. Then she went through the process of taking down information needed to request the certificate by mail: a copy of her driver's license, a check for $15 and a self-addressed stamped return envelope.

She thanked the young lady for her help, then asked one last question. "In the case of adoptions, what process should be followed to determine if records will be made available?'

"Those are confidential and only available to the adopted child. You can call 445-7876 for information on what procedures to follow. Is there anything else we can help you with?"

"No. You've been a great help." Rachel hung up the phone and returned to the dining room where she shared this new information with Dan. Both were intrigued with the turn of events.

"Looks like you need to ask a few questions in Orange," Dan told her.

By the time she arrived back in Texas, Rachel thought through several scenarios that might explain the somewhat strange information she found in Virginia. Each played over and over in her mind, only to simply make no sense.

The drive from the Houston airport to her parents' home in Orange passed quickly as she thought of questions to ask without upsetting her father. He was so protective of the Stark name and simply wasn't interested in anything that would cast a shadow on his father.

She couldn't help but think her grandfather created this situation. "Why" was what she couldn't figure out. Why would a town that didn't exist be listed on a birth certificate filed when a child was 19 years old? Where were the adoption records that should have been attached to the papers filed in 1925?

Between Dayton and Liberty, she remembered it was the same route she often took 20 years earlier when she lived in Humble. The sight of a familiar Dairy Queen brought a smile to Rachel's face as she thought of Clemmie, a woman who had worked for Nita and Lutcher Stark for years, then continued on the payroll until the 1960s when she "retired."

Whenever Clemmie came by their home, it was never dull and stories about the "good ole days" punctuated the conversation for hours at a time. Although photos revealed she was slender and quite attractive in her younger days, Clemmie grew heavier as she aged, with her hair shorter and tightly curled. You would never see her wear purple, she loved anything fried, had a marvelous sense of humor and it was rumored she enjoyed an adult beverage or two on special occasions.

Even as the children became adults, Clemmie was always there to impart wisdom, tell tales or offer unsolicited advice. One of her favorite sayings, "Honey, you ain't lived until you've been a nigger on a Saturday night," always elicited laughter as

Clemmie recalled tales of the Drag Theater and Drag Kitchen that she and her husband, Charlie Rosenthal, operated for years on Second Street. It was the place to be in the 40s and 50s, with acts like Ike and Tina Turner before they gained a national following. Occasionally she would sneak Rachel in upstairs so she could watch from the projection booth, peeking through the opening at the best entertainment in town.

Rachel remembered trips Clemmie made to her home and those of her sisters as each married and had children of her own. It was then they sometimes wondered if Clemmie was perhaps departing from the truth as she started telling them – almost in a whisper – that Lutcher was really their dad's father, that Homer was not adopted.

The statements were not taken seriously, for Homer always responded that Clemmie's memory wasn't what is used to be. And since Clemmie never expanded on her statements when they questioned her, no one gave it much credence.

Rachel did recall that Clemmie accompanied Nita on the trip to pick up Homer and Bill when the adoption was arranged. Now she wished they spent more time talking about the trip, how they traveled, their conversations en route, how Nita reacted when she held those tiny babies in her arms for the first time. But Clemmie was dead, finally passing away three years after Nelda and Eunice offered to pay for a new treatment to cure her arthritis – an electroshock treatment that had nothing to do with arthritis and everything to do with turning the faithful friend into a vegetable-like state where she spent her final days. Clemmie was starting to talk too much, in hindsight a sure sign her days were numbered.

Lost in thought, Rachel missed the exit and had to take the turnaround at the Sabine River and drive back to the Luby's cafeteria on Interstate 10. There she was meeting her parents for a late lunch and the chance to tell them all about her trip.

They were waiting in the foyer, her father anxious to get in line and beat the crowd. At 1:30 in the afternoon, Rachel wasn't sure what crowd he expected but decided to simply kiss them hello and grab a tray.

Somewhere between her chopped steak and chocolate cream pie, after updating them on Dan's family and the trip to Williamsburg, Jamestown finally entered the conversation.

"Daddy, have you ever been to Jamestown?"

"Yeah, about two years ago – drove there the day after the reunion of the USS Richmond crew."

"What did you think?'

"Not much there," he laughed.

"Did that seem odd to you? I mean, didn't you wonder where the buildings were?"

Homer shrugged his shoulders, took another bite of bread pudding, and replied that he just figured it had changed a lot since he was born. But, yes, he thought it strange.

Rachel took a deep breath, then paused before asking one last question.

"Did anyone ever tell you Granddaddy was really your father?"

"Well, you know there were rumors when we came back from the war," Homer said. "But I just figured that's all they were – rumors. If they were true, Dad would have been the first to tell us. And you know, I always figured it didn't make any difference one way or the other. He's my father no matter what."

Friday dawned and Rachel woke early to visit the Orange County Courthouse and locate the missing attachment for her dad and uncle's adoption papers. It was as much a mystery to the young woman in the County Clerk's office. No one seemed to have a clue as to the whereabouts of the document.

As she pulled out of the courthouse parking lot, Rachel realized she was only a few blocks from Nelda's offices and decided to pay her a visit. They had a good relationship, and the older woman always seemed pleased when her granddaughter stopped by.

Entering the Stark offices, Rachel waved to the security guard and said hello to Norma at the reception desk. She knew it was almost 10 o'clock and the entire staff would soon be taking a coffee/Coke break. It was tradition. Right on time, the little bell rang and everyone headed for the kitchen area at the rear of the former bank building. Work came to a complete halt.

Nelda overheard her visiting with Norma and came to her office door, a smile on her face, one hand in the pocket of her jacket and the ever-present cigarette in her right hand. Rachel walked the short distance, gave her grandmother a quick hug and kiss on the cheek, and the two disappeared into her private office.

Although never one to chitchat, Nelda inquired about her granddaughter's trip and patiently listened as Rachel told her about her stay at Andrews Air Force Base and touring the national monuments in Washington, D.C. She kept it short, because her grandmother was not known as a listener and was always more comfortable when she was in control.

Rachel went straight to the point, telling her about the questions surrounding the birth certificate and adoption papers.

"Do you know who Daddy's real father is?" she finally asked, not sure what Nelda's reaction would be.

"Well, you know," began Nelda, "that's a very good question. But one of these days – after I'm gone – you come back and check at the office. They might have some papers you'd like to see."

It was more than Rachel could have hoped for. Not anything definite, but why would Nelda say anything at all if she didn't know something? And why wouldn't she tell her if she knew?

Nelda was 87, but in good health, and Rachel hoped her grandmother would have a change of heart and eventually produce the records she had mentioned. The older woman stood and moved from behind her desk, indicating the conversation was over. Rachel knew the routine and said goodbye, promising to come by the next time she was in town.

Between rumors about the true identity of Homer's biological father and the existing documents, or lack thereof, the trip to Jamestown had simply created a puzzle. A puzzle based on both facts and fiction. Yet one thing was certain: Rachel loved puzzles and the difficulty simply made the challenge even more appealing. Now she just had to find the missing pieces.

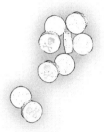

CHAPTER 5

"Oh what a tangled web we weave,
When first we practice to deceive!"
— *Sir Walter Scott*

Where would someone look for answers to Homer and Bill's adoption and the mysterious lives of Nelda and Eunice? There were several possibilities: newspaper clippings, interviews with those who knew the Stark family in the past, the courthouse. The most likely, yet time consuming, would be reviewing the hundreds of thousands of pages copied during the earlier lawsuit regarding Nita's estate.

Rachel recalled the reluctance of Maxwell Shaw, the lawyer who represented both Bill and Homer's families, when the case was over and they asked for the return of the documents. It seemed strange at the time that he even cared what happened to them. Although highly recommended and rated as one of the top lawyers in the United States, he ran up more than $1 million in expenses only to tell them there was no evidence of fraud. Nita had been married to Lutcher for almost 30 years, yet the lawyer said very little of the property they shared was community and her estate was indeed small.

Rachel remembered how impressive Shaw seemed at first, only to wonder a couple of years later why he was so anxious to settle when the families preferred to take their chances in court. Threats he made to make certain no one else would touch the case, plus concerns for Homer's welfare, forced Rachel, Ramona, Rebel and Jake to settle after months of rewording the release to their satisfaction.

Homer and Bill's families split the hefty expense tab presented by Shaw, and both agreed they wanted possession of the copies. After all, the price tag for copies alone was almost $200,000. The lawyers had assured them there was really nothing there, just an incredible amount of detail that included meticulous accounting of every penny spent by the Starks. Rent payments, insurance listings, drug store receipts, ledgers from the early 1900s. They obviously kept exceptional records and there was nothing to indicate Homer and Bill were denied anything that was Nita's.

Apparently, the myriad of boxes contained only a glimpse into the first half of the 20th century. A snapshot of Orange and a way of life that had long since passed. One of these days the families might want to go through them.

As far as Rachel was concerned, one of these days had arrived. Six years had passed since her cousins Bill and Randy irritated Shaw by actually showing up to transfer the documents from his 71st floor office to a rental truck parked below. They made trip after trip on the elevator to eventually take possession of the copies, then drove back to Orange where the boxes had remained undisturbed.

Today, Rachel and her cousins would drive to the storage unit so she could take a few boxes back to College Station and begin reviewing them. Temperatures were warm as they climbed in Randy's pickup truck, renewing conversations that began weeks earlier when the idea of examining the documents first was discussed.

It was good to see her cousins. While Rachel and Randy were only months apart, Bill was two years older. The brothers looked nothing alike. Bill was tall, blonde and slender. Randy was short, dark and not so slender. Both had operated a sports store years ago, but now Bill was in some kind of insurance and Randy was rebounding from bankruptcy. Personalities differed as well, with Bill on the serious side and Randy more the jokester.

The failed lawsuit had been a disappointment, not only with the final results but the manner in which the families were treated during the process. Like outsiders with no rights at all to question motives or actions of Nelda and her willing associates. It seemed strange that Nelda's attorneys, who at first seemed pleased Homer had no intention of joining the lawsuit, actually advised him to participate or his children would receive nothing. He refused, but eventually Nelda persuaded him to assign his interest in his mother's estate to his kids. A year later, shortly after Nelda's attorneys refused requests for her deposition, Nelda quit talking to Homer. The two had since reconciled and their relationship was back to normal. Homer was again a frequent guest in her office and home, and Nelda looked forward to taking Homer and Becky to dinner each week.

If nothing else, Rachel wanted to find out more about life in the Stark family and, like everyone always dreams, write a book. Lutcher and Nelda seemed like a strange couple to her, especially after she had children, then grandchildren, of her own. That was possibly the first indication her grandparents were anything but normal.

From what she had observed, Nelda was the complete opposite of Nita. Bought her clothes at Griffin's menswear, picking up a couple dozen Sansabelt slacks at a time and topping them off with those loose-fitting tropical shirts. Never saw her with a purse, only a man's wallet. Other than the local weather, the only television show she watched was "Murder She Wrote." To the best of her knowledge, Rachel didn't recall Nelda working in a soup kitchen or chairing any fundraiser.

Perhaps by examining the past she would discover some clues to the present. That was her theory anyway. Bill and Randy said they looked through some of the documents years earlier, but had not yet spent any extended time trying to see what was there. One thing they did know for certain was the lengthy index did not match the boxes, something that would make it extremely difficult to find documents in anything close to a timely manner.

The storage units were located on the edge of town and Randy's red truck pulled up to the entrance, allowing him to enter the access code. As the gates swung open, they drove down the first corridor, then took a right to the farthest section. Unit D213 was directly in front of them. The three stepped out of the truck, still talking about the efforts of Shaw to prevent them from taking the copies. Randy worked the combination lock at least half a dozen times, not certain of the final number, then it popped open and he raised the door.

There before them was one fully loaded 10' x 10' storage unit. Floor to ceiling, wall to wall, there were boxes stacked almost solid except for a slight opening in the center near the door. Rachel was surprised at the sight, while Randy and Bill took it in stride. After all, they were the ones who put them there in the first place and recalled in detail how much trouble it had been.

"This is the so-called index," said Randy, crawling over the boxes near the front to reach one stacked about five high. "It doesn't match anything we could find, kind of like they wanted to make it as tough as possible to locate one document or another."

He opened the box and pulled out an extensive listing with box numbers in the righthand column. The problem was that not one box number matched the correct item on the index.

Bill illustrated the point by taking another box, cross-checking it with the index, and showing Rachel there was nothing remotely close to the contents listed for that particular number.

"Kind of makes you wonder what they were up to," said Bill. "They didn't like it at all that we took them, but I just figured we paid for them and they were ours."

Rachel was still amazed at the sight of all those boxes. Somehow she thought they would pick up five or six and it would make a significant dent in the number stored. Never good with distance or size, she had completely underestimated the number of boxes necessary to hold 400,000 documents. At least, that's the number they paid for.

The cousins randomly selected 10 or 12 boxes and loaded them in the back of the pickup, then Randy replaced the lock to secure the unit before climbing back in the cab and heading for Homer's house.

"Looks like you'll be busy for a day or two," Randy joked.

For the next two months, she spent most of her Saturdays sitting next to a box in her garage and carefully trying to catalogue what she found. To date, the ones she examined revealed an interesting variety of items. Some held ledgers from 1917-1921, while others had detailed information on the extensive art collection now housed in the Stark Museum of Art. The most interesting boxes to her, however, contained a number of lawsuits against her grandfather and the wills of Frances Ann Lutcher and Miriam and W. H. Stark.

Written in pencil more than 70 years earlier, the ledgers were hard to read and even more difficult to understand. There were several different companies, apparently all operated by the Stark family. Some names she recognized, others were unfamiliar. The most interesting feature was the handwriting of the entries in the ledger. What beautiful cursive lettering on every page, almost perfect script with no erasures or corrections.

The listing of art was disappointing since it had been a center of controversy during the lawsuit. Apparently none of the impressive art collections were acquired during Lutcher's marriage to Nita, even though Rachel had been told by Clemmie that Nita selected many of the European pieces and encouraged Lutcher to add to the Southwestern selections. Without exception, each page detailing an oil, etching or watercolor included an acquisition date from the 1940s to the mid-1960s. Clearly after Nita's death in 1939.

The wills and lawsuits were fascinating, painting a picture of her grandfather quite different from the one her father had drawn since she was old enough to remember. While Homer always talked so highly of his dad, never even hinting of a dark side, the documents in Box 23C and 34A were not exactly complimentary. Homer's version of the modest, astute businessman who dedicated his life to education and improving the quality of life for those less fortunate wasn't all that Rachel discovered as she meticulously went through page after page in each box. There she found a man being sued by his own cousins, not just once but on several occasions. It was difficult to comprehend that her grandfather could possibly have done what they claimed, but she eventually came to believe he had.

As executor and primary beneficiary of Frances Ann Lutcher's estate, he may have pretty much cheated the Brown family out of significant assets. A document pre-dating his grandmother's death by five years was filed after she died, stipulating the sale of more than 140,000 acres – 300 square miles – of property in East Texas to Lutcher for $1 and other consideration. Rachel noted that signatures of all witnesses on the sale document were on Lutcher Stark's payroll. Another claim questioned Lutcher's refusal to pay a one million dollar bequest from his grandmother's estate to Carrie Brown, the younger sister of Lutcher's mother. There were other suits, seemingly justified, and totally at odds with the character and qualities Homer so admired of his father.

The wills were a window into Lutcher Stark's world. There he made his fortune, not by actions or decisions as a businessman. Her grandfather actually inherited the vast majority of his wealth rather than earned it through his business acumen, and Rachel wasn't certain he had even done that honestly. As executor and primary beneficiary of the estates left first by his grandmother and then his parents, Lutcher Stark ended up with at least 75 percent of the fortune originally created by his grandparents.

Rachel thought of Edgar Brown, the "other rich man" in Orange, and her grandfather's first cousin. She often saw Mr. Brown when she accompanied her dad to work. "Linden," the Brown yacht, and Colonel Byrd's "Silver Moon" were the largest boats in Orange, impressive in any setting – even more-so when compared to others docked at the Sabine Yacht Basin. When she questioned why her grandfather and Mr. Brown did not get along, Homer said he thought they had a misunderstanding or "something like that." Now she knew.

The wills reflected a side to Lutcher Stark that Rachel had neither seen or suspected. She always thought how wonderful her grandfather was, how much he did for the community. Lutcher Stark High School was his namesake, leading one to believe he must have done something to be recognized in that manner.

Yet here in W. H. Stark's will was a simple bequest to three elderly women – $30 and $125 each to two of his sisters, a third payment of $25 to his brother's widow – to be made on a monthly basis for the remainder of their lives. Attached to the will was an interoffice memo indicating one of the sisters had died and Lutcher was now questioning his tax liability if he made payments to the two remaining women, now 75 and 80 years of age. Rachel read the memo a second time, especially the part about the women depending on the money and her grandfather's reluctance to provide for them. It was hard to believe this was the Lutcher Stark she thought she knew. W. H. Stark left more than enough money to cover the small monthly checks, but his son justified depriving them of the monthly stipend because of estate taxes. Rachel noted Lutcher drafted the memo shortly after his father's death, taking care of business while his mother was grieving from a broken heart. She died unexpectedly and was buried only six weeks after her husband's death.

The final box contained ledgers, nothing more. After a cursory review, Rachel placed it next to the others and took a moment to look through her notes. Interesting, if nothing else. Maxwell Shaw was right about these boxes. There certainly appeared to be no fraud involving Nita's estate. In fact, there was nothing about Nita in any of the boxes. But it was a start, and lots more boxes were waiting in Orange.

The call came around six in the morning. Nelda had been taken to Diagnostic Hospital in Houston, apparently complaining of stomach pains and related aches. Homer said she was resting comfortably and they would be running tests for the next few days.

It was August and Rachel was only a few months from retirement after 30 years in the Texas public schools. With 63 sick days at her disposal, she offered to stay with her grandmother in the hospital, but Eunice politely declined. As the days extended into the following week, however, Eunice was anxious for a break and accepted an offer from Becky to stay with Nelda for a couple of nights. Homer provided the transportation, driving Becky to the hospital and spending an hour or so visiting with Nelda, then returning to Orange with Eunice. The trip was uneventful, but Homer was not pleased to see Margaret Sadler, a close friend of Eunice's, waiting on the porch as they drove up. He was uncomfortable around them and thought it disrespectful of the relationship Nelda and Eunice had maintained for years.

Less than 48 hours later, Homer returned Eunice to Houston and drove Becky home. Nelda was improving and expected to be released by the end of the week.

"Miss Nelda seemed to be feeling much better," Becky told her husband. "She was actually glad I was there, and we had a good time visiting with each other. Did you know she was the only girl in the boys band your dad sponsored?"

"How can a girl be in a boys band?"

"I have no idea, but she was. In a way, I felt sorry for her. Even though I don't really understand her... uh, lifestyle, it couldn't have been easy growing up that way. Not in Orange, Texas."

"Did the doctors figure out what was wrong?"

"Whatever it is, Dr. Gregory seems to think medication will take care of it," said Becky, "but he's concerned Eunice is not administering the medication properly. Said the best medicine for Nelda was to see more of us. I'm glad she won't need surgery because that would scare her to death. Wouldn't surprise me if she was back in the office next week."

The remainder of the trip was filled with observations Becky had made during her hospital stay with Nelda. She told Homer of several visitors who came to see Nelda, with most of them the subjects of unkind comments upon their departure. It was actually entertaining, she said, to listen to Nelda's impressions of the individuals or couples who stopped by the room.

"I don't think she liked any of them. In fact, I know she didn't. All she talked about was what they wanted from her, or thought they should have. One couple...not sure who they were, but they had an Eastern accent and seemed to have known her from years ago... upset Miss Nelda the most. They asked about buying some art they admired when they were in Orange, even wanted to purchase Roslyn Ranch at a discount. Can you believe that?"

"What did she say?"

"She told them she wasn't dead yet," laughed Becky. "Then she seemed to take particular delight in telling them she had given the ranch to you."

Homer smiled. Miss Nelda really meant well, and he did appreciate her gift of the ranch. Now if her office would just take care of transferring title to him so they could drive up next year and enjoy the place. He was looking forward to spending the summer there and having his kids and grandchildren enjoy his favorite spot in the world.

CHAPTER 6

*"One who condones evil is just as guilty
as the one who perpetuates it."*
— *Martin Luther King, Jr.*

It was a cold day in Texas when they buried Nelda. Normally moderate weather in December was near freezing with brisk winds underscoring the need for a coat.

Visitation the previous night had been strange. No one really knew who was to receive condolences. The lesbian lover, the stepson, or the cronies who had aided and abetted Nelda's activities all these years.

Eunice's "friend" came dressed in some of Nelda's clothes. A retired accountant who had been closely acquainted with Eunice for more than 30 years, Margaret Sadler was the subject of many arguments between Nelda and Eunice. Homer's family marveled as she worked the crowd, seemingly impressed with her elevated status now that Nelda was out of the picture.

The funeral services planned by Eunice were not at all what Nelda would have preferred. The casket was open during visitation, not closed. Graveside rites were public, not private. Most noticeable of all was how Eunice surrounded herself in the funeral home's family room with members of the Bencken-stein clan, her late husband's relatives – a group that was never welcome at Nelda's home. They turned a somber affair into a family reunion, talking and laughing while "mourners" filled the pews.

Flowers lined the chapel walls, prompting a smile from Homer and Becky who were aware of Nelda's dislike of most arrangements. Only the color green interested Nelda, and was reflected in the lack of blooming plants or seasonal displays of color at any of the properties she owned.

Local television reporters and a photographer from the Orange newspaper jockeyed for position at the funeral of the richest person in town. Controlling a billion dollar fortune while keeping the lowest of profiles and making minimal effort to give back to the community, she was considered by many as perhaps the meanest person in Orange. That helped to explain the lack of sincerity and display of grief by anyone attending, even Eunice who rather enjoyed the spotlight.

It was an interesting group. Most were on the Stark payroll and a few others kept an eye on the casket, almost like they half expected it to open. An elderly woman on the front row ap-peared quite pleased that her trip from Houston was worth the effort. She had not seen Nelda since 1935, the day her younger brother died of a ruptured appendix on the hospital steps when Nelda, the hospital administrator, refused admittance since the family had no money. Seeing was believing, and Nelda was definitely dead.

No emotion. No tears. No fond farewells. And certainly no stories of warmth, humor or kindness were repeated by the presiding minister, a young man who never met Nelda, yet stood in front of the packed chapel and struggled to come up with something acceptable. What he failed to grasp was that no one really cared. Most of those seated in front of him were employees more concerned with their jobs than Nelda's destiny.

The 77-year old Homer Stark, quite possibly her only true friend, had the best reason to celebrate her death but was instead saddened and almost felt sorry for her. She apologized to him only a year earlier "for all the wrongs she had done him," but Homer was gracious and accepted her word that she would keep her promise to set things straight.

Departing for the graveside service at Evergreen, Homer kept turning around as if looking for something. Eventually he smiled and admitted to Becky he was almost certain a Brink's truck would follow her casket. If anyone had figured out a way to take it with you, Nelda would be the one.

Most gathered at the cemetery stood back from the seated area under the green tent, but a young woman who arrived late leaned her bicycle against a headstone near the burial site, took an empty seat on the back row, and seemed quite comfortable until she was escorted away. Graveside services were brief, and Nelda would be interred in the Childers family plot between Ruby and their mother. It was less than 50 yards from the Stark mausoleum, or "a good chip shot away" according to Homer. Eunice once again sought to be the main attraction as she reigned over the site from the front row, constantly looking at her watch as if she was being inconvenienced.

As he sat quietly listening to the preacher comment on the weather, the town, the future, Homer could not help wondering about stories he had been told since Nelda's death four days earlier. He glanced at Eunice, thinking how inappropriate it was to have Walter Riedel bring Margaret to the hospital in Houston only hours after Nelda died. He recalled the many tales he had heard since Monday. Stories that remained dormant for decades finally emerged as employees, neighbors, former classmates, nurses and others he didn't even know had something to share with him.

The first call came from Charles Kinney, a retired Stark Museum guard who operated a kennel often used to board Bullet, Homer and Becky's golden retriever, when they went to visit the grandchildren. An Army veteran with two Purple Hearts, Kinney had served his country as well as the Stark Foundation, but occasionally made comments to Homer indicating there was more going on than most people suspected.

When *The Orange Leader* published a tribute to Nelda on the afternoon she died, it was more than Kinney could stomach and he immediately placed a call to Homer. Years of service at the museum gave him a front row seat during the lawsuit over Nita's estate. The story he told Homer included everything from changing data on records of items now held by the Foundation to an almost surreal effort to hide computer discs by moving them from one location to another. All in an effort to evade the law, or at least the petition for discovery.

Conversations with Anna Jean Cathey, the records registrar for the museum, gleaned valuable information as Kinney learned the movement of items was deliberate and intended to keep Homer and Bill from discovering the truth. Acquisition dates were altered from the original to reflect dates following Lutcher's marriage to Nelda, while the true information was hidden from Pandwick Services, the company hired to copy information produced by the Stark Foundation for the lawsuit.

"It's just a travesty what that woman has done to your family," Kinney told Homer. "And I'm not the only one who knows it. Clay Newberry will tell you the same thing. He was assistant chief of security and Nelda fired him when she thought he told someone what was going on."

A foundation employee and a servant in Nelda's home called as well, offering to help but knowing their jobs would be eliminated should they be found out.* The information they provided gave Homer an insight into just how badly Nelda had been treated in her final days by Eunice.

It was almost like a rush on confession, with calls coming from across Texas and as far away as Florida. Somehow they felt better telling him what they had learned or witnessed years before. Nelda was gone. She could no longer threaten, intimidate, blackmail or harm anyone. But there was always Eunice.

Speaking of Eunice, he noticed she didn't even linger at the gravesite but walked directly to the limo. The Benckenstein family was coming to her home after the service. She took a sudden turn and walked in Homer's direction, pausing to invite him and Becky, Jake and Rachel, to come by her house for refreshments.

Other than curiosity, there was no reason to go. Becky said they should stop by because it was the right thing to do. From the moment they arrived at Eunice's front door to their departure about 20 minutes later, no one mentioned Nelda's name. No one seemed unhappy or even sentimental; in fact, they seemed quite the opposite. A total stranger wandering in would have thought a celebration was going on rather than people paying their respects upon the death of a loved one.

In the house, shadows appeared on the wall where beautiful oil paintings once hung. Originally on loan to Eunice when Lutcher was alive, sometime after his death they became permanent fixtures in the living area and now were nowhere in sight. Possibly among those items crated and shipped to her native Oklahoma in recent years.

Eunice was the perfect hostess, making sure each of her guests tried the cajun chicken or saved a spot for one of several desserts. A nurse from Galveston was sitting quietly on the ottoman in the living room, not quite sure how to describe the scene she witnessed. She liked Nelda and was offended that no one seemed concerned about the deceased.

As Homer and Becky waited in the car for Jake to rescue Rachel from a rather lengthy conversation with Peter Benckenstein, Walter Riedel arrived. The man who had worked for Nelda since the 70s and advanced to become one of her key advisers seemed a little rattled and uncomfortable around Homer, saying little and heading for the front door to join the group inside.

It took Homer by surprise, for he had rather enjoyed his many visits with Walter when he came by to see Nelda, then later when she was ill and he had coffee with Walter to talk about how things were going in general and the transfer of the Roslyn Ranch to Homer in particular. Although Walter always seemed nervous, afraid he would make a decision only to have Nelda return to the office and turn her temper in his direction, Homer thought Walter was competent and trustworthy. Becky, on the other hand, would remind him of how often Nelda wanted to fire Walter, only to have Eunice remind her she couldn't fire "that boy down the hall" since "he knows too much about our business."

Homer and his family returned home, took a few more phone calls and had a couple of longtime friends stop by to express their condolences, then follow with a less than positive story about Nelda and/or Eunice. A woman who claimed to be an acquaintance of Nelda's at Texas State College for Women (now TWU) called from Florida to make certain the "witch was dead." Several other calls came that evening, each expressing a universal sentiment that the world was a much better place.

The following morning, a newspaper headline in *The Orange Leader* revealed why Walter appeared nervous. He lied. Rather than tell Homer the truth, he simply told him the will would not be read until the following week. In reality, Walter had actually filed the document at the courthouse between the services and Eunice's party.

There it was in black and white, a banner headline on the front page: Nelda had died and Homer would receive $1 million. Although he was grateful for the gift, once again he was being treated as an outsider and not extended the courtesies one would expect for a family member. Eunice and Walter were left the house, its furnishings and jewelry. The Foundation would receive more than 99 percent of her wealth, but you would not know that unless you read deep into the story. Again the estate was undervalued. A Stark tradition since 1924 designed to keep the public from knowing the immense wealth hidden behind the office walls. No one would guess Nelda left an estate valued at more than $500 million.

The Roslyn Ranch wasn't mentioned, but no one at Homer's house expected it to be in the will. She had given it to him

18 months earlier, yet Walter failed to transfer the property. He assured Homer it would eventually be straightened out.

The phone rang and Becky heard Homer talking to what appeared to be Eunice, judging from the conversation. She could hear him thanking her for the invitation, but explaining the jazz group he wanted to hear at the theater was not on the schedule until the following month.

"Well, I'm not sure she can go, but I'll get her for you," said Homer, calling Rachel to the phone.

Facial expressions were priceless as his daughter entered the room. Homer was grinning, quite proud of himself for getting out of the invitation. Becky was in agreement. The last thing she wanted to do was act normal around Eunice. Jake was glad his dad had suggested Rachel, for Lord knows he had no interest in going anywhere with Eunice. Rachel was clearly not happy to be the chosen one.

"Hello," said Rachel, pretending she had no idea who was on the line, then acting surprised when Eunice invited her to the evening's performance at the Lutcher Theater. Although she planned to return home that afternoon, Rachel decided to stay and see for herself how Eunice mourned her grandmother.

"It's a southwestern music concert and I know you'll enjoy it," said Eunice, adding that she would be by at 6:45 to pick her up and making it clear not to be late. Rachel thanked her and hung up, now almost looking forward to the prospect of accompanying Eunice and two of her friends to the theater.

At 6:35, ten minutes early, Eunice came by. Luckily, Rachel was ready and the foursome headed to the theater and arrived at the theater parking lot five minutes later. The concert didn't start until 7:30 and there was plenty of time to get to their seats. Certainly no crowds that early in the evening.

She had never been to the Lutcher Theater, so Rachel took time to pay attention to the details of a facility that had literally been built twice in less than 15 years at costs exceeding $20 million. Something about the construction, the marble, the flaws in the design. As she glanced at the program, Rachel realized it was not a southwestern concert, but a holiday program featuring a children's choir from neighboring Beaumont and two soloists with remote ties to the area.

According to Eunice, their seats were among those on the row Nelda purchased each year. Rachel remembered a bank employee who told her unused tickets were often given away by Nelda's office, but with the understanding no Blacks would be allowed to use them. She found the statement easy to believe, especially since Nelda had angrily refused to give Texas Woman's University "one red cent" after they named an African American to serve as President of her alma mater. A promise she kept until the day she died.

On the way to the theater, Rachel overheard Olivia Mayfield ask Eunice about a tribute to Nelda planned that evening. At least they would acknowledge her grandmother's contributions, but as the performance began Rachel could distinguish no moment of silence, no appropriate remarks commenting on the death of Nelda Stark, nothing that even resembled memorializing her grandmother.

The entire evening was uneventful, although Rachel had never seen Eunice move as fast as when the audience gave the performers a standing ovation. Before she realized it, the three older women had taken advantage of the clear aisles and were making a quick exit. Up the aisle, across the foyer, down the stairs and out the door. Rachel followed, but was amused to see the car already moving in reverse as she tried to open the back door.

As they dropped her off at Homer and Becky's house, Rachel thanked Eunice and walked toward the garage. She turned and watched the car as it backed over the lawn, a sure sign driving in reverse at night was not often done by the occupants. But she also thought about all the questions that had been asked in recent days, questions that seemed to raise the same issues that surfaced eight years earlier in the lawsuit. She could almost hear Bob Dylan singing words from one of her favorite songs from the 60s, "Something's happening here; what it is ain't exactly clear."

Morning brought a phone call from Walter, asking if he could stop by to see Homer for a few minutes. He had something for him.

"Sure, Walter. Come on over. We're always glad to see you," said Homer, thinking perhaps Walter had just been under too much pressure the last few months. Surely that was the explanation for his behavior in recent days.

In less than 10 minutes, Walter rang the doorbell and Becky ushered him into the living room while Homer finished getting dressed. They talked about routine topics like the weather or holiday plans, never mentioning Nelda's funeral or will.

"Walter, how in the world are you?" asked Homer, extending his hand and welcoming the visitor to his home. "How about some coffee?"

"Coffee would be great, black – no sugar or cream."

The two men walked into the kitchen, Walter trailing Homer and appearing a bit nervous. You could usually tell from his habit of constantly adjusting his glasses. Becky offered a kolache, but Homer was the lone taker as the three took a seat at the kitchen table.

"Know you are busy, but we were going through a storage area in the office yesterday and found some things about your mother that you might be interested in."

Walter continued with the story, explaining he had no idea Nita had been so active in the community or the state. He described a large number of press clippings, magazine articles, family photos, letters and other documents that Homer might find interesting, and Walter offered to let Homer go through them in the near future.

"All the years I worked for Mrs. Stark, I never really knew much about Nita. I think you'd enjoy seeing them." He then produced a large silver pitcher engraved with Nita Hill Stark, the 1925 champion of a putting tournament in Somerset, Maine.

"Also thought you might like to have this," offering the silver trophy to Homer. It was a nice gesture on Walter's part and one that struck a sentimental chord with Homer as he grasped his mother's treasure.

"Really appreciate it, Walter. I had no idea it was down there... and I'd love a chance to see the pictures. Somewhere along the line, I guess I just figured everything about my mother was thrown away."

Walter assured him there was lots to see, even offering to let Rebecca review the materials so she would have a better understanding of Nita for the family history she was writing.

As he stood to leave, Becky walked over and gave him a hug to thank him for the gift. Homer set the trophy aside and walked him to the car, only to return minutes later with a satisfied look that underlined his faith in Walter.

"You know, Becky, I don't know why Miss Nelda didn't like that man. I think he's going to do the right thing now that she's gone. He even asked me if Rachel would like to join him next month for a scholarship dinner in College Station. First time I can recall a family member actually representing the Foundation."

Five weeks passed and Rachel had indeed received an invitation from Walter to attend the dinner recognizing UIL scholarship recipients at Texas A&M. It was scheduled that evening, but she still wasn't sure she should go. She had seen Walter twice since he visited her father, and each time he appeared sincere. Yet she had developed strong suspicions about him when he refused to let her see Nita's papers and photographs – saying "the lawyers needed to wait until everything was appraised." How ridiculous.

Her second trip to the office was to see Eunice about one of Nelda's handkerchiefs. Rachel's youngest son, Patrick, was getting married a week later on February 19, her grandmother's birthday, and Eunice had offered to give one to the bride as something old. It was a nice gesture and Rachel promised to come by and pick it up when she was in town.

As she waited for Eunice in the outer office area, Rachel visited with the receptionist and was surprised to hear almost every word of the phone conversation Eunice was having with Peter Benckenstein. It seemed unusual that they were discussing a lawsuit that ended almost 10 years earlier, why Nelda put Homer's son on the Foundation Board, and the fact that no one had proven any fraud.

Typical of the hearing impaired, Eunice spoke loudly and anyone within the open office area could hear every word. So much so that Walter suddenly appeared and looked extremely nervous, trying to engage Rachel in conversation so she wouldn't hear what was being said. He excused himself and went to "tell" Miss B that Rachel was waiting. The conversation with Peter came to an abrupt end, and Eunice appeared from her office and walking fast, as was her nature, toward Rachel.

"My goodness, Rachel. I do apologize for keeping you – and also for forgetting to bring the handkerchief. Do you want to follow me over to Nelda's and we'll get one for you?"

Rachel followed Eunice in her car the four blocks to Nelda's home. While Walter inherited the house, Eunice was given all of the contents –including handkerchiefs.

It seemed almost strange to enter her grandmother's home for the first time since Nelda died. Other than a few boxes in the porch area, little had been touched. Rather than staying on the ground floor, Rachel was motioned to the second level by a maid who indicated Eunice had already gone upstairs.

She was 54 years old and had never been on the second floor of her grandmother's house. All she ever saw was the stairway and had no idea what was really up there. Nelda had told her stories of skating in the attic after her father floored it, but it was hard to picture her grandmother doing anything fun.

Yet as she reached the top of the stairs, sprawled before her was an indoor skating rink. Rachel smiled, thinking how much fun it would have been to use it when she was growing up. She could almost picture Nelda skating at top speed as a young girl, circling the room over and over or playing a form of indoor street hockey with the neighborhood kids.

Eunice called her name and Rachel saw her yards away going through an old chest, one of two that were stored there along with a small number of older pieces of furniture that had seen better days. One chest was Nelda's, the other belonged to Ruby. Each had not only pieces of fabric, napkins, and clothing, but handmade cards and self portraits probably made as gifts for Mr. and Mrs. Childers.

As Eunice concentrated on searching through the contents of the chest, an enclosed room added in the attic caught Rachel's eye. She wandered toward it and peeked in, only to find a large cedar closet that seemed bigger than the downstairs living area. There she found her grandfather's clothing, from suits and sport coats to hats and the wonderful collection of bow ties he often wore. As if he still lived there and not one hanger had moved from its position. Along the other walls, and on shelving in the middle of the room, were items such as framed photographs, western ties, souvenirs from towns in New Mexico and Colorado, luggage and a hundred other memories from happier times.

"Rachel, how is this?"

Eunice appeared behind her with a napkin, possibly thinking Rachel would not be able to tell the difference in the fabric weight. She was wrong, as Rachel asked if they could find one that was lighter. Both searched the trunk, but there were only napkins and Christmas towels.

"The napkin will do just fine, Miss Eunice. And I do appreciate your willingness to let us have it."

"Happy to help, dear. When we have time, I want you to come back and we'll pick out a piece of silver for each of the kids – yours, Ramona's and Rebel's. They should have a piece of the family silver."

It was a gracious offer and Rebecca was truly surprised. Eunice had never been one to give away anything of value, and she wouldn't this time either. She thanked her and headed to her parent's home, anxious to tell them about the second floor discoveries and the phone conversation between Peter and Eunice.

Finally deciding she should join Walter, if for no other reason than to observe, Rachel arrived at the Texas A&M Student Rec Center at straight up 6 o'clock, hurrying from the parking lot to avoid being too late. No one noticed she was slightly tardy as other guests were still arriving and no formal program had started. Student honorees and sponsors of the various scholarships were visiting throughout the large banquet room, with University Interscholastic League officials from Austin mixed in the conversations.

Walter spotted her and moved quickly to welcome her and make the introductions to the Stark scholars and other sponsors with whom he was acquainted. It was a casual affair, befitting the barbeque on the menu. Everything went well and Rachel enjoyed the opportunity to visit with the students, taking an interest in the program as introductions of each student were made along with hometown, major field of study, ties to UIL events.

When the program ended, she thanked Walter for his invitation and wished him a safe trip back to Orange. He asked her to wait a moment and walk out with him. It was only a short distance to the parking lot and Walter's car was near the front, only two cars away from the sidewalk. As Rachel said goodbye, Walter struck up a conversation in the parking lot that would last more than two hours – from 8 o'clock to almost 10:30.

"Rachel, is your dad mad at me?"

It was the farthest thing from her mind, especially since Homer rarely was mad at anyone.

"Mad? Not to my knowledge. Whatever makes you say something like that?"

"Well, I'd heard he was upset with me about the ranch… that it wasn't in the will."

"Walter, we never expected it to be in the will. She gave it to him before she even became sick. You were supposed to take care of it, but for whatever reason you didn't get it done. But Daddy's not mad, just frustrated."

He explained how the lawyers were trying to figure out a way to get the Colorado ranch to Homer, one he had been promised on several occasions but as recently as the year before she died. Rachel asked about a recent case in Montana, one where the judge awarded a ranch to Charles Kuralt's mistress even though it wasn't in the will. Intent counted for something farther north.

One topic led to another: Stark family history, the future of the Foundation, rumors about untimely deaths and illnesses, Shangri La, the last lawsuit. It proved to be an interesting combination of subjects, especially considering Walter was the one bringing up most of them. As they discussed the number of homosexuals on the payroll or doing business with Nelda, Rachel couldn't resist asking Walter if he, too, was gay.

The accountant clutched his chest and fell back on his black Ford Expedition, which saved him from suffering a direct hit on the pavement. "Oh, no, not me," said Walter. "Not everyone in Orange goes that way."

Regaining his composure, Walter talked at length about the unsettling information coming out since Nelda's death.

"There's just so much that was done wrong, but we're going to straighten it out. You can count on that. We'll find a way to get that ranch to your dad."

"He would appreciate that very much," said Rachel. "The only thing he wanted was the ranch and a chance to run the Foundation so it would really make a difference in Orange. He's never been after the money."

"I know. Before she died, Miss Nelda discussed plans with me to add more family members to the Board. That should be easy enough to do."

"Daddy would like that very much, Walter. You know, of all the things they did to him, the worst thing they ever did was take him off the Foundation Board. It was his connection with the family..."

"Rachel," Walter interrupted. "That meeting never happened."

"What do you mean, never happened? You seconded the motion."

"No. It never took place. I didn't realize until I was reviewing the minutes this month to prepare for the Annual Meeting that they had done that. We were just told he resigned."

Standing in the middle of the Aggie student rec center parking lot, with people walking by throughout the entire conversation, seemed like a rather unusual place to learn of the power play that removed her father from the Board. Only a few days earlier, Rachel had reviewed the notification letter sent to Homer years ago, complete with the official minutes detailing the motion and who made it. A letter from the Attorney General's office citing a conflict of interest was attached, along with minutes signed by Clyde McKee and Eunice Benckenstein. It proved so upsetting to her dad that she kept the letter in the small fireproof safe in her home, where it remained since he first gave it to her. They had agreed to put it aside for the moment, only to revisit it if her dad asked.

Rachel had taken note of Walter's body language. He did a lot of lying that evening, especially when he talked about the future. It was almost as if the entire conversation was designed to bait her and see what Homer's family was thinking. Yet she was quite comfortable with the results. She watched when Walter responded to questions to see if he looked to the right – often when someone is simply recalling facts, as opposed to the left – an indicator he was lying. Seems like he spent a lot of time that evening looking left.

When she commented on removal of her dad from the Board, it apparently caught him offguard as he looked directly at her and responded without hesitation. He was telling the truth about the non-meeting. Why in the world would he ever make up something like that?

When Homer refused to join any lawsuit against his father, why would lawyers for Nelda and the Stark Foundation advise him to transfer his interests to his children, then use those actions to remove him from the Board two years later. And then lie about it. Knowing Homer was not a party to the lawsuit, and that his children were involved only at the suggestion of

Nelda's own attorneys, why did the Attorney General's office contend it was a conflict of interest? And if by some stretch of the imagination it truly was a conflict, why did they reelect him to the Board during the lawsuit, only to remove him after it was settled?

What were they trying to hide? It was time to look at some more of the boxes. And probably get a lawyer.

Both employees no longer work for the Foundation.

CHAPTER 7

*"Study the past if you would
define the future."*

— *Confucius*

Lawyers. Not exactly high on Rachel's list of respected professionals. Probably not even on the list, now that she thought about it. Somehow her son Patrick was one of them and she recalled the day he broke the news to her that he wanted to be an attorney.

"If that's what you want to do, it's fine with me."

Patrick was taken back by her response, fully expecting a lecture or expression of disbelief. He knew his mother well and she had passionate feelings about the legal profession, especially after Knox and Henderson, supposedly among the best in the business, had taken advantage of her father earlier in the lawsuit to straighten out Nita's estate.

But she surprised him and took it graciously, telling him "it would be nice to know there was at least one honest lawyer in the world."

He was only one year out of law school, but she needed to talk to someone, just in case things did not work out as Walter led her to believe. Perhaps Patrick could recommend a lawyer to advise them.

She left a phone message, asking him to suggest someone to help them sort things out, but mentioned she would be out of town for a few days. If he needed her, she'd be in Orange going through boxes.

It was an uneventful trip despite Memorial Day traffic, with Travis – her small dog – sleeping most of the way and reacting with customary excitement as the car slowed to exit at 16th Street. They had made this drive countless times, with the dog seemingly knowing to the minute how long it took to travel the distance from College Station.

Randy was sitting outside with Homer, trying in vain to feed the squirrels and doves only to see them scatter with the sound of the approaching car. They were awaiting Rachel's arrival to update her on activities of the last several weeks. Although they talked daily after the boxes were moved from the storage shed to Aunt Ida Marie's home, Rachel was anxious to see for herself what her cousins had found.

"Hey, cuz, did you have to scare all the birds away?" Randy said in a teasing and good natured manner. Only three months apart in age, they remained close over the years and seemed to enjoy the rare occasions when they saw each other.

"Surely feeding birds is not the highlight of your day," said Rachel. "Thought you'd be glad to see me."

"I am. Just had to give you a hard time. Uncle Homer's keeping me busy supplying him with pecans and birdseed, so I'm actually looking forward to doing some work."

"Whoa. Wish I had a tape recorder to play that one back," said Homer. "Don't hear Randy talk too much about working."

"Certainly would cause heads to turn, but give me a few minutes and I'll get him started on our little project," countered Rachel. "Then you can get back to your computer or the television while we check out some of those family stories we're hearing about."

She walked down the driveway to retrieve Travis, then disappeared in the house to leave her suitcase and tell her mother hello before leaving for her aunt's home. Ever since Nelda's death, it seemed like each day brought something unusual to consider as people and paperwork led to new discoveries of old issues. Somehow she thought these boxes would add to that list.

Homer laughed as Rachel tried to climb into Randy's red pickup truck as the oversize tires elevated the chassis far out of her normal reach. The only thing more comical was Randy trying to get in. He was the same height as his cousin, but there was more pressure on him to step up gracefully, or at least like he'd done it before.

Headed north on Highway 87, it was only a short distance to Aunt Ida Marie's home. One left turn on the dirt road that circled in front of the house and they were there. A beautiful contemporary home built 30 years earlier when Uncle Bill was still alive, it backed up to a small lake that provided a relaxing backdrop from any room across the rear of the site. Randy and Rachel went in through the side door near the kitchen, but there was no sign of her aunt or cousins. A small guest room on the left had taken on the appearance of a remote storage area with several of the boxes stacked along the floor next to the twin beds. Folders were neatly stacked along the top of a dresser.

They cut through a sitting area adjoining the back porch and turned right toward the bedroom area, but not without noticing several dozen boxes placed four or five high against the wall lining the hallway. By now, they could hear voices and sounds of a copy machine followed. There in front of Rachel was a large bedroom converted to a work area. A king size bed had file folders in separate stacks, more boxes lined either side of two walls, and an open closet door revealed even more documents organized on shelves and in file cabinets that filled one long wall. The copy machine and a fax topped a makeshift table converted out of even more boxes.

Rachel was impressed with the amount of effort and work that had obviously gone into transferring hundreds of thousands of documents into this showplace of a home to actually see what secrets they might hold. A voice from across the room called her name, but she almost didn't see Linda. Her youngest cousin was sprawled on the floor near the window, carefully going through papers in a box marked "Correspondence: Stark Library at UT." At almost the same moment, Ida Marie stepped out of the closet and flashed a smile upon seeing her niece. Bill entered from an adjacent room and could not resist teasing Rebecca.

"So, you finally showed up to help. Lord knows we can use it."

"Can you believe all these papers?" asked Rachel. "Where in the world do you start?"

"Doesn't really matter," replied her aunt. "The index they gave us is useless – even the contents listed on the box aren't even close to accurate. The kids have been going through them and marking the outside with what they really contain."

It was a true group effort as each tackled a box, patiently reviewing the contents to uncover any clues which might support the rumors circulating around town. To date, there had been some rather interesting items but nothing directly related to Nita's estate. Two boxes were filled with drug store receipts, noting every carton of cigarettes, tissue or candy purchased for more than 30 years. Another held an assortment of receipts: caddy fees at the country club; lawn care for the property in Austin; groceries in Colorado; Rotary Club dues; assorted nails and screws for the office.

Hundreds of pages listing Miriam Stark's book collection and its donation to the University of Texas were interesting to read, not only for the sheer volume and value of the items, but the correspondence between Nita and the University librarian at Texas as plans were made to properly display the books in a special library housed in the Tower. Every detail seemed to be worked out by Nita, from the purchase of furniture, rugs and lamps, to the selection of drapes and placement of outdoor benches and chairs for those who chose to take advantage of pleasant weather on an adjacent patio.

Assorted pieces of correspondence – from different decades and on a variety of topics – seemed strangely out of place in one box. Yet they yielded some of the more interesting subjects. Letters offering football tickets to the IRS regional director; memos listing priceless art loaned to Eunice for display in her home; handwritten letters from H. J. Lutcher to his wife as he spent weeks at a time in Louisiana; receipts from John Sealy Hospital when Nelda was hospitalized in 1958 with cancer;

correspondence from one Stark employee to the accounting department indicating a judge had been placed on the payroll, complete with rent and phone, in return for "his looking the other way."

As afternoon became evening, hardly anyone noticed. They were too busy reading and sharing the more interesting items with each other. Rachel thought it was almost like eating Cracker Jack – the caramel popcorn treat so popular when they were younger – promising a surprise in every box. Eventually, they had to stop for the night and Rachel promised to return early the next morning.

With orange juice, coffee and kolaches in abundance, they were off to a fresh start. Same room. Same routine as the day before. Today they would focus on several boxes containing files of fine art sorted by artist. They were similar in format to files found in the boxes at Rachel's house, but covered different artists. Each profile detailed the item number, artist, subject, condition, price, date of acquisition, framing, and special notations when necessary. From western art and the Old Masters to valuable rugs and Indian artifacts, there was a listing for each item to trace its way into the Stark family.

Ida Marie interrupted their work at noon to insist they break for lunch. None of them realized hours had passed since they arrived and a hot meal and iced tea sounded attractive to anyone who had downed nothing but donuts and candy bars for most of the morning. They stood and stretched before moving into the kitchen area, but Randy and Rachel took a few moments to walk outside if for no other reason than to enjoy the sunshine and a light breeze coming off the water.

"What do you think?" Randy asked Rachel.

"Kind of early, but have you noticed anything kind of strange?"

"Strange in what way?"

"Well, actually there could be any number of things, but the strangest is not what we've seen, but what we haven't seen."

"I don't understand. What do you mean what we haven't seen?"

Rachel leaned on the railing along the short pier, looking into the distance, before responding.

"Have you seen much of anything about property Nita owned? I mean, jewelry, art, checking accounts, cars, savings bonds, royalty payments, anything that had her name on it?"

"Now that you mention it, seems like the only times we see her name are in letters or memos about one project or another," said Randy.

"You've been through more boxes than I have," Rachel replied. "Have you seen much about her anywhere? ...they were married for almost 30 years and you'd think at least one piece of art was hers."

"Don't forget. Max Shaw told us the western art was purchased after Lutcher married Nelda. And the inventory supports that."

"I know, I know. None of the boxes – these or the others at my house – show any art purchases during his marriage to Nita. But something doesn't make sense about that. Remember the day Nelda died and Mr. Kinney told us that they had hidden records from us?"

"Yeah. I know that's what he said, but he must have been wrong," Randy said. "All the Remington, Russell and Dunton records I saw weren't bought until the 1940s at the earliest. The only thing I know for sure is that I'm starving."

Rachel was certain that last statement was a strong signal to move toward the kitchen. They found Bill and Linda halfway through the grilled chicken, rice and broccoli attractively placed on each dinner plate. Within moments, it was quiet as they focused on the food and enjoyed the silence broken only by an occasional fish breaking the surface of the small lake.

Ida Marie was absent at lunch. They found her seated quietly in the study, a room hardly touched since the day her husband died 21 years earlier. She sat comfortably in his overstuffed leather chair, looking out the windows, almost willing him to appear. Pictures of his family, a golf score card, souvenirs of the past were scattered across the desk and bookshelves.

"He loved this room, this setting." Ida Marie spoke first, as if giving permission for her children and niece to join the conversation. They preferred to let her talk, and she shared story after story of their courtship, their wedding, their life in Orange, his death from cancer at age 56. Each had heard them before, but this was the time and place for a refresher course.

"Bill and Homer were such good young men, I often wonder how this all happened," she said, referring to the turn of events that took place while they were overseas. "I don't think they saw it coming at all. Nelda and Eunice just took control. It was as if Lutcher had no sons, no ties to the past."

Rachel suggested there had to be a reason the two women could take control of a man as powerful as Lutcher Stark. "I don't know what it is, but perhaps those records will be able to tell us."

They returned to the boxes and started anew, this time focusing on file after file of land transactions, lease agreements and information on companies they had never heard of before. Real estate transactions, offers to buy or sell, leases to trappers and logging companies. It was more factual than the other documents, lacking few interesting moments as they took several hours to complete just half a dozen boxes, long enough to call it a day and head for home.

The next morning, Rachel awoke to the loud arrival of Randy's diesel truck. She pulled the pillow over her head and prayed he would turn off the ignition. Almost anything would be worth a few more minutes of peace and quiet, but she knew it was time to get up and dressed. As her feet touched the floor and she reached for her everpresent terry cloth robe, the sounds disappeared.

Thank God, she thought and looked upwards. The diesel roar was gone, but so was Randy. He had stopped by only to let her know they'd have to postpone the boxes for a day or two. Something had come up and he'd be gone until late that afternoon. She had the day off. Only problem was there was lots to do and Rachel wanted to get as much behind her as possible before returning home. Whatever Randy was doing, it allowed Rachel the chance to go through a huge Bengal Guards scrapbook her mother kept under the bed. Easily three feet wide, it took up the entire twin bed when she opened it to take a trip back in time when Orange and Lutcher Stark were in the national spotlight. There were newspaper clippings from Chicago, New Orleans, Austin, San Antonio and photo layouts from *Life* magazine. Many of the pictures featured "beautiful Becky Havens," now Becky Stark, since she had served as drum major and gained notoriety as the national baton twirling champion two years in a row. The fact she was both gorgeous and photogenic made her a popular subject, prompting one reporter to admit "the only thing I can think of is to ask for her telephone number."*

Mixed in the clippings were occasional stories about Nita and Lutcher, including the gift to the University of Texas, the death of Nita's father, the purchase of uniforms for the Longhorn band, and even details of a slide show Nita presented to women's groups regarding a 1927 tour of Europe. An envelope in the back of the scrapbook contained photos of Bill and Homer as toddlers showing them at play on a wooden roller coaster by the carriage house of the W. H. Stark home.

Somehow the photos and news stories seemed sad, almost cruel reminders of how life took a dramatic change for the worst. Rachel found herself studying every photograph, every image of Lutcher Stark, trying to pick up some clue that might explain his "other side." Yet he appeared perfectly happy, totally in charge, and quite an admirer of the people he fondly described to one columnist as his three bosses – Nita, Bill and Homer. One particular picture, taken when the new high school stadium built by Lutcher Stark opened in 1940, showed the multimillionaire standing proudly between his two sons. Another article quoted Lutcher extensively as he spoke about his greatest role in life, as a father to such great young men.

That afternoon Homer surprised them with a special showing of some old, really old, films he had professionally reconditioned in Houston. All were taken at the Stark family's Roslyn Ranch in Colorado during the late 1930's and showed a glimpse of the lifestyle enjoyed by family and friends. While the images of vintage photos and a two-hour visit there in the 1970's provided a frame of reference for Rachel when Homer talked about Colorado, the movies added motion and life to those they portrayed.

"You ready?" Homer asked. He had patiently pulled out his old 16mm projector, set up the screen, carefully threaded the film and darkened the room. It was showtime.

Sounds of the film moving from reel to reel, coupled with the light flickering as the frames fed through the projector, added to the atmosphere. Becky laughed when she saw Homer cutting up for the camera, while Bill took a more serious approach in mounting a horse. Images of adults going in and out of one of the cabins – the Rose Cabin, according to Homer – showed activity as a car was loaded and the couple paused before climbing in. Lutcher came into the picture, apparently adding his goodbyes before the departure of his guests, but the next frames were memorable as a slim, striking woman in a polka dot dress approached them in the most gracious manner Rachel had ever witnessed. Her smile was truly stunning as she effortlessly managed to make saying farewell almost an art. It was Nita and would be the only time Rachel ever saw her in motion. All the still photographs pictured a poised woman with an elegant demeanor, but the addition of movement transformed Rachel's opinion of her grandmother. Now she could see the warmth, the charm, the absolute beauty projected by this woman.

"Mother was something else. Not sure how she managed to get through that month," said Homer, recalling that summer vacation.

"What do you mean?" asked Rachel.

"Two weeks after the Hills left, she was on her way home for the last time. It was the summer she got so ill that Dad had to arrange for a private train to get her back to Orange. We thought she was doing so much better once we arrived in Colorado, but I think she just wanted everyone to enjoy themselves and not worry about her."

The doorbell rang about the same time the last movie ended. Randy was back and had little to say about his whereabouts for most of the day. Whatever it was, he wouldn't be able to help with the boxes for a few days.

"That's fine, we'll just get together when you can," said Rachel.

"Hey, you don't have to wait on me. I know you need to get back to work tomorrow. Why not take more of the boxes with you and go through them at home?"

That sounded good to Rachel. She wanted to take a closer look at some of the files they had already reviewed, plus there were others her cousins suggested she would find interesting in a lot of ways. A few they had spent little time with, only stopping to label which topics were contained in particular boxes.

She followed Randy to his mother's house, mentally trying to decide which boxes she wanted first. It didn't take long to locate those on her list. Anything to do with tax returns, foundation records, estate inventories, audits and the drug store receipts.

"Drug store receipts?" asked Randy, obviously puzzled by her request for those boxes.

"Remember when you told me pills, rat poison and empty capsules were included in those receipts – and that there seemed to be something strange about that?"

"Yeah."

"Well, it's more than strange. Maybe it was nothing, but then again, maybe not."

The following weekend, Rachel was anxious to revisit the dozen or so boxes she had added to others stored in her garage. This time she was alone and there were no distractions. With any luck, she would have soon a better idea if there were any family secrets.

A card table and folding chair became the center of her world, with a fan circulating the air inside the garage and a plastic cup with ice cold lemonade on the floor within easy reach.

The first four boxes contained Lutcher Stark's personal audits covering most of the 1940s and 1950s, very detailed documents with an almost endless list of property he owned. From real estate to rental property to leases, every piece of real property was entered in the neat and systematic way of the financial community. Stocks and bonds were also itemized. Her first inclination was to hurriedly glance through them, but she decided to be more selective and spend more time with the audits for specific years. 1956, for example, was when he sold a significant portion of his Louisiana lands to John Mecom for approximately $15 million. It was duly noted in the audit, along with hundreds of pages of balance sheets and notations explaining one item or another. By the time she finished reviewing the fourth box, the day was almost over. Rachel was tired, but pleased with the progress she thought had been made. Not so much with any startling discovery, but because she simply knew more about her grandfather's business.

Morning found her ready to tackle more boxes, a task she actually was looking forward to as she grabbed a quick breakfast and returned to the garage. First was a single box with 990-PF's – the equivalent of foundation tax returns, to be specific. Records of 1979, 1987 and 1988 were separated in file folders which contained not only a copy of each year's report, but the working papers used to prepare the form.

Taking them in sequence, Rachel spent more than two hours glancing through the 1987 submission. She had never completed anything other than the usual 1040 for her personal income tax, so a form this complex and detailed was a challenge. From calculations to determine required giving to lengthy listings of assets and liabilities, it was anything but light reading.

She recalled Walter's comments regarding Foundation contributions. What was it he had told her? "Nelda did not want to give more than she had to, and preferred using monies on Foundation projects where they had complete control of the dollars."

It had been part of the long conversation in the A&M parking lot, and the same explanation when she spoke with him again. While she was trying to understand the process, he was revealing much more than the procedures to follow. Keeping his words in mind, she noted the Stark Foundation's required giving in 1987 was set at $2,273,630, with more than a quarter of a million dollars left unspent.

Under operating expenses, the Foundation reported $2,010,153. A breakdown of those costs showed $1,172,472 spent on the Stark Museum; $213,677 on the W. H. Stark Home; and a $476,904 grant for the Lutcher Theater. Combined with $147,100 in what was classified as "other contributions, grants paid," the reported total was exactly $263,477 short of calculated expenditures.

So far, Walter seemed to be right on target as almost 90% of the Foundation dollars were being spent in the same office charged with oversight of the projects. Is it charity if nine of every ten dollars is spent on yourself?

Other pages listed question after question with reference to one particular requirement or another, while others documented salaries of the five highest paid employees, legal fees, accounting and investment fees, or information relative to attendance at the museum or theater.

Near the back, however, she found some pages obviously out of sequence according to the page numbers. Here was a list of property acquired by the Foundation during 1987: four items covering 361.75 acres, all in Orange County. Rachel looked at the parcel description included for each and noticed names of J. B. Childress, Lizzie Higginbotham, O. M. Thomas and James Watson. They seemed vaguely familiar, but she couldn't quite recall why they should mean anything to her. Her question for the moment was why the Foundation would buy property in the first place? What would they use it for? From whom did they buy it? Why was the book value more than market value – $369,456 to $126,616 – for property purchased that same year?

A three-ring spiral binder placed nearby was once again used to record not only information she found interesting, but questions she might want to follow up on in the future. A red ink pen used only on occasion underscored items of the greatest importance, including a notation to borrow Jake's "Handbook for Private Foundations." If she was going to go through these documents intelligently, she needed to have a clear and objective understanding about foundation governance.

The 1988 documents were similar to the year before and raised the same questions. She set it aside and pulled out the 1979 version. How were they different?

For starters, the fair market value in 1979 was listed at $39,530,727 – enough to qualify it as one of the major foundations in Texas. The 1987 FMV was $73,655,532, about 54% higher according to Rachel's $5.99 solar calculator. It seemed like an error at first glance. In spite of the substantial increase in assets during the eight-year period, required giving only increased approximately $59,000 – from $2,214,166 to $2,273,630. This was definitely a red-line question.

The next three boxes were the most interesting of the lot, at least when it came to family history. Two contained nothing but items related to the Roslyn Ranch, including newspaper clippings from the *North Park News*, the Colorado weekly paper that served the Walden and Rand areas. Rachel scanned the pages, looking not only at articles regarding Nita and Lutcher Stark, but even the display ads and the news style of the day were interesting to her journalistic side. Mixed in the boxes were magazine and catalogue listings for Stickley furniture, the Mission style manufacturer synonymous with quality. It was interesting to see Nita's handwritten notes in the margins, indicating which items she selected and for which cabin or room.

Correspondence between Lutcher and Hank Kerr, the ranch manager, provided a snapshot of life on the ranch. Approval of invoices for groceries, supplies, baling equipment, repairs on the tractor or one of the other vehicles. Letters in the boxes revealed that those initiated by the ranch manager were usually short, possibly requesting permission to buy a piece of equipment, while those from Lutcher were longer and specific. He not only told Hank what he wanted done, but why and how. Souvenir postcards, travel maps and correspondence from the Stark offices in Orange were included.

The third box, containing tax returns from decades ago, seemed to be part of a larger group she had not yet seen. Rachel looked hurriedly through it, noting they covered both Texas and Louisiana business and personal returns. She decided the tax rate was either much lower then or someone was cheating the government, writing a note to herself to spend more time on these documents.

Next was a collection of letters related to the gift of Miriam Stark's antique and art collection to the University of Texas. Apparently there had been a change of heart after Lutcher's marriage to Nelda. Correspondence dated in the early 1930's indicated Miriam had been persuaded by her son to donate the materials to the University rather than display them in Orange. "To do so would allow more people to enjoy your collection while providing a resource for students and faculty" according to Lutcher's letter. The gift was to include $150,000 from the Stark family to properly house the items. Yet in the late 1940s there were letters from Lutcher Stark to his Houston attorneys seeking advice on reversing his position. One to the University of Texas even withdrew the $150,000 as he claimed financial reversals would not permit the cash donation originally pledged as part of the gift.

In 1953, he officially rescinded the collection from his alma mater and news clippings attached to the letter confirmed his actions. Rachel read the articles again, one from the campus newspaper and another from the *Austin American Statesman*. Both were based on the same facts: the gift in 1937 from Mr. and Mrs. H. J. L. Stark to the University of Texas was rescinded in 1953 by Mr. and Mrs. H. J. L. Stark.

How interesting, she thought, realizing that they were actually talking about Nita and Nelda, two different wives. Although certainly no lawyer, she felt if Nita and Lutcher gave the gift in the first place, Nita's half should have gone to Bill and Homer when it was rescinded. Yet it was Nelda who claimed the art and antique treasures for herself.

After walking Travis and enjoying being outdoors even for 15 minutes, Rachel returned to the boxes. She looked to see which ones included the drugstore receipts, the ones she asked Randy to locate for her. There were three with that notation, so she accepted the fact it might be a long afternoon. She was right.

More than four hours later, she was still collating papers in an effort to put them in chronological order. Her cousins had been absolutely correct. There were receipts for prescriptions, rat poison and empty capsules. But she also noticed a lot of items listing phenobarbital. In different strengths and in large quantities. At least it seemed that way.

Late afternoon she was interrupted by a call from the family doctor in Orange. She left a message earlier to see if he knew anything of interest regarding all the drug store purchases.

"Dr. Eastman, thanks for returning my call. How are you?"

"Can't complain. Seems I'm too old to play much golf, but doesn't take too much effort to watch it on television. What can I do for you?"

"I've been going through a lot of documents from years ago and wondered if you could explain a few things to me. To help me understand one of the medicines that keeps turning up."

"Sure, what is it?" said Dr. Eastman.

"Phenobarbital."

"Been around a long time, known as the preferred drug for epileptics."

He proceeded to provide more information, explaining it could only be used under the strict supervision of a medical doctor. While it was effective for up to 12 hours, it usually peaked at about eight and had proven highly effective at transforming epilepsy patients into a trance-like state to prevent convulsions.

"But why are you asking about phenobarbital? No one in your family is epileptic."

"I know, but all these records show multiple purchases of that drug in different milligram sizes and for several hundred at a time. Is there another reason people buy them?"

"No. But you need a prescription and that makes it virtually impossible to buy them in amounts you are describing."

"What if I told you Nelda was the one buying them from her own drugstores from the 1940s until right before Granddaddy died in 1965?"

"Then I'd have to say she was up to no good. And, I'd have to suspect Lutcher was her target. It would explain his behavior over the years and she sure as hell wasn't taking them or giving them to Eunice. Were there any prescription receipts?"

"Yes, lots of them, but we don't know what they are. Both drug stores burned and the records with them."

"Then I can't help you with those, but you could probably get phenobarbital over the counter back then. Some people used them as sleeping pills, but they can cause confusion, especially for older patients. I don't think anyone thought about putting a limit on how many you could buy at the same time."

She thanked him for the information, promised to come by the next time she was in town, then returned to filing the receipts with even more motivation to complete the task as soon as possible. Once in order, she hole-punched and placed the receipts in two four-inch binders, the first with records from 1937-1954, the second covering 1955-1971.

Even a complete stranger should be able to notice the pattern. Before Lutcher's marriage to Nelda, drugstore receipts for the Stark family included typical items such as hand cream, muscle balm, tissues, candy, ice cream and cigarettes. Starting after their marriage and continuing until just before Lutcher Stark's death in 1965, Nelda purchased large amounts of phenobarbital and prescription drugs delivered along with cigarettes and candy. Plus the standard favorites of the average American family: rat poison and empty capsules, with a few syringes mixed in with the order.

Rachel put the last box in place and walked into the house, thinking nothing could possibly surprise her now. Then the phone rang.

"Dr. Eastman, what a treat. Can't believe I get to talk with you twice in one day."

"Uh... Rachel, I've been thinking since we talked."

"Yes, sir," she said, waiting for him to continue.

"About Nelda. You know she never made a secret of how much she admired German doctors?"

"Actually, she mentioned that to me one time. Can't even recall what in the world we were talking about – World War II history, I think – and she brought up something about how they developed new procedures, or treatments, or something like that. I didn't really understand the connection, just that she was impressed with their work.

"Dr. Eastman?"

"Yes, I'm here. Have you ever heard of Operation T-4?"

"No, sir. What is that?"

"A code name, one for a Nazi policy back in the 30s and 40s used to murder children who didn't meet their Arayan standards. A few adults were included, if I remember correctly."**

"What does that have to do with Nelda?"

"They used phenobarbital, but it was also called Luminal back then."

"It could be used to kill a person?" asked Rachel.

"An overdose would slow bodily functions, sometimes resulting in a coma. It's been used by some to commit suicide, so obviously it could kill someone if it fell in the wrong hands. Like the Germans. Or Nelda."

Excerpt from newspaper article describing Becky Havens: "...She's slim and athletic, and she's got witchery in her fingertips. She can twirl a baton on the tips of her four fingers. She can handle a pair of them so fast you see nothing but a sheen in the sun. Under the direction of her supple hands, the cold steel seems to take life, and spring about like a thing possessed..."

**Many of the German medical staff members involved in the project were transferred to Nazi concentration camps during WWII to continue this practice.*

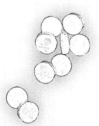

CHAPTER 8

*"The character of every act depends upon
the circumstances in which it is done."*
— *Oliver Wendell Holmes, Jr.*

A small community 28 miles north of Orange, Call was set among part of the thickest timber sections in the area. It was a scenic trip along Highway 87 as Homer drove Rachel to visit Jim Henderson, the man who helped raise him as a youngster and kept him out of trouble as a teenager. Perfect spring weather for a drive in the country.

To be honest, he thought Jim died years earlier, only to learn two weeks ago that he was enjoying a comfortable retirement less than half an hour away. The elderly gentleman phoned Homer one morning, giving him a hard time about a shotgun promised a lifetime ago during a summer in Colorado. Soon after the conversation ended, Homer went back to his office, unlocked the gun cabinet and pulled out the weapon in question. He could hardly wait to see his old friend and took Becky that afternoon to surprise Jim, the first time they had seen each other in more than 35 years.

It was during a phone call from Rachel that Homer mentioned Jim Henderson to her for the first time, responding to a question about where he had been all day.

"Jim Henderson? Who's that?"

"Clemmie's first husband."

"First husband? I thought Charlie was her first husband." Rachel never thought Clemmie was married more than once, much less divorced. No one seemed to get divorced in those days.

"Yeah. She and Jim were married for a long time, spent summers at the ranch when we went up each year. Jim followed after me, his brother, C.W., was in charge of Bill."

"Guess I just never thought about it. And Clemmie never mentioned him that I ever remember," said Rachel.

"He's a really nice man. You'd like him. And you'd love his stories about Dad. He may be 98, but he's sharp as ever."

It was all the invitation Rachel needed to convince her dad to take her to visit Jim. She thought he might have some of the answers about Jamestown. After all, Clemmie said she and Nita picked up the boys at the orphanage. He was married to her then and could remember the details.

The prospect of talking to someone who might be able to set her straight about the trip to Jamestown kept Rachel up all night, anticipating his responses to questions left unanswered. Whatever they were, this was a man who had firsthand information and she couldn't wait to meet him.

A left turn off the highway took them two miles on CR 524. There Homer slowed and turned right into a gravel driveway of a small, well kept frame home. Whoever lived there took wonderful care of the home and, if you could judge by the gorgeous flowers and plants surrounding the porch, had a master's touch when it came to gardening.

Homer opened the gate, gave the two dogs a friendly pat and went up the steps to the front door. He didn't have to knock. Jim was sitting in a green wingback chair just inside, waiting for Homer to arrive. His granddaughter Betty opened the screen door and gave Homer a hug, happy to see him.

Introductions were made, coffee was poured and Rachel waited patiently as the two men talked about hunting, fishing and other important things in life. You would have thought the pair was planning an overnight camping trip, when neither one had shot a gun or cleaned a fish in years.

Jim looked younger than his age, but couldn't get around much anymore and wasn't able to walk at all without assistance. He was dressed in khaki pants and a long sleeve sports shirt – just like Homer. While he may move slower in his golden years, Rachel thought, he could talk a blue streak. What a perfect pair they must have been back in the 1930's, exploring the mountains and creeks of the Colorado ranch. Rabbit Ears Pass, Thunder Mountain, Last Chance Gap, Grizzly Creek and dozens of other landmarks that became regular stops as they explored the high mountain country.

"Yes, sir... Mr. Homer was some kind of shot. We'd be driving through the field in Colorado, him standing in the back of his pickup, me trying to keep from driving into a ditch, and he could still hit a rabbit on the run," said Jim, continuing to spin a few tales about life on the ranch and some misadventures both men seemed to easily recall.

"But there were good times at home, too, didn't seem to matter where we were," Jim recalled, flashing a smile Homer's way. "Your daddy could hit golf balls just as good as rabbits. Remember when we'd take Mr. W. H. to play golf at the country club?"

"Not sure it was really golf, but Grandpapaw sure did have a good time," chimed in Homer. "Wonder how many times we hit the ball and he had no idea?"

"Were you playing with him?" asked Rachel.

"Nope. But we had to help him out," said Homer. "He couldn't see much at all – was probably legally blind – but loved to play golf. Never was much good at it, but enjoyed the game so much that Dad built the course so he'd have a place to play whenever he wanted to."

"You should have seen Mr. Homer," said Jim. "Couldn't have been more than nine or ten years old and he'd help the ole man line up his shot. Then we'd wait, hoping he'd hit the ball on the second or third swing. On a good day, Mr. W. H. might do it, but other times we kinda helped out."

Homer explained the customary ritual that involved standing opposite his grandfather and hoping the club connected with the ball. When it didn't... and that happened more often than not because of the older man's failing eyesight... Homer would step in quickly with a putter, swing it lefthanded and most of the time hit the ball, taking pains to time it just behind Mr. W. H.'s swing to avoid being hit by the older man's club.

"Yep, he never figured it out," said Jim. "Mr. Homer, he'd hit the ball, and Mr. W.H., well, he'd be all smiles thinking he hit it, then we'd start down the fairway, talking about what a good shot that was. Mr. Homer'd grab the ball he hit with the putter as we walked past it, I'd drop another further down, and no one was surprised when the second shot came with a ball that turned up halfway to the green."

Another cup of coffee and it was Rachel's turn. After asking about Jim's family and what Clemmie was like years ago, she brought up the trip to pick up Bill and Homer. Clemmie told her long ago she accompanied Nita, but she never said how they got there.

"Mr. Henderson…"

"Jim," he said, correcting her.

"Jim," said Rachel. "When Clemmie and Miss Nita went to pick up Daddy and Uncle Bill, how did they go? I mean, did they take the train or drive?"

"They took the brown Rolls Royce," he replied without hesitation. "Murray was driving and Clemmie rode up front with him on the way up there to the Settlement Home. Mr. Lutcher and Miss Nita were in the back, but the nurse rode with them from Tennessee. Jes' like yesterday. I can still remember how excited we were to hold those boys for the first time."

He never mentioned Jamestown or Richmond, but Tennessee.

"Tennessee? Is that where they went?"

"Yes, ma'm. Drove up straight to the Settlement Home in Gatlinburg and brought those boys home. That nurse was something else, I'll tell you for sure. Had us hopping when she got here.

"Insisted on doing things a certain way with those babies. Giving us orders – all of us, even Mr. Lutcher. I remember when she was leavin', she turned and told him – with all of us help standing there – to be sure and tell the boys who their father really was when they were older."

"What did she mean by that, Mr. Henderson... uh, Jim?"

He looked at Homer, who laughed softly and shook his head as the mystery finally unraveled.

"Well, you know. Everybody pretty much knew Mr. Lutcher was the father. We just didn't say it out loud."

He volunteered some of the details Clemmie shared with him, entertaining them with his southern accent and charming imitations of Clemmie and her often scandalous – for those days – comments.

"Yeah... she was something else, that Clemmie," said Jim, flashing a broad grin. "That woman had a way of saying just what was on her mind... never at a loss for words. But Clemmie had Miss Nelda pegged before any of us.

"Remember that day Miss Ruby told her Nelda was trying to kill her?" he said, looking directly at Homer. "Clemmie came straight home, scared white of that woman, and told me we wouldn't have to worry about seeing her in heaven because a seat in Hell damn sure had her name on it."

From the trip to Tennessee and Clemmie, they moved to stories about life working for Lutcher Stark. It was clear Jim respected his longtime boss and enjoyed a close relationship with the man despite the obvious differences between them. He recalled conversations and situations that portrayed happy times as Homer and Bill grew up. Plus others that certainly stretched the imagination.

"That man could come up with the strangest things – something no one else would ever think of," said Jim. "Remember those flag blowers he made us drag around for the bands?"

"Flag blowers?" asked Rachel.

"Yes, m'am. Flag blowers. Mr. Lutcher was always way ahead of everyone else. 'All in the details' he would say.

"So he decided he always wanted a breeze when the flags were flying. Indoors or out, didn't matter, they just looked better that way. He'd have us plug in those blowers at the base of the flags.

"Still remember him saying if God was too busy to take care of the wind, we'd just bring our own."

In an attempt to explain to Rachel the lifestyle of her great-grandparents, he told her of fine china place settings trimmed with 24K gold. Place settings that would become so warm in the searing summer heat in Orange that servants put them on ice to keep the gold from melting. Other times, Jim was instructed to follow Mr. W. H. home from the office with large baskets full of hundred dollar bills. Somewhere around $400,000 that he would take down to the basement each Friday afternoon and return to the bank on Monday morning.

"It was during the Depression and Mr. W. H., he didn't trust the government with his money. He just brung it home with him each weekend. Told me if the house ever caught fire, I was to head for the basement and get that money out first. He'd take care of Miss Miriam."

There were lots of stories about Lutcher. Mostly ones that brought a smile to your face, like the incident with the Conn's delivery truck that Jim began telling with obvious delight.

"Yes, sir. He sure made old man Conn mad that day, but Lord knows Mr. Lutcher warned him often enough," said Jim, turning to ask Rachel if she remembered Conn's Furniture Store.

"Sure, but I don't remember anything about Granddaddy and a truck," she said.

"Well, not everyone knew about it, but word got around mighty fast. You know that vacant lot across from Shangri La – the one right at 16th Street and Park Avenue, almost directly in front of the main gate?"

Rachel nodded.

"Well, sometimes when business was slow old man Conn would just pull his delivery truck up on that piece of land and leave it parked there. Kind of like a billboard.

"I know for sure Mr. Lutcher asked him nice not to do that anymore, but Mr. Conn kept letting his drivers park that truck on your granddaddy's land."

"Why was that funny?" asked Rachel, kind of surprised by Jim's laughter in telling the story.

"Oh, it wasn't funny one bit, especially to Mr. Lutcher. One day he jes' had enough and when Mr. Conn came to get the truck for a delivery it was fenced in."

"What do you mean, fenced in?" asked Rachel.

"I mean fenced in. Mr. Lutcher told us to put up a cyclone fence all the way around that truck. He took it down a few days later, but I promise you the truck was never parked on that lot again. We must have laughed about that goin' on a year, especially whenever we saw Conn's truck coming down the street."

Next was the tale of railroad tracks used to reinforce the Shangri La fence. "Yep, he put those tracks up right behind the fenceline where 16th Street used to deadend at Park, right at the curve in the road. Did that in broad daylight, too.

"Mr. Lutcher got tired of hot rodders missing the curve and plowing into his fence, taking out a few plants along the way. So he put in those steel rails – and wanted everyone to know it. Yes, sir. No one's run into that fence for almost 50 years now.

"And that man loved the number 13... said it brought him luck ever since he bought Miss Nita that Hupmobile back in the early days, just before they were married."

"Dad always had 13 for his license plate, but I don't think that was the license plate on the Hupmobile," said Homer.

Jim smiled, pleased that he could enlighten his guests.

"Right. But you know Mr. Lutcher. He was deadset on having 13 for that car, being his favorite number and all, and 'specially because it was for Miss Nita. So he made arrangements for Nita to have $193 - 1 + 9 + 3 = 13$. Then he decided to go one step further when he placed the order since they sold them by vehicle number, you know... as they were making them, that's when he placed the order for #5813."

"So he took the one with 13 at the end?"

"No, sir. He wanted that one because it was 13 either way – you could add 5 and 8 to get 13 on the front end. He was real pleased with himself on that one... said he was double lucky when Miss Nita said 'yes'."

The stories took a different tone after Nelda entered the picture.

"You know, before he married that woman we got along great. He'd call me over in the mornings and we'd just sit out on the porch, drink our coffee and talk. She put a stop to all that, even called me over one time and told me, 'Jim, you just remember you're nothing but a nigger to me. You stay away from Lutcher'."

Rachel thought it was an awful thing to say, especially when Jim explained how Nelda cut his wages – and those of others loyal to Lutcher – until they were forced to look elsewhere. He worked for the family 48 years when he finally left to work for the Brown family. As Jim said, "if she couldn't rule you, she got rid of you – one way or the other."

"Mr. Homer, did you tell her about Shangri La?" he asked.

"No. Haven't said anything about it. You tell her."

Secrets about Shangri La? Rachel was confused as the conversation went from coffee on the porch to her grandfather's gardens. The private retreat was originally called the Fifteenth Street Farm* when Nita and Lutcher acquired it in the early years of their marriage and plans were drawn for a new home near the lake the year before she died. Although opened to the public on spring weekends in the 1950s, the magnificent private gardens had been in a state of disrepair since Nelda assumed ownership when Lutcher died. She cut off the water, plugged the well and only allowed the grass to be mowed.

"What about Shangri La?"

Jim glanced at the floor, then launched into the story he told Homer for the first time only days earlier.

It started when Lutcher Stark turned 70. Sometime that spring Nelda began bringing him out to Shangri La each morning around eight and locking him behind the gates, "leading him in like he was her prisoner."

"She'd come back at lunch with a sandwich and a Coke and we'd have to help her find him. We'd do the same thing again a little after 5 when she came to pick him up."

"What for? What did he do there?" she asked.

"He didn't do nothin'. She would give him these little white pills and he wandered around and didn't seem to know where he was. We had orders from her not to unlock the gate or give him anything else to eat or drink. And you know, it gets hot here in the summertime.

"Once he went over to the fence near Fuller's Texaco station on 16th street** and begged the high school kid that works there to give him some water. But most the time he couldn't even talk, just sat around on the ground or next to a tree."

Rachel was taking notes, but having trouble understanding how this happened. As Jim continued with more instances of the pills and the day Nelda fired one of the employees for giving Lutcher a cup of water, Rachel tried to make sense of what she was hearing.

She calculated it was 1958, the same time his power of attorney was assigned to Jules David, the insurance agent whose family handled the Stark accounts for years. In fact, his grandson still handled insurance for the Foundation even though he was on the Foundation Board. The document surfaced in one of the boxes and she thought it strange that her grandfather's distinctive signature was not the one at the bottom of the document. Several weeks later, her cousins told her of all the land and mineral lease transfers entered in the public records in Orange County during that same year. Transfers from her grandfather's name to Nelda, Eunice, or Clyde. Not just one or two items. Pages of entries that seemed to never end. Until now, Rachel couldn't understand why her grandfather would allow such a thing. He probably had no idea. All that phenobarbital delivered to Nelda was being used to control Lutcher. While he was given pills and locked in Shangri La, they were stealing lands that had been in the family since the 1800s. Apparently with court approval.

The thought of Shangri La, her grandfather's favorite place in the world, being used as a holding cell for him was unthinkable. Yet Jim Henderson was a man of character and an impeccable reputation for being truthful. He had no reason to lie and every reason to tell the truth.

117

It was a quiet trip back to Orange. Homer never said much anyway, and Rachel was too busy thinking to start a conversation. Less than a mile from the house, though, she asked if her dad would drive by Shangri La along Park Avenue. She wanted to take one more look at the topic of the afternoon's conversation.

He drove down Sunset Drive, took a left and there it was directly in front of them. Another left and Shangri La covered all the 252 acres on the right until they reached the signal light at 16th street. The lush green acreage had not changed since that morning, nor had the gates at the greenhouse. But she saw it through different eyes and it no longer reminded her of pleasant memories.

When they returned to the house, Becky was waiting to see how Rachel reacted to the new information Jim had provided. Rachel made a couple of comments as she passed her grandfather's portrait hanging in the entry hall, then walked into the breakfast area and started going through some of the boxes scattered on the floor and in the chairs.

"Now what are you looking for?" asked Becky.

"Those three-ring binders. You know, the big green ones I used to keep all the drug store receipts from the boxes. Do you remember seeing them?"

Becky knew exactly what her daughter was trying to find, but neither was able to locate them. It seemed improbable that two large binders could just disappear from the room.

Homer walked by, realized what they were searching for, and suggested his office.

"Why there?" asked Rachel.

"Because that's where I put them this morning. You wanted me to make some copies and we left for Jim's before I could finish."

Soon the binders were back in the breakfast room and Rachel opened the one marked 1955-71. There she found what she was looking for. One receipt after another for phenobarbital, increasing in frequency around 1958 and disappearing from the receipts completely in the summer of 1965 – shortly before Lutcher Stark died.

Lutcher Stark never suffered seizures and was in good health until Nelda entered the picture. Never diagnosed as an epileptic. The phenobarbital explained how her grandfather could seem perfectly fine one day, then "drugged and off the wall" the next. "Up to no good," Dr. Eastman had said of Nelda. What an understatement that turned out to be, even though he did tell her of Nelda's interest in the German experiments involving that particular drug. But no one connected Nelda directly to the pills until today.

She brought the binder into the den and told her parents that the pills Jim mentioned produced the same results as the phenobarbital listed in the receipts.

"Phenobarbital?" said Homer. "What are you talking about?"

"The pills Jim mentioned today. You know, the small white ones he saw Nelda giving Granddaddy when they first got married and again in Shangri La. It explains why he acted so strange sometimes when you would go see him and he didn't know who you were."

Homer was taken by surprise. It was the same medication Dr. Pearce told him Nelda was giving his dad in the hospital the summer he died.

After James Hilton's "Lost Horizons" was published in 1933, Nita and Lutcher Stark named the private retreat Shangri La. A few years later, Franklin Roosevelt created a presidential retreat during World War II and named it Shangri La. The name was changed to Camp David when Dwight Eisenhower named it for his grandson.

**Ironically, the area bordering the gas station is almost exactly the same location where the Stark Foundation placed a sign that proclaims "Be Kind to Your World" next to Shangri La.

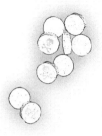

CHAPTER 9

"Each time a man stands up for an ideal, or acts to improve the lot of others, or strikes out against injustice, he sends forth a tiny ripple of hope."
— **Robert F. Kennedy**

Evergreen Cemetery served the citizens of Orange County well for more than 162 years, providing a final resting place for thousands who witnessed changes in Orange from a lumber town, to shipbuilding, to the establishment of Chemical Row, to today's version – a town without a destiny, lacking much of an economy or a downtown. Somehow having a funeral director as Mayor seemed appropriate for Orange as it faced tough times.

The graveyard provided an interesting mix of eras, with blockade runners and pioneer settlers buried among war veterans spanning years from the Texas Revolution to Vietnam, along with the community's most prominent citizens and those who aspired to be.

Near the center of Evergreen's 12 acres and 15,000 gravesites was the Stark mausoleum. Or more accurately, the Stark-Hill-Lutcher mausoleum. The granite structure with its bronze door and elegant stain glass windows was an accurate reflection of the style popular with the wealthy years earlier. It stood at a 90 degree angle from the Brown mausoleum, with only 40 feet separating the final resting place of the two families.

Homer, Jake, Rachel and Rebel arrived around 7:45 that bright Saturday morning in late April, a little early and a lot anxious about the exhumation scheduled that day. Michael and Patrick, Rachel's sons, followed in a pickup truck, carefully looking around as they turned into Evergreen to make sure there would not be any last minute attempt by the Stark Foundation to stop them. No one was in sight.

Both vehicles pulled past the family mausoleum before stopping, allowing easy access to the walk that extended from the gravel drive to the door. Everyone got out but Homer, who stayed behind the wheel of his Landcruiser, thinking quietly about exhuming his father's body. It had not been an easy decision, but one that made sense to help solve the mystery surrounding his birth and adoption. Before his visit with Jim Henderson, he never really cared to discover who his birth parents were, but time and circumstances had presented the strong possibility that Lutcher Stark was more than his adopted father.

The distinct but muffled sound of cars approaching caused everyone to glance toward the gate. There came the two black Suburbans from the Dorman Funeral Home as they entered the property and slowly navigated the turns, showing respect for the location as well as Homer's mindset.

Traffic was picking up on Jackson Street along the cemetery. Jake spotted Randy's car, Bill's truck and a van bringing additional men to help with the exhumation. Everyone who was supposed to be there had arrived with minutes to spare.

Homer exited his vehicle and walked over to thank the Dormans for their assistance. Standing in his khaki pants and light blue shirt, Stetson hat in place and loading his pipe as he talked, he showed little of the nervous tension that had followed him for days.

"You boys know what you are doing, but I just want to make certain we leave this place the way we found it," said Homer. "I know it won't be an easy job, but I'd really appreciate your taking time to do this right."

"Don't worry, Mr. Stark. Everything will be fine," said the elder Dorman.

"Great. I'm having enough trouble sleeping as it is, and sure don't want anyone dropping my dad's casket this morning."

Homer shook their hands, walked directly to the tall bronze door, unlocked it, and moved silently inside to spend a few moments alone with his deceased parents, grandparents and great-grandparents. It was almost like he was asking permission to invade their space with the equipment on hand.

Rebel broke the silence and stepped inside to take a few pictures, documenting the interior before any attempts were made to remove the casket. In her customary style, she gave Homer a hug and told him everything would be okay.

"Granddaddy is probably up there just wondering what took us so long," she laughed, causing Homer to crack a smile and follow her outside.

"Bet we are drawing a crowd in heaven," replied Homer.

"Looks like we're drawing a crowd down here as well," remarked Jake, motioning to the City of Orange police car stopped at the gate before slowly pulling away. He would circle the block three or four more times before completely disappearing from the area.

"Ain't that something?" said Randy. "The crime rate must be dropping for them to find nothing better to do than cruise around a cemetery in the daytime."

Jake laughed and let Rebel in on what the others already knew. The Foundation "owned" the police department, at least according to a couple of workmen who had warned the Stark family only a week earlier after Rachel requested a police report.

Within moments, Roland Wolfford – president of the Evergreen Cemetery Association – exited the tiny building across the street and began walking toward Homer's family. Since the office was not normally open on Saturday, his appearance was a surprise.

"Homer, Roland Wolfford with the cemetery association. You and Becky went to school with my older brother Lyle and he speaks very highly of you both. Let us know if we can help with anything."

"Appreciate that, but I think we've got everything under control," said Homer. The two started talking about high school days as work began to remove the caulking around the marble in front of Lutcher Stark's casket, made even more difficult since it was on the top row. Almost from the start, it was clear the job would take much longer than the 20 or 30 minutes estimated by the funeral home to remove the panel.

Randy, Bill and Jake took turns talking with each other and rotating inside to judge the progress of the first phase of the exhumation. Michael and Patrick stayed close to Homer. Rachel pulled Rebel aside and the two started walking east down a dirt road, away from the mausoleum and toward the far side of the cemetery.

"Where are we going?" asked Rebel.

"Miss Nelda's buried down here. Thought you might want to see where she is, plus I want to check her gravesite. When I was here at Christmas, no one had done anything to remember her. Kind of sad when you think about it. All that money and no one to care."

"Not even Eunice?"

"Nope, not even Eunice. Or Walter, or Clyde, or Roy. They all got rich off her, then didn't even bother to trim her gravesite or leave some flowers. Someone told me once that the way people treat the dead is merely a reflection of how they treat the living. Guess this proves that theory. "*

As they walked carefully between rows of tombstones scattered unevenly throughout Evergreen, Rachel explained that Miss Nelda's grave was next to Ruby's, and both sisters were buried near their parents and a younger brother who died when he was six years old. They arrived to find the site pretty much as Rachel remembered it, yet there was one thing that was not apparent when she visited during the colder days of December.

"Look at Miss Nelda's grave," Rachel told Rebel.

"What about it?"

"See anything kind of out of the ordinary? Different?"

"What are you talking about?" said Rebel.

"The only place the grass is dead is over her grave."

Sure enough, the green grass of an April morning was growing over the entire Childers plot – everywhere but above Nelda. Her gravesite – the standard 42" wide, 10 feet long, and of course 6 feet under – showed no signs of life.

"Spooky, isn't it?" said Rebel.

Rachel acknowledged her sister's comment and the two walked back to their dad's car, leaning against it as they waited. It had been more than an hour and the crew was still carefully, almost painstakingly, working to remove the seal. One of the men appeared outside and talked briefly with Mr. Dorman, then the two approached Homer and explained that they would be back shortly. After almost 40 years untouched, the seal had proven a formidable opponent and a quick trip to retrieve additional tools was necessary.

For anyone driving by, it might have appeared to be a rather normal scene in the cemetery. A family waiting for a loved one to be buried. Workers preparing the site. Only those who paid attention would realize how truly unusual it was in Orange to exhume a body, much less that of Lutcher Stark.

"What do you think? " asked Rebel.

"About what?" replied Rachel.

"About what we're doing. Do you think Daddy is all right with it?"

"He would never have done it on his own, but then I've come to believe they brainwashed him into thinking he was so lucky to be adopted by such a good family. As if he really wasn't entitled to anything. Even Uncle Bill seemed to believe so, but that changed."

"What do you mean?"

"Well, when Aunt Ida Marie and I were talking a month or so ago, she told me Uncle Bill was really quiet one afternoon soon after Granddaddy died. Didn't say much at all, just kind of retreated to his study and stared out the window."

"But that's not unusual after a death in the family."

"No, but what he said was. He told her that after the first 20 years of his life, he had no idea how he would ever repay his father for everything he had done for him. But after the last 20, he figured they were even."

Rebel seemed surprised, but even more so after Rebecca pointed out her uncle's grave on a plot adjacent to the mausoleum.

"You see Uncle Bill's gravesite?"

It took only moments to survey the area, but Rebel thought it looked like most of the other gravesites in Evergreen. The cemetery was not known for manicured lawns or attention to detail, but her uncle's seemed better kept than most.

Almost as if reading Rebel's mind, Rachel filled in the blanks.

"The reason his grave is cared for is no thanks to Nelda. Aunt Ida Marie takes care of it. After he died, Nelda gave strict orders that her crew was not allowed to mow or edge around Uncle Bill's grave – even though they were here anyway to take care of the mausoleum's exterior. She even put a short white picket fence between the two plots to make certain they knew exactly where their maintenance area stopped and started."

"How mean," said Rebel, silently wondering how her grandmother would be so cruel to her uncle's family.

"I know. The fence stayed there for 20 years. Daddy called Walter after Miss Nelda died and asked him to take it down. Enough was enough."

While they talked, the equipment arrived. Jake motioned for Rebel to bring her camera to take more pictures, this time of the removal of the marble panel that protected the casket. A flurry of activity followed as the workmen prepared to lower

Lutcher Stark's bronze casket and carefully carry it outside to a metal gurney to transport it to the waiting Suburban.

Jake, Michael, Patrick, Randy, and Bill joined the workmen in lifting the heavy casket and struggling slowly toward the doorway while balancing several hundred pounds of bronze in tight quarters. Homer stood silently in the drive as the scene unfolded, while Rebel and Rachel were motionless nearby.

But just as the casket hit daylight, bells of the First Presbyterian Church rang magically from the sanctuary several blocks away. Whatever doubts Homer had earlier dissolved instantly as broad smiles replaced looks of concern on his family and those assisting them. "What A Friend We Have In Jesus " had never sounded so good.

It was 10 a.m. and no one had paid attention to the time until the rich sounds of the bells pierced the silence. Glances of approval were exchanged as several heads turned skyward and there was a noticeable change in pace as the casket was placed in the rear of the first Suburban for an uneventful trip across town to the funeral home.

Rachel and Randy followed in the second Suburban as planned, while Homer and other family members returned home to await reports once the pathologist flown in to obtain samples completed his assignment. From using a funeral home with no known connections to Nelda Stark to hiring an out of town doctor for the testing, the Stark family preferred not to take any chances. Not anymore.

Once they arrived at the funeral home and the casket was moved inside, the doctor explained the procedures he would be following, what to expect with regard to both time and results, the sounds of the saw and drill that would be used to obtain evidence, plus the chain of custody involved to transport samples to the DNA lab in New Orleans. He gave Rachel and Randy the option of viewing the examination, but cautioned them on whether they might want to simply remain close by.

It was an easy decision. They sat quietly a few feet away from the casket, wanting to be nearby out of respect for their grandfather. Occasionally, Randy went outside for a cigarette and Rachel called to check on the family.

Time passed slowly, at least for the cousins who had fought for this opportunity. Once Walter refused to turn over the adoption information after Nelda's death, the family felt they had no other way to determine if Lutcher Stark was indeed the biological father of Homer and Bill. It had no bearing on the Foundation, but it would surprise no one if the Stark Foundation lawyers began their stall tactics again.

A hearing to determine if Homer Stark's family could proceed with the exhumation had been held three weeks earlier in Judge Ben Wilson's Orange County courtroom. It lasted only 45 minutes and the request was approved following testimony outlining the efforts that had been made through other sources.

Point by point, the family addressed each of the concerns raised by the judge. Conversations with employees and long-time residents of Orange, the trip to Jamestown, the seemingly falsified birth certificate, missing adoption papers, Nelda's own words, Walter's reluctance to provide other documentation. The family presented each issue and made its case, with no one from the Stark Foundation there to disagree or object.

It would be the next day when the Stark Foundation reopened the Lutcher Stark estate, named Eunice Benckenstein as executor, and filed a complaint to block the exhumation. The attorneys even visited Homer's lawyer and said they had arranged a private hearing with the judge, a hearing that the judge later said he had no knowledge of and refused to schedule.

Rachel remembered Patrick's comments when the Foundation raised no objections for testing to determine paternity, but under no circumstances would they approve efforts to identify drugs in Lutcher Stark's body.

"That's kind of like the police showing up at a house with a search warrant and someone telling them to look anywhere they like – just don't check the hall closet."

Randy had returned and she repeated Patrick's words to him. Both needed a good laugh as more than four hours had gone by since they took a seat in the area adjacent to the casket.

"Hey, Mom. Any news yet?"

The welcome sound of Michael's voice echoed in the large room as her oldest son strolled through the side door. A small paper sack in one hand, a phone in the other.

"Patrick's on his way, but said to give this to Dr. Nyen. It's the DNA sample from Papaw."

The doctor parted the curtain and entered the room, introducing himself to Michael and thanking him for the paper sack and the contents it held. A few q-tips used to swab inside Homer's mouth were neatly stored in a ziplock bag, all the DNA evidence needed to determine any relationship between the adopted son and his father.

"I'm almost finished with the samples, then you can return the casket to the mausoleum. Do you have any questions before I finish?"

"I know you can't predict what the results will be, but can you tell us anything about what you found?" asked Rachel.

"Given the number of years since Mr. Stark died and the condition of the body, it has been a very slow process but I was able to obtain some samples," Dr Nyen said. "Wouldn't get your hopes up on the drug testing, though. Phenobarbital can be found in the brain tissue, but it may be expecting too much to think it will show up 40 years later. Tried to get the best DNA samples we could from his teeth, but he had gold fillings in most which limited what could be used."

He went to complete his work and arrangements were made for the return trip to Evergreen. Once Lutcher Stark was back where he belonged and everything was in order, the family relaxed and felt comfortable that it had done the right thing.

Whatever the test results showed, there was a lot of quiet confidence that evening to indicate the family would be okay either way. It really didn't matter to Homer.

"Lutcher Stark was my father, whether it was biological, adoptive, or both," he declared. "I'm more interested in the drug tests. Now that's where things could get interesting."

As Randy strolled in the room from the kitchen, a cup of coffee in hand, he couldn't resist chuckling at his uncle's comment.

"Yep, Uncle Homer. Those bastards fed him everything from rat poison to phenobarbital to who knows what was prescribed in those records that burned to the ground with her drug store. With any luck at all, something will turn up in those tests."

"That's the problem, though, Randy," said Homer. "Luck hasn't been on our side for more than 70 years."

After Homer Stark's death in 2008, his children inquired as to whether the Stark Foundation would be maintaining the family mausoleum since none of Homer's children lived in Orange. They were assured a crew would be at the cemetery every two weeks to take care of the area around the site where H. J. Lutcher, W. H. Stark, and H. J. Lutcher Stark are interred with their wives. To date, that has not happened. Nelda Stark and Ruby Stark's graves are also unattended.

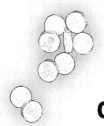

CHAPTER 10

*"The trust of the innocent is
the liar's most useful tool."*

— *Stephen King*

It was a short trip as Homer drove from Evergreen cemetery to the Port Authority of Orange, an impressive two story building on the riverfront. Rachel went along for the ride as her dad took flowers for Nita's grave, a Mother's Day tradition.

Somewhere between Polk and Border Streets on the trip to Evergreen, she had questioned Homer about the Louisiana lands supposedly owned by her grandfather.

"Supposedly?' asked Homer. "I'll show you supposedly on our way home. You have to remember that Dad owned hundreds of square miles of that state, plus who knows how much of Texas."

"But how do you know? There was hardly anything in the boxes, even the index, to show sales or leases in Louisiana. Just because you went hunting on property didn't mean he owned it."

Wearing a Stetson hat and smoking one of his favorite pipes, Homer almost bit through the stem as his oldest daughter cast doubt on his father's holdings. He had heard enough and decided it was time to teach Rachel a lesson, even if she was more than 50 years old. Once the flowers were delivered, the pair turned right out of the cemetery and right again on Border, they drove less than two minutes before crossing the railroad tracks and turning in at the Port Authority sign. From there it was a short distance to the portico extended from the stucco and brick structure. In its previous life, the building was headquarters of the Lutcher & Moore Lumber Company. Built in 1915, the mission style structure was solid and obviously well maintained as Rachel squinted in the sunlight at the building her father said was hurricane-proof and haunted as well. Huge palm trees bordered the property and orange trees – the first she had ever seen in Orange – lined one side of the parking lot.

Homer didn't say a word, just opened the car door and walked around to the front entrance of the building. Rachel followed suit, wondering to herself what this building on the Sabine River had to do with Louisiana, other than the fact you could see the neighboring state across the river.

She followed her father to the covered walkway and started up the steps to the main entrance. But Homer stopped a few feet behind her.

"Rachel, here's your land," he said, looking down at the granite extending the length of the walk. She joined her father and glanced down at the floor. There she saw a map, actually several maps, detailing holdings of the lumber company. The one they stood on identified parcels of land in Orange County, with Shangri La, the Neches River, Sabine River, and other landmarks clearly identified. Above it, near the main entrance, was a second map of the Joyce Tract with Mud Lake, Rabbit

Island and miles of canals etched in the stone. To the left of the entrance, along the walkway, was a much larger map with holdings in East Texas and West Louisiana clearly marked. She paused to study each of the renderings and noted the towns, rivers, creeks and railroads that were integral parts of the pictures.

As if he were reading her mind, Homer started explaining the importance of the railroad, the rivers, the roadways – all key ingredients to transporting the timber, providing access for trappers and oil companies.

"You know, each time I see these maps are like the first time," said Homer. "Takes you totally by surprise to see how much property was controlled by one family, one man, actually. And this doesn't even include land held by the Lutcher & Moore Cypress Lumber Company."

The words "Lutcher & Moore Cypress" jarred Rachel back to the present, recalling those words on correspondence from H. J. Lutcher to his wife, Frances Ann, while he worked the family business from an office in Lutcher, Louisiana. Until this moment, she thought the company name on the stationery was just part of the main Lutcher & Moore offices. She never considered one was a Texas corporation, the other regulated by Louisiana laws.

Homer was pleased his daughter was suitably impressed with the maps. It wasn't so much that she ever truly doubted him, but in the face of such overwhelming documentation presented by attorneys for the Foundation, how were you to know the truth? They must have taken extraordinary measures years ago to be so confident no one would discover what really happened.

A historical marker near the entrance caught Rachel's eye and she took a moment to read it. Everything about it seemed routine on the surface until she reached the last sentence: "The company ceased operations in the early 1930s."

She never recalled visiting the lumber mill as a child, but it was a fixture on the way to the yacht basin her father owned for 20 years. Countless conversations on trips to Homer's office, whether to fish from the dock or make extra money polishing the chrome on client's boats, seemed to automatically include a reference to the Lutcher & Moore property as they made the curve.

"Daddy, when did the lumber mill close?"

"Seems like it was in the late 1950s. I remember Dad was mad as hell because he'd just built the first electric mill in the country and Nelda wanted one of Eunice's stepsons to run it. Edwin Benckenstein, I think was his name."

"You think it was his name?"

"Well," said Homer, starting to laugh. "Dad rarely called him by his real name because he stayed so mad at him. He had a nickname for him that I couldn't repeat because it would reflect poorly on his mother. Let's leave it at that."

"So what does that have to do with when it closed?"

"Dad found out he was losing lots of money when he went over the books one night, fired Edwin and came out here and closed the plant. Put a chain and padlock on the front gate at midnight and never went there again."

"In the 1950s, correct?"

"Yes, but what difference does it make?"

"Probably none, but it seems strange that the historical marker claims it stopped operations in the 1930s."

Homer walked over to the marker and read the brief inscription.

"Why would they say that? Everybody in town knows that's a lie. Hell, lots of them worked here in the 1940s and 1950s."

"But how many of them came out here when the historical marker was dedicated? I'd almost bet it was done in the dark of night with no invitations to family members or those who might actually stop to read the marker."

Homer admitted he had never known the marker existed, a strange statement by itself since Lutcher & Moore had been a family business for more than 75 years. At the very least, he should have been on the guest list.

Father and daughter left the way they came in, through the gated entry and across the tracks that had been so essential to the location years ago. The trip to the cemetery, to Nita's gravesite, opened new windows with the side trip to the lumber mill site. Rachel now had plenty of reasons to explore the neighboring state, and there was no time like the present.

With retirement came time, allowing her to spend weekdays in Orange rather than limiting it to weekends or holidays. Rachel unfolded a Louisiana map and started to highlight specific parishes to visit. Using notes from the Lutcher & Moore visit to guide her, she made a short list of which ones to explore, with Cameron – the only one mentioned in Nita's will – at the top.

It was not yet daylight when she and Jake backed out of the driveway, drove silently by Eunice's home down the street, and continued to MacArthur Drive and Highway 87 to Port Arthur. As they approached MacArthur Circle, it seemed almost sad to see, even in the darkness, shadows reflecting the changes to their hometown. Gone were the town's outdoor movie theater with its impressive painting of Shangri La across the entrance, the Tower Restaurant with the best hot chocolate in town, the strip shopping center that seemed so modern in the 60s, the Pines Motel owned by their neighbors, and Zack's Burger House where all the teenagers hung out during high school. Now there was just a potpourri of businesses that seemed to change frequently and a feeling of depression created by the disappearance of days from long ago.

Brother and sister said nothing, not a word, until they reached the Rainbow Bridge at the eastern gateway to Port Arthur, the highest bridge in the South when it was built in 1938 with a vertical clearance of 177 feet – enough for the tallest Navy ship to pass underneath, not that it ever did. The huge span over the Neches River provided a panoramic view of the entire area as Jake's pickup neared the highest point just as the sun peeked over the horizon. In the distance was Sabine Lake and the low lying areas that marked a part of the Stark holdings. They stretched for miles to the east, while in the other direction refineries stood like sentries as they descended into Jefferson County where oil production created a prosperous economy. White billowing smoke from the tall, slender stacks and tiny lights outlining buildings of every size that dominated the property almost gave it a festive atmosphere at dawn.

"Just look at that," said Jake, motioning to the water below and in the distance. "Hard to imagine what in the world Granddaddy was thinking. That man loved the marsh, the outdoors, yet he turned it into chemical plants and contributed to one of the worst areas to live in the whole country. What a legacy."

Rachel knew he was right, but hoped her grandfather simply had not realized the havoc he unleashed on the area as he provided land for Chemical Row in Orange. It may have been good for the economy, not to mention his pocketbook, when DuPont, Goodyear, Firestone and others built on Stark and Brown lands in the early 1950s, but it certainly carried a high price as health and environmental issues surfaced in later years.

"Yeah, can you believe people still go fishing and crabbing along the highway at the base of the bridge – with Bailey's landfill right there? Always thought they should put some kind of sign up, you know, to warn people."

"What are you talking about?" she asked, glancing back to find the small area was now out of sight.

"Bailey's. That little fenced-in area just to the right of the bridge. That's not just a landfill, but was one of the most toxic areas in Texas, if not the whole damn country. Years ago – when no one really knew what they were doing – toxic waste was dumped in that area with no thought of the consequences. No regulations to follow, no precautions to take."

"But they cleaned it up, right?"

Jake laughed. "Well, let's put it this way. The government eventually spent some Superfund money trying to, uh… I believe 'mitigate the threat' was the term they used. Only problem is when you have such large quantities of chemicals in the system with no liner, what do you think? Especially with hurricanes and tropical storms stirring up the waters each year. Plus it was going to take longer and cost more than they thought, so they didn't get as much done as they planned."

"So it's dangerous to fish there?" asked Rachel.

"I'm saying I wouldn't fish there, especially when people are catching fish with one eye or scabs all over. Just look it up on the internet... google 'Bailey's Landfill' and if you're okay knowing there was arsenic and benzene at that location... and you trust the government... then go ahead and fish."

Minutes later they turned east on Highway 82 and crossed the Pleasure Island Bridge over Sabine Lake to Cameron Parish. More than 1400 square miles in size, it was the largest parish in Louisiana, yet perhaps the most remote. Some referred to it as the Louisiana Outback, a vast unspoiled wilderness with miles of beaches and four wildlife refuges. Fish and game were abundant, both in the low-lying areas and along the Gulf of Mexico waters. Fur bearing animals, cattle and a virtual storehouse of oil and gas added to the wealth of the area. It was a sportsman's paradise with 284,000 acres of both fresh and saltwater marshes, plus a bird sanctuary.

"What's the secret?" asked Rachel, focusing on the marshland to their left.

"Secret to what?" countered Jake.

"All my life I've heard you and Daddy talk about the Joyce Tract, about Cameron and Holly Beach. Almost as if there were something magical about hunting here. So what makes it so special?"

"It may not look like much to most people," he said, "but you're looking at land so unique you wouldn't find it anywhere else on the North American continent. Without getting too technical on you, it has everything to do with location – being west of the Mississippi where silt deposits carried to the ocean have created a fertility in the area unmatched in the United

States or Canada. I mean, you can't even imagine what it was like to hunt here, to have more species of ducks and geese – 34 was the number I was told – than maybe anywhere in the world.

"And the sound, the sight of them was enough to take your breath away."

He knew his sister still did not understand, so he motioned to the sky and pointed to the horizon.

"Dad would tell me stories of so many ducks getting up from the marsh that they resembled a black, waving cloud as thousands appeared and were so thick in flight it made it seem like nighttime. And the noise, the roar of those beautiful birds, would always announce their arrival.

"Some sportswriter from Chicago called it the 'winter Palm Beach bird resort.' Governors, senators, businessmen…they came from all over to hunt this land. They'd just board one of Granddaddy's speedboats in Orange to make the trip. About the only way you could get here back then. "

Jake asked if she remembered Ma Ferguson.*

"The Governor of Texas?"

"Yeah, that's the one. She was invited to go duck hunting in Cameron Parish – think it was her second term – and made the boat trip to the camp set up deep in the marsh.

"She didn't last long. Story goes there was a card game going on the first night and at some point Granddaddy came in and just randomly checked the guns as he walked across the room. He had this rule that loaded guns were not allowed inside.

"Anyway, one he picked up was loaded."

"And that was the Governor's?"

"Yep, short trip for her. Dad told me she was sent back first thing in the morning."

He continued with stories of how Lutcher Stark purchased and controlled almost 163,000 acres of the region, then dredged more than 149 miles of canals that crisscrossed the property to not only make it more accessible for hunting, but open it to the muskrat trade."

"Muskrats?"

"Don't laugh. It may not seem like much, but fur was big business. Shoot, one year Louisiana produced almost twice as many pelts as the whole country of Canada.

"You know, they just used dynamite to create those canals and worked their way across the marsh, taking in more than 500 square miles – some of it running right up to the edge of the Gulf of Mexico."

Jake slowed as they neared Johnson Bayou before arriving at Holly Beach, a favorite destination of Homer and Jake's when they went hunting back in the 50s. Beachfront cabins, an occasional restaurant and a gas station were pretty much the sum total of the area, but it held memories of good times with great friends years ago. The rustic beauty of Cameron Parish included not only the beachfront property, but cheniers in the surrounding area. Former beaches, over time they had become isolated from the sea by strips of marshes. With groves of majestic oaks with Spanish moss, punctuated by dewberry and blackberry vines in the spring, areas such as Grand Chenier, Front Ridge and Chenier Purdue portrayed a totally different look from the surf and beach communities.

Cameron, the seat of local government in the parish by the same name, was a few miles down the road and required a ferry to navigate the Calcasieu Parish channel separating the town from the western part of the highway. It only took a few minutes to make the crossing, then Jake drove into the small community as Rachel looked for signs of a courthouse.

"You should have asked someone," said Jake, irritated that his sister hadn't bothered to even get the address of the building.

"It can't be that difficult," she responded. "How many main streets can a town this size have?"

After driving the length of town with no success, Jake glanced at his sister and couldn't resist commenting. "Apparently they have enough to confuse us."

He drove back through Cameron, slower this time, and both spotted the flagpole set back from the road behind a smaller building fronting the highway. Jake turned on the side road and there it was in a wooded setting: the Cameron Parish Courthouse, just as it must have appeared when they built it in 1937. It was one of the few buildings left standing after Hurricane Audrey devastated the town in 1957.

Three stories high with the main entrance on the second floor, they climbed the two levels of stairs and seemed comfortable with the surroundings they found inside. A uniformed policeman in the foyer directed them to the records division to their left, where they found neatly organized volumes of records dating back to the 1870s. Long, slanted counters running the length of the room dominated the center of the room and allowed easy access to documents.

It was a new adventure and Rachel wasn't certain how to locate the various information, so she asked for help from the small brunette at the desk in the outer office. With her slight Cajun accent and a broad smile, the young woman gave a quick tour of the area and instructed both sister and brother on procedures to follow, location of different documents, and the all important "how to use the copy machine" directions.

"Now what?" asked Jake. "What's the plan, or do we even have one?"

"Of course there's a plan. We just may need to make it up as we go along," she replied, laughing at her brother's expression. "First, we need to find Nita's will that Granddaddy filed, then check to see if there was any other property in his name."

Within minutes, they located the will plus additional affidavits and a petition for tutorship of Homer and Bill. All filed in December 1941.**

"You know, somehow I thought Granddaddy would have more on his mind after Pearl Harbor than filing documents in a remote area," said Jake. "But here he was, the whole world at war, and he was more interested in selling a piece of property valued at less than $10,000."

"I can tell you one thing I've learned about Granddaddy. He didn't do anything without a reason," Rachel said. "In fact, the more I learn about him, the more I realize he moves in predictable patterns. December was always a big month for him at the courthouse, probably because fewer people were paying attention during the holidays."

With copies of the documents made, the two began working their way through Vendor and Vendee indexes. Selectively looking under family names like Stark, Lutcher, Brown – or company names like Orange Cameron Land Company or Del Dixie, and covering each era from the 1900s to the present. Once familiar with the format, the two were identifying documents to copy fairly quickly. Four hours and 52 minutes later, just shy of 2 p.m., they were paying for the copies and anxious to begin the trip home.

Conversation had been limited in the records room. Not only were they busy reading through the volumes and locating documents, but both agreed not to say much until they were safely in the car – out of range of others who might be linked in some manner to the Stark Foundation.

"Damn, I'm starving," said Jake as Rachel climbed in the truck and he started the engine.

"Is that all you can say after all the records we found?"

"All I know is you can read through the documents on the way home…even at the restaurant if you insist. But I've got to have something besides candy bars to eat."

He turned out of the courthouse parking lot on Highway 87 and went back to a seafood restaurant they saw earlier that morning. It was a good choice, even more so based on the people who dined there.

"There's just something about Louisiana that's hard to beat," Jake said, commenting on the friendliness of the people, their work ethic, spicy foods, humor and even the music. "The more I'm around them, the more certain I am they are the happiest people in the world."

Rachel agreed and they talked about family friends from Louisiana whose memories remained strong decades later. Jimmie Moncieus, Tom Kelly, Sam and Isabel Barton, Charlsie, Hebert, Thibodeaux and others who always had a smile, a story or a joke to share, not to mention the Cajun cuisine.

As the ferry landed and they returned to Orange along the beach road, Jake pointed out everything from pelicans to Mud Lake and the Sabine Wildlife Refuge. While the pelicans were the state bird and always interesting to see, Mud Lake and the Refuge had been part of the Stark properties.

"Why weren't they listed in the records?" asked Jake, realizing as he passed the markers and road signs that no documents they found mentioned the 1956 sale of the Joyce Tract to John Mecom. It had been one of the few times they recalled their father upset as Lutcher Stark insisted on selling the Louisiana lands promised to Homer.

"I'm not certain, but it wasn't an oversight. Too many of those boxes and too little detail about Louisiana to suit me," said Rachel, looking out the window and trying to understand how these hundreds of thousands of acres simply disappeared from the books. "If I were a betting person – and you know that I am – I'd have to say it has something to do with Louisiana law. Here everything was community property, regardless of how you acquired it. Yet all Nita owned in the entire State of Louisiana when she died was a small parcel of acreage in Cameron Parish. Or at least that's what Granddaddy swore to as executor. These records should prove, one way or the other, if he was an honest man."

Miriam A. Ferguson was the first woman governor of Texas. She served two terms, 1925-27 and 1933-35.

**Although Nita left her estate to Homer and Bill, Lutcher served as executor and guardian. In Louisiana, guardians were known as tutors.*

Henry Jacob Lutcher

Frances Ann Lutcher

Miriam Lutcher Stark
with grandsons Homer and Bill

William H. Stark

Carrie Lutcher Brown

Dr. Edgar Brown

Carrie Lutcher Brown with her son and daughter-in-law,
Edgar and Gladys Brown, as they christen the
"Dr. Edgar Brown" tug in Orange on January 13, 1941.

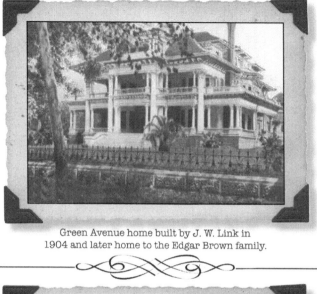

Green Avenue home built by J. W. Link in
1904 and later home to the Edgar Brown family.

F. H. Farwell home on Green Avenue served as model for
current Lutcher & Moore office building constructed in 1915.

1908: Lutcher Stark's room at The University of Texas.

1929: Lutcher & Moore's celebration marking
the birthday of W. H. Stark.

1930: Family photo of H. J. Lutcher Stark,
first wife Nita Hill Stark, and twin boys Homer and Bill.

1924: Photos of twins
Bill and Homer

1939: House at Roslyn Ranch, Colorado

Homer's horse "Pal"

1939: Homer Stark fishing in the newly-built lake at Roslyn.

1938: Bengal Guards rehearse in gym/band hall. Note William Herbert Dunton's painting ("McMullin Guide") centered on back wall.

1939: Bengal Guard drum majors modeling new western uniforms with Longhorn logo designed by Nita Hill Stark.

1939: Bengal Guards perform at Soldier Field for the Chicagoland Music Festival.

H. J. Lutcher Stark

Nita Hill Stark,
first wife of H.J. Lutcher Stark.

Ruby Childers Stark,
second wife of H.J. Lutcher Stark.

Nelda Childers Stark,
third wife of H.J. Lutcher Stark.

Bill Stark

Ida Marie Stark

Homer Stark

Becky and Homer Stark

1928: Sunset Grove Country Club

1940: H. J. Lutcher Stark enjoying a billiards game with sons – Bill (left) and Homer, at their home on 10th Street in Orange.

1940: Becky Havens Stark, first girl to lead The University of Texas band.

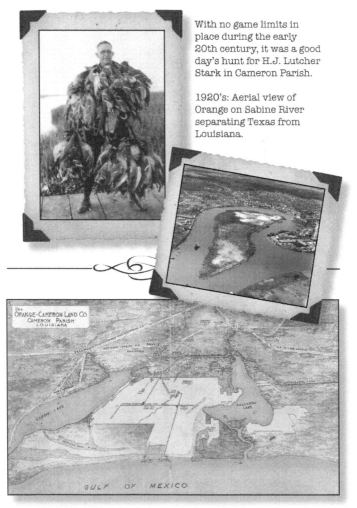

With no game limits in place during the early 20th century, it was a good day's hunt for H.J. Lutcher Stark in Cameron Parish.

1920's: Aerial view of Orange on Sabine River separating Texas from Louisiana.

1924: Map showing Cameron Parish property purchased in 1918 by H. J. Lutcher Stark.

1943: Navy Day parade in downtown Orange.

Opera House/ Holland Hotel

1940s: Lutcher Stark driving in Shangri La. The license plate forecast his future.

Photo Credits: Pictures of Edgar and Carrie Lutcher Brown, courtesy John S. Brown, Jr. Special thanks to Dr. Howard C. Williams (hcwilliams.com) for photos of the christening of the tug; aerial view of Orange; the Link and Farwell homes; Sunset Grove Country Club; the Navy Day parade and the Opera House/Holland Hotel. All other photos were provided by the Homer and Bill Stark families.

CHAPTER 11

"Now we got here in the State of Louisiana what's known as the Napoleonic Code. You see, now according to that, what belongs to the wife belongs to the husband... and vice versa..."

— **Stanley in Streetcar Named Desire**

From the moment you crossed the state line, you expected Louisiana would be different. The welcome sign was in both English and French (Bienvenue en Louisiane), a clear indicator you were now traveling in new territory. Jazz, gospel, zydeco and Cajun music offered a spirited background for the unique culture of the nation's 18th state. Not only did Louisiana have an official flower (the magnolia), bird (the brown pelican), and insect (the honey bee), but it had a State dog – the Catahoula Leopard.

Regardless of how often she crossed the Sabine River in the last 50 plus years, Rachel guessed she never really paid that much attention to Louisiana. The people had always been friendly and the food rivaled the nation's best offerings, but somehow she failed to appreciate the unique features of her neighbors to the east.

Their legal system, different from the other 49 states with its basis in the Napoleonic Code, was at the top of her list to explore.

Since the trip to Cameron Parish, she enlisted Randy's aid to investigate public records in some of the more than 60 parishes – rather than counties – in the state. Calcasieu Parish was their first stop since Lake Charles was located less than an hour from Orange.

Half a day later they had copied hundreds of pages, including an 82-page document for the Boise Southern sale in 1970. Forty million dollars worth of Louisiana land held by Lutcher & Moore was sold five years after Lutcher Stark's death. Since the same sale included at least two other $40 million transactions – for property in Newton and Orange Counties – it seemed the $10 million value placed on his estate had been a trifle low.

"Let's see. $120 million for part of his holdings," said Randy as they left the courthouse. "Pretty good return on your money."

"I have a feeling we're going to find a lot of unusual things in the next few days," said Rachel. "Did you see that affidavit about W. H. Stark? The one filed 40 years after his death? What was that all about?"

"You're asking me? All I know is it seems strange to file something like that after the man's been dead for decades. "

Rachel started to laugh, stopping to readjust her grip on one of the boxes holding the copies produced that day.

"Now what's funny?" asked Randy, juggling the box he was carrying.

"Did you see their faces as we kept making copies?"

"Yeah. I don't think they get too many people making…
what was it, more than 900 copies?"

"Something like that. How many more do you think we'll
find?"

They reached the truck and Randy was still calculating his
guess, taking into consideration neither cousin knew what they
would find as they followed I-10 across Louisiana.

He fired up the diesel engine on his pickup and exited the
parking lot, turning left on Lakeshore as they made their way
to the interstate. It was only a short distance as they stopped
at a red light before following the curve to the access road and
heading west to Texas.

"Ten thousand," said Randy.

"Ten thousand what?" asked Rachel.

"I think we'll find 10,000 documents before it's over.
We've got 62 more parishes to check and haven't even started
in Texas."

His cousin hesitated before speaking, then agreed with
him. Two parishes and more than 1400 documents to date.

Heading east again the next morning, they left by 7 with do-
nuts, coffee and juice providing a healthy start as they used
Interstate 10 as the primary link to the three parishes – Jeff
Davis, Iberia and St. Martin – they hoped to cover that day.

With Randy driving and Rachel reading through papers
copied in Lake Charles, the cousins kept a lively conversation
going for much of the drive. It seemed there was always something to talk about since Nelda's death five months earlier.

"What did Jake say about the Board meeting?" asked Randy,
referring to the annual meeting of the Stark Foundation Board

held the previous day. Nelda had appointed Jake to the Board two years before she died, and this was the first meeting since her death.

"Not a whole lot," responded Rachel. "It was business as usual, saying little and doing less, but he thought it odd no one mentioned Nelda. Wouldn't you think someone would say something, even if only acknowledging she died or the fact she would no longer be there?"

"That's strange, even for them. Who did they elect to replace her?"

"No one. Didn't even mention it. Apparently, they just went over the agenda and so-called report, broke for lunch, then returned for a presentation on how to properly run the foundation."

"And who in the world did that?"

"The esteemed legal team of Dyke and Spencer," said Rachel, laughing at the thought it had taken 39 years for the Foundation to talk about the legal and ethical way to operate. She continued telling Randy how an outline of procedures and background information were given to Jake, along with a copy of "Handbook for Private Foundations."

"I went through some of it last night and couldn't figure out why they would openly discuss what they had not done for so many years. It's almost like they were giving us a roadmap of where to look for their mistakes," she added.

Before Randy had a chance to respond, the exit at Jennings came up quickly and he turned his attention from foundation operations to locating the courthouse. Signs identified the city as the "Cradle of Louisiana Oil," but it was better known for its rich farmlands covering more than 300,000 acres. With a population of just over 11,000, the town was conveniently located midway between not only Lake Charles and Lafayette, but Houston and New Orleans.

With a turn here and a turn there, and a couple of red lights in between, the red brick courthouse was fairly easy to find but lacked the imposing stature of buildings the cousins expected to house government records. The interior was more like a school library than the records areas in Cameron and Calcasieu, but it held the same large books they needed to review for Vendors and Vendees.

Randy and Rachel now had a routine to follow, each carefully locating the section covering dates from the first entry to those shortly after Lutcher Stark's death in 1965. From there they focused on familiar names – those of family members, business associates, or any of a dozen businesses or corporations controlled by Lutcher Stark. Lutcher, Stark, Brown, Benckenstein, McKee, Moore, and Falwell were the most likely suspects.

One after another, they opened a book, found the section they wanted to review, closed the book, and went on to the next. It moved rather quickly since they found nothing of interest to even bother copying. Less than an hour later they returned to the car and headed east to Lafayette.

"Man, I can't believe we didn't find anything," said Randy, steering the truck onto the freeway at a pretty good clip.

"Just remember this area isn't known for timber, so I doubt Mr. Lutcher was even interested in this part of the state," replied Rachel. "We may not find much in the others today, but that's the beauty of it. If we didn't look, we might miss something really important."

"That's for damn sure," said Randy. "It still seems strange to me that there wasn't more in Cameron Parish. I know we got a lot, but there was a lot of land in the Stark family that just doesn't show up anywhere. Remember that map in your dad's office?"

She did. It had hung in that room for more than 50 years, clearly showing the holdings between Port Arthur, Texas and Cameron, Louisiana. Almost all of it owned by Lutcher Stark. Somehow none of it had shown up in the records they located.

Lafayette was soon on the horizon, partially due to Randy's lead foot and the fact he had made several trips there before to meet with Billy Clyde Cavanaugh, his family's attorney. He was familiar with the city and had no trouble locating Billy Clyde's office for a quick visit before departing for St. Martin-ville less than 30 miles away.

"Hey, man!" exclaimed Billy Clyde as Randy waltzed into the office unannounced.

Rachel watched as the two went through some ritual hand-shake and seemed amused about a comment that was obviously an inside joke. By all accounts, she would normally expect lawyers to be a bit more formal, but Billy Clyde was different. Young, ambitious and a bit outspoken at times, he loved to talk about Louisiana law. It was a subject that was definitely fasci-nating when you realized the obvious disparities separating it from the other states.

At 5'10 with jet black hair, dark eyes and an infectious smile, he was an attractive young man determined to right what he described as "the biggest scam of the 20th Century."

"Yes, sir. You get me some kick-ass documents to go with all those shenanigans they pulled over the last 60-something years, and the State of Louisiana will be more than willing to explain how things work on this side of the stateline," said Billy Clyde, with his voice becoming progressively louder as he ended the sentence.

He was still excited about the prospects of righting a wrong, and that was enough motivation to inspire the cousins to find more ammunition to help when their lawyers sat down in the next few weeks with the Stark Estate/Foundation to discuss the unusual matters that surfaced since Nelda's death.

Billy Clyde walked with them to the parking lot, giving them instructions on a short cut to Highway 31 to St. Martinville. Moments later, they were bound for the beautiful historic town, deep in the heart of French Creole country known for the Evangeline oak in Longfellow's poem.

"Ever been there?" asked Rachel.

"Not that I remember," said Randy. "But it seems we studied something about that poem when we were in high school – didn't we take a field trip?"

"I think one was planned. A hurricane or something came up and our class never made the trip. Too bad. We might have learned something useful back then.

"Speaking of learning something – did you know Nelda was the last person to see Miriam alive?" asked Rachel.

"What do you mean, I didn't know she had anything to do with her death…"

"Remember Murray, the chauffeur who worked for Miss Nita?"

"Yeah…"

"Well, two of his kids are still alive and I visited with them when Larry, the last surviving son, was here to visit his sister – they went to high school with Mother and Daddy, plus they spent summers at the ranch when they were growing up."

"So what does that have to do with Miriam?" asked Randy, still trying to negotiate the road as well as the conversation.

"I'm getting to that.... both told me what Daddy said years ago... the whole town was sad when Mr. W. H. died, and Miriam just took to her bed... broken hearted and all. Not sick, just sad and still grieving. Well... Murray's wife was helping inventory the Stark house since everything in it was going to the University of Texas. Then – out of nowhere, right in the middle of the afternoon, Eunice appeared inside the back door off the kitchen and told everyone to leave the house immediately– just drop what they were doing and get out."

"What does that have to do with Nelda?"

"Mrs. Murray didn't leave, she stayed behind to finish sorting some papers at the desk in the area just under the front staircase, but as she sat up in the chair she caught a glimpse of Nelda – hurrying upstairs with her black bag. You know, that one she always carried with her."

"Yeah, right. The one she used to make people think she was a nurse."

"Exactly. Anyway, Nelda went up to 'take care' of Miriam and the lady died that night."

Randy cocked his head, glanced at his cousin before looking back at the highway, then had to laugh.

"You gotta be kiddin' me."

"Nope. Mrs. Murray was absolutely positive what she saw. Nelda was treating Miriam and wasn't at all qualified. And the woman wasn't sick in the first place. Lutcher and Nita were in

Austin when it happened, and you know they would never have left town if she had been ill."

Again, Randy took his time framing his response before asking "Well, if she wasn't sick, what did it say on the death certificate? That would be the place to look, right?"

"Heart failure. And even though it was the law to conduct an autopsy if the death occurred at home, they didn't do it – which makes you wonder how they knew it was heart failure if they didn't check things out."

"Let me get this straight," said Randy. "You say Nelda killed Miriam?"

"No, I'm saying she was the last person to see Miriam before she died. But when you consider the woman was not sick to begin with, that Nelda arrived at the house in rather strange circumstances, plus the fact she wasn't trained at all in the medical field, and an autopsy was never done even though it was required by law, doesn't it kind of make you wonder what was going on?"

"But why? Why would Nelda want Miriam out of the way?"

"Probably figured no one would think anything of it if Miriam died a few months, even a few years, early. Lutcher would have total control of the family fortune and all Nelda had to do was get rid of Nita and make her move."

"But he married Ruby after Nita died," said Randy.

"Yeah – and that was a surprise to Nelda and Eunice," said Rachel. "But it didn't stop them. She just got rid of Ruby – Larry said Nelda even got rid of her own mother when Mrs. Childers realized how Ruby died."

"Wait a minute – you mean she killed her own mother, too? How in the world would Larry know that?"

"Servants see and hear everything, and they talk to each other. Larry said Mrs. Childers overheard Nelda and Eunice bragging about how everything fell into place after they took care of Ruby. She confronted them and next thing you know, she's in Evergreen next to Ruby."

"Whoa, let's hang on just a little second," said Randy. "Seems funny they'd say something like that if Mrs. Childers was home. And that house was so small you'd know if she was there."

"That's exactly what I asked Larry," said Rachel. "But he explained that Mrs. Childers wasn't in the house – she was outside working in the flower bed just below the windows where they were talking. Pretty easy to hear every word since the windows were open. No air conditioning back then."

Rachel added that the maid told Larry she believed Nelda used the oleander to poison her mother. Mrs. Childers became ill that evening and died a week later.

"Oleander?" asked Randy, still trying to sort out what he just heard. "Those flowers that grow all over town?"

"Yeah, the whole plant – flowers and all – is apparently one of the most poisonous in the country."

"Nelda grew her own poison in the backyard?" asked Randy, almost laughing at the thought.

"Some of it," said Rachel. "Guess it came in handy for emergencies when she didn't have time to call the drug store or have Mrs. Scofield bring in supplies from the hospital.

"With the drugs and enough information to blackmail Granddaddy, the only people standing between Nelda and all that money were Daddy and Uncle Bill. And, like Larry said, 'that woman thought everyone was disposable' and made sure Granddaddy never was close to his sons again."

Randy seemed somewhat stunned, then grinned, flashing that mischievous look perfected over the years.

"Cuz, I do believe one thing. ..."

"What's that?"

"If Hell ever opens a branch office, and I'm not saying it hasn't already happened, it would be in Orange, Texas with Nelda in charge."

The two-lane highway entered the city limits and Rachel pulled out the map Billy Clyde's office had printed from the internet. As they neared the downtown area, both looked for Virginia Street yet couldn't help but appreciate the architecture and ambience of the small town. Block after block showcased a different look, with paint and wrought iron trim teaming with impressive arches and wooden borders around doorways and windows.

"Certainly doesn't look like Orange," Randy observed.

"That's for certain, but it makes you wonder what Nelda, Eunice and Clyde were thinking when they practically turned Orange into a ghost town," said Rachel. "Why do you think they did that? If you look at the pictures from the 1940's and 50's, there were lots of good things about downtown. Remember the toy store on the corner, across from the newsstand and just down the street from the Strand theater? And the Holland Hotel or J. C. Penny's?"

"Yep. The Lone Ranger and Roy Rogers for a nickel on Saturday morning. Those were the days," said Randy.

"Turn left here. I think we just passed Virginia."

Indeed they had, but Randy made the block and they turned into the parking lot adjacent to the courthouse. Up the steps to the main entrance, they found an outer foyer with several employees assisting customers. Continuing past those desks, they entered the parish clerk's office and found an extensive area filled with documents. Row upon row of counters with ample shelving along the walls filled with indexes. More than they had imagined based on previous stops.

"Surely there is something here," said Randy. "I mean, look at all these books."

"Well, you know the drill. Let's get started. Do you want to check the Vendor or Vendee listings?"

"I think I really shine at getting copies made and operating the vending machines," he replied, half joking yet serious.

On that note, they agreed to start with the Vendee listings and covered the same names as before. Occasional entries were found tracing back to the Lutchers and W. H. Stark or Miriam Stark, but little if anything seemed to have Lutcher Stark or Nita's name attached. Even the Brown family had several transactions listed. They found no listing for John Mecom with regard to the $15 million purchase of the Joyce Tract in 1956.

A candy bar and Diet Coke later, they moved into the Vendor section and repeated their efforts to track family names. A few transactions surfaced, but nothing significant.

"There has to be some record of the Joyce Tract sale," Randy said. "But I'll be damned if we can find it."

"It has to be here," said Rachel. "Somewhere in Louisiana there should be a recording of the transfer, don't you think?"

"Absolutely, but what name would they use?"

"You're right. We've been looking for Mecom and they probably listed it under something else. Let's look again in the Vendor books, but this time check under the sale date and see how they listed the buyer."

Moments later they had the answer directly in front of them.

"The Largo Company. Who would have thought it?" said Randy. "I don't ever recall any mention of it by that name, just Mecom. No wonder we never found it earlier."

Apparently John Mecom had several partners when he purchased the large land tract in Cameron Parish, plus surrounding areas. As they skimmed the lengthy document, it was apparent they should copy first, read later in the interest of time. Randy took it over to the desk and turned in the slip of paper indicating the pages to be copied. The clerk added it to the others they had requested to be duplicated and indicated it would be at least an hour before they would be ready.

"Now what?" asked Randy. "Think we should keep looking?"

"Absolutely," said Rachel. "You never know what we might find."

With no other names to check, they picked up a couple of indexes– "C" and "D" – and decided to explore them by reviewing names to see if any seemed familiar. The goal was to check the years 1911-1939, the time period when Lutcher and Nita were married.

Page after page, the two examined the entries of each index, hoping to find something, anything regarding their grandfather. They had moved from 1911 to 1938 in the "D" volume when they spotted an entry for Dibert, Stark and Brown.

"Who is Dibert? And what is Dibert, Stark and Brown?" asked Rachel.

"Got me," said Randy. "Never heard or seen that name before."

With the volume and page number written on a post-it note, they located the appropriate book and returned to the counter in order to review whatever transaction was listed.

"Well, look what we found," said Rachel, skimming the pages that detailed the 1938 dissolution of Dibert, Stark and Brown. "Lutcher and Nita's interest was about 35% when the company folded and land holdings were distributed to the stockholders. Looks like about 30,000 acres in St. Martin, Assumption, Terrebone, and LeFerrouche went to Lutcher and Nita."

"So what happened to that land?" asked Randy.

"I have no idea – doesn't appear to go anywhere at all," said Rachel. "It would have probably been in Lutcher's name, but I don't remember seeing anything about that acreage today."

Randy agreed, pointing out that the whole investigation had pretty much produced one mystery after another. Yet at least they were starting to find documents related to the holdings in Louisiana – something that had been conveniently left out of discovery documents produced during the 1988 lawsuit.

They added the newest find to the copy list and glanced at the clock over the main desk. It was 2:45 in the afternoon and half an hour later they were on the road, with more than 300 pages to add to the "collection" as Randy called it. Next stop was New Iberia, but they only located one document and headed west to Texas.

"So what's on the list for tomorrow?" asked Randy.

"Vernon and Beauregard," said Rachel, without hesitation.

"That was quick. Something I should know?"

"Nope. Just think it's worth looking there since both parishes were involved in the Boise Southern sale, but didn't have any real estate listed in the document we found in Calcasieu Parish."

Twelve hours after they arrived home, Randy was back in Homer's driveway with coffee in hand. They had agreed to drive to Leesville first, home of Fort Polk and the Vernon Parish courthouse.

Avoiding Interstate 10, the cousins headed north on Highway 87 to Deweyville, then turned east to the Louisiana line. The two-lane highway took them over the Sabine River as they drove over the first of several small bridges –"crossings, if you asked me" said Randy – and through the piney woods that characterized the border along the river. Thick stands of pine forests dominated both sides of the road as it cut through 18 miles of Calcasieu Parish before heading north to Leesville.

"Did you know when we were growing up that he owned so much property?" asked Randy.

"No. Looking back, I guess I didn't think about how much money or land he had. Never really thought about whether he was rich or not. The house he lived in was small and he drove a Chevrolet like anybody else. He was just our grandfather and we didn't get to see him that much anyway."

"Lots of things we didn't know unless someone told us, and no one really talked until Nelda was six feet under," said Randy.

Rachel gazed at the countryside, then told her cousin about a conversation with Clemmie's nephew about how tough Orange was years ago, especially if you were black.

"Homer Delarue told me stories that certainly weren't in any history book I ever read. About curfews, random shootings and hangings, just miserable treatment of Negroes in the 20s and 30s. People riding by in trucks and taking shots at them."

"Well, not to excuse it, but I think Orange was pretty much like a lot of southern towns in those days," came Randy's reply.

Conversation continued on a lighter note for the rest of the trip as they exchanged stories about growing up, life after high school, and commented on the passing images of life in Louisiana as Randy's red pickup moved at the maximum speed the law allowed.

As they approached Leesville from the south, it was immediately obvious a military base was nearby. Signs, vehicles, American flags and uniformed personnel sent the message. Closer to the downtown area, Randy looked for the street leading to the courthouse and impressed even himself when he saw it soon enough to turn right and head straight for their destination.

"Good job," laughed Rachel, acknowledging one of the few times they found a courthouse on the first try. "Now let's find a parking place."

Construction around the building indicated a new courthouse was being built, but the current one looked good to them. With a tote bag filled with notepads, index cards, pens and a magnifying glass, they headed downstairs to the Clerk's office to begin their search.

"Wow! This is one big room," said Randy, looking around at the vast area that housed the history of Vernon Parish. A small area to the left housed the Vendor and Vendee books, while the larger one that covered 80% of the giant room had neatly organized records dating back to the 1800's.

Rachel checked with the young woman at the information desk to verify the procedures and learn about the copy policy. To date, each parish had a different rate and preference for requests to make duplicates. Vernon was no different, but seemed to be the most reasonable and helpful of the ones they had visited.

"Yes, ma'm, you'll find almost anything you need to get started over here," said Carla, the attendant at the help desk. "Any questions, you just ask them. Can't find it, don't understand it, whatever. You just let me know."

Little did she realize how much help she would be as Randy and Rachel immediately discovered several long documents to copy. With post-it notes again marking the ledger pages, Rachel wrote each volume and page number on request forms that Randy took to Carla. The process would continue for more than four hours as the cousins found more information than they could have anticipated.

The largest document, and the first they located, was the Boise Southern sale in 1970. The same transaction that covered 82 pages in Lake Charles numbered 320 in Leesville. While individual tracts of land were missing in the smaller version, every piece of real estate was detailed in the longer one. Including multiple examples of property that was transferred from Lutcher Stark's estate after his death to Lutcher & Moore.

"So much for being truthful," thought Rachel, referring to Nelda's claim that the only property he owned in Louisiana at his death was the Big Lake acreage in Cameron Parish. A claim still made by Nelda's lawyers.

Randy returned to the counter where they were methodically making their way through the alphabet of individual names and corporations that had become their guide to tracing property. Leases, purchases and sales of everything from timber and oil to real estate seemed to be everywhere they looked, regardless of which family name or corporation they used.

"Can you believe this?" he asked. "We could stay here the rest of the week and still not finish."

"True," said Rachel. "But we can always come back. I think Carla has several people in the back making copies – probably at least a 1000 different entries. I'd still like to make it to DeRidder and see what Beauregard has to offer, wouldn't you?"

"Damn right. That was home office for Boise Southern, so I'd bet there was a lot of timber in that parish."

They checked in with Carla and she advised them it would be an hour before all the copies requested would be ready. A quick trip back the way they came to the local Dairy Queen for a hamburger, then the two returned to the courthouse, paid for the copies and were on their way to DeRidder.

The Beauregard Parish courthouse was two blocks off the main highway, near the library, with parking limited to a rather small lot in front and parking spaces lining the streets around the building.

Up the front steps to the second floor, they had no trouble locating the Clerk's office. It was just to the left, through a set of double doors, but significantly smaller than the one in Vernon Parish. They followed the same procedure as they checked with the front desk for directions and policies. Once the ground rules were established, they set in motion the system that had served them well: review the indexes for specific names, cross check with volume and page numbers of identified documents, then turn in requests for copies.

With the clock at twenty till four and time running short, there was little conversation as both cousins worked to locate as much as possible before closing time. Diet Coke and candy bars kept up their energy level as they finally checked each name off the list and turned in final requests for copies.

A college student working part-time had been assigned to help them, but explained there was no way to complete the hundreds of requests that same day. Randy offered to come back the following week, but they would stay until five and take whatever copies had been completed at that time.

"What a haul," said Randy. "I think we worked so fast here that I'm not entirely sure what we are even having copied."

He went outside for a cigarette, leaving Rachel behind to review her notes and wait for the copies. She started flipping through some of the Vendor indexes out of curiosity, ending up with the one marked "U-V-W." None of the names on the list started with any of those letters, but it was interesting to look if for no other reason than the exquisite penmanship.

Less than 10 minutes passed when Randy returned through the double doors. As Rachel looked up, he knew immediately something had happened. He crossed the room, keeping his eyes focused on his cousin, almost as if something surreal was occurring. As he approached Rachel and the index she was reading, her right hand simply pointed to the left column with the words "United States of America" beautifully written down the side of the page. The second column, the one identifying the Vendee, had "H. J. Lutcher" opposite each of the 30 entries on that page.

"What's this?" asked Randy.

"Land patents. Issued in 1877 to Mr. Lutcher by the United States and, in some cases, the State of Louisiana."

"Why aren't they listed under Lutcher Stark?"

"Because they weren't filed until 1964, 1970 and 1991. They just kept them in the vault, I guess, making it virtually impossible for anyone to know since they weren't included in the public records for more than 100 years. Tax bills would still be sent to the Stark offices, regardless of who was in charge. No wonder they didn't show up in Nita's estate. They intentionally delayed filing them so there was no trace."

"So, you're telling me these 30-something entries were kept from us?" asked Randy.

"No," Rachel said, starting to turn the pages. "I'm telling you that 26 pages with 30 entries each were kept from us."

CHAPTER 12

"Power is the ultimate aphrodisiac."
— *Henry Kissinger*

At home in College Station, Rachel put down the newspaper, picked up the phone and dialed the number written in her address book. She had thought about calling several times earlier, but hesitated just long enough to change her mind.

On the third ring she heard a familiar voice say "Hello."

"Mary Anne, it's Rachel. Hope this isn't a bad time to call."

"Rachel?" came the voice with the charming Southern accent. "Your mother called me a few weeks ago. It was just like yesterday catching up with all the news in Orange."

"Judging from what Mother said, it sounded like you were the one catching us up on the news," laughed Rachel.

The two women talked for almost an hour about their younger years before addressing the reason for the call: Mildred Gallagher's recollections of Nelda and Lutcher. She worked in the Stark offices for years, along with husband Frank Gallagher, one of Lutcher Stark's closest associates. The Gallagher's two children – David and Mary Anne – were classmates and friends of Rebel and Jake, and close enough in age to have known Rachel when they were growing up.

"Did your mom tell you about our conversation?"

"She certainly did. And I have to admit that, even after talking with others who knew Nelda, it was hard to believe she could be any worse," said Rachel. "Obviously, I was wrong."

"You really should talk to Mother. I know she can tell you a lot more about what really went on back then," Mary Anne said. "Why don't you call Saturday when she comes over for her weekly visit?"

Rachel pictured the 92-year old Mildred who now lived in an assisted living complex, but spent weekends at her daughter's home and going out to dinner before returning to her apartment. From all accounts, she seemed to be mentally sharp and willing to shed light on the past.

"Actually," she began, "I was hoping it would be all right to visit in person. The telephone has its advantages, but it would be more fun to see you in Little Rock."

Mary Anne's response was immediate as she not only agreed, but began planning for the weekend. Rachel and Becky would drive to Little Rock, Mildred would join them, and the guests from Orange would be staying in the extra room at Mary Anne's home.

Moments after they said goodbye, Rachel dialed her parent's number in Orange.

"Okay, I owe you dinner," she said as her mother answered the phone.

"Told you that's what she said. She is a really sharp lady, always has been."

"I know, I know," said Rachel. "But when you really think about what she told you, most normal people would think it a bit odd, even for Nelda. Mary Anne mentioned it again when we talked, assuring me the facts haven't changed over time. Mildred tells the same story today that she did 30 or 40 years ago."

"So are you going to call Mildred?"

"Nope. We're driving to Little Rock this week, so pack your bags."

Two days later, Rachel and her mother left Orange and headed north to Arkansas. In between stops for gas and food, Mildred and Frank Gallagher's relationship with Nelda and Lutcher was the main topic of conversation for the first half of the 400-mile journey. That and what Mildred shared about firsthand accounts of others in and out of the office.

Becky Stark's memory was amazing as she recalled stories, incidents, situations...whatever you might call them...that took place more than 50 years ago. She could remember individuals, their family members, who said what, where someone sat in school, what instrument a classmate played, who was related to whom, and countless other observations that might seem trivial on the surface but offered keys to understanding both past and present.

"What did Mary Anne say about the million dollar offer?" asked Becky, knowing Rachel had lots of questions when her mother first told her the story.

"Exactly the same thing Mildred told you, just adding a little more detail," said Rachel, thinking about her reaction when she first heard about Nelda offering Mildred a million dollars for each of her two children – on the condition she divorce Frank. It simply didn't make sense. Anyone could take the money and simply remarry. Rachel couldn't imagine her grandmother giving millions of dollars away. More importantly, why? Why would you even think of doing something like that?

Almost word for word, she told her mother what Mary Anne described. How Nelda came by the Gallagher's home one evening, saying she had an offer to make Mildred. Mary Anne could hear them talking in the bedroom and peeked in as Nelda offered Mildred a million dollars each for David and Mary Anne. Money that would be put in trust until they were 21 years old on the condition they left Orange and had no contact with their father. Mildred said nothing at first, shocked at such a proposal.

"When she refused and told Nelda to leave, Mary Anne ran from the doorway and into the living room,"said Rachel. " She heard both women still arguing before Nelda left and stormed out the front door without closing it behind her."

"Did she say why Nelda made the offer?"

"Frank may have just been the next name on the list. He was one of the few she hadn't fired yet. But she made his life so miserable at the office that he had a drinking problem. Nelda told Mildred she wanted the family to leave him so he'd just self destruct. Mildred will tell us more."

Neither woman said anything. Perhaps they were trying to picture what would possess someone to act that way, or maybe they were just counting their blessings.

At Texarkana, they took Interstate 30 to Arkansas and what promised to be happy days with old friends. It was only a couple of hours to Little Rock and the pair decided they would spend the night in a motel when they arrived and locate Mary Anne's home the next morning.

Miles of freeway weaved through the pine forests and scenic countryside of southwest Arkansas, almost as if untouched by the fast paced and often unsightly advance of civilization. The mood picked up as they agreed to talk about anything but Nelda for the rest of the evening, fully aware she would be the topic for the next two days.

Little Rock was a welcome sight after the eight-hour trip, with both mother and daughter anxious to turn in early after dinner and a quick phone call to touch base with Homer and check on Rachel's dog. Morning couldn't come soon enough.

In rush hour traffic in a town neither had visited in recent years, highway numbers, street names, construction areas – each added to the delay before they found 1212 Winding Creek in the fashionable northwest section of the city. Before they had a chance to reach the front porch, Mary Anne appeared at the door, all smiles as she walked quickly to greet them and help with their luggage.

"You made it! Mother's going to be so thrilled to see you."

Becky Stark hugged the young woman and began a conversation that lasted well past their entrance into the home. With luggage put away, the three gathered in the kitchen for coffee and conversation. Photo albums were exchanged, with pictures of children and grandchildren, graduations and proms, vacations and hunting trips spilling over the breakfast table. Laughter filled the room as pictures of Mildred and Becky at the Tacky Day golf tournament at Sunset Grove presented them in a new light, one that clearly showed a sense of humor when it came to fashionable attire.

"We do need to get Mother. She would love this so," said Mary Anne, wiping tears as she continued to laugh at the old photographs. A quick phone call and they were off to pick up Mildred and return for lunch, plus the rare opportunity to listen to tales only the two older women could recount.

Mildred was ready to go, probably long before they called. Anxious to see her old friend, she wasted no time getting dressed and waited by the large window in the lobby. Her face broke into a broad grin as she saw Becky walking toward the office and the two women hugged as they met for the first time in more than 20 years. Arm in arm, they followed Mary Anne to the car and talked the entire drive home.

Old friends, family updates, special recipes long forgotten. The conversation covered it all. They were just getting around to Nelda when they reached the house.

"Honey, we have so much to talk about," Mildred told Becky. "It seems the older I get, the harder it is to believe they have gotten away with it for so long."

Mildred selected a favorite wingback chair in the living room that was placed near another upholstered in a coordinated fabric. Becky sat there while Rachel and Mary Anne took the couch.

"Long story, for sure. But it all began years before Lutcher ever married Nelda. Joyce Broussard – you remember her, Becky, couple of years older than Nelda but still lives in Orange, knew what they were up to when Eunice and Nelda made that vow in college."

Mildred began telling the story. One that dated back to when Eunice and Nelda were attending Texas State College for Women, about a plan to marry wealthy older men with grown children, then take over their fortunes.

"You have to be kidding," said Rachel. "I thought they didn't even know each other until Eunice moved to Orange to teach school."

"That's what they wanted everyone to think," continued Mildred. "But they didn't count on Joyce moving back years later and sharing the college secret with others in town. By then, they were on their way. Eunice's husband died shortly after they were married – complications from toe surgery in New Orleans, I believe is what she said – and Nelda married Lutcher.

"She didn't like anyone to be close to Lutcher, so her first steps were to distance him from his friends, his business associates, especially his sons. Anyone who was a threat to her had to go. It was the most calculated takeover I do believe I'd ever heard of. No one could stop her. Not even Lutcher."

The stories continued for more than an hour, with Becky adding details to Mildred's as they talked of individuals or events from the 1940's. Especially interesting to Rachel were tales of Nelda pursuing Lutcher, going with him to nightclubs in Lake Charles and pretending to enjoy herself. Or accompanying him on trips to the marsh. Although Nelda disliked boats and couldn't swim, she pretended she liked the water until they were married.

"Why, that woman ran after him like nothing you've ever seen. When he finally agreed to marry her, she insisted the ceremony take place the next day. A Thursday. Who in the world gets married on a Thursday? Happened so fast that we couldn't believe it. The whole office was in shock, even more so later when she insisted on setting up her own office and gradually took over the books."

Rachel and Mary Anne sat speechless. Becky urged Mildred to tell them more.

"Oh, my. It was hard to believe, growing up in Orange and finding out firsthand about lesbians in the Stark offices," replied Mildred. "But Lutcher Stark himself was in the rather unusual position of warning the secretaries to stay away from Nelda and Eunice."

"Granddaddy did what?" interrupted Rachel.

"He warned us about them. I remember it clear as day when he pulled me aside and said to be careful of Nelda and Eunice – they liked 'threesomes'. I swear I thought I would faint when he told me that. Everyone seemed to know about Nelda and Eunice, but I had no idea they were recruiting for their team."

That was all the women needed to break out in laughter. A multi-generation laugh that was almost uncontrolled before subsiding, only to start again when they pictured scenes that must have generated daily conversations around the office years ago.

"I don't know about you all, but I could use a drink," said Mary Anne, moving toward the kitchen with an amused look on her face. She returned with something for everyone as the conversation continued.

In her absence, Becky and Mildred resurrected the infamous million dollar offer and were discussing similar offers made by Nelda in days that followed.

"She simply wasn't going to give up trying to destroy Frank, but eventually she withdrew and left us alone. At home, anyway," Mildred said. "The office was a different story. She didn't even try to hide her hatred of us and Lutcher was helpless to stop her."

"What do you mean?" asked Rachel.

"Your grandfather had no control over her. Whatever she had on him worked most of the time, and when it didn't she'd just whip out those pills and he'd sit and stare a lot. I remember when she wanted Lutcher to change his will and Frank was there, trying to make her understand that he couldn't disinherit the boys, especially all that Louisiana property that was protected by the forced heirship law. Not to mention Lutcher was obviously drugged and too out of it to make any changes."

"So what happened with the will?" said Rachel.

"That, my dear, is an interesting question," responded Mildred. "The will they probated after his death was brought to the hospital a couple of weeks before he died, but dated to coincide with the one Nelda and Clyde burned. They asked George Kelly, one of the Stark lawyers, to bring the new will to Galveston along with a notary from the office.

"Not long after that I overheard Nelda laughing about the problems getting that signed in the hospital. They had to hold Lutcher's hand and move it across the page. Did it a couple of times to get it right. About the time they were finished, in comes Bill to check on his dad. Ten seconds earlier and he would have caught them."

Mildred continued with the story, explaining that Mr. Kelly, a longtime judge and highly respected attorney who joined the Stark staff in the 1950s, was haunted by any role he might have played in helping Nelda take property that belonged to the boys. So much so that he committed suicide, a self-inflicted gunshot to the head in his home down the street from the Gallaghers.

"Or that's what they said happened," said Becky, picking up where Mildred left off. "The strange thing was Nelda and

Jo Scofield, the hospital administrator, were there and cleaned up the scene before calling the police. No police report was filed, no note was found, no autopsy was performed.

"George's wife left Orange within a year of his death. She hated Nelda and Eunice, swore they'd never control her, and spent the rest of her life in Dallas."

Mary Anne had been a listener for most of the day, but even she had to question the new storyline being told. There had to be a police report when someone died, especially if the crime scene was tampered with and, in this case, completely cleaned. What were Nelda and Mrs. Scofield doing there when he shot himself? Where was Mrs. Kelly? Why did he do it? Did he do it?

There were lots of questions to consider, especially with the unlikely presence of one of the richest women in the United States. The Orange police force had no report. Not one notation in their records indicating the death by gunshot had occurred.

"We don't do suicides" was the response of the officer on duty when Rachel requested records of the incident.

"Makes you wonder if it really was self-inflicted – or if Nelda was just nervous he was going to tell Homer and Bill about the forged will," said Mildred. "Or if he really shot himself, what did he tell Nelda before he pulled the trigger? Something had to be really wrong to cause Eleanor Kelly to leave Orange behind and never look back."

The women dwelled on memories of Eleanor, recalling her years as secretary to Lutcher Stark before marrying the handsome former judge and attorney when he joined the staff. She knew more than most about what happened in those offices, enough to question Nelda's actions or motives the night George Kelly died.

Mildred recalled one conversation when Eleanor disclosed how Nelda and Clyde McKee, her attorney, misdirected proceeds from a $25,000 life insurance policy that should have gone to Homer and Bill. During the months after Lutcher died, the policy was found in a box, overlooked for years. It named Nita Hill Stark as the beneficiary, which meant Homer and Bill should receive the money as her heirs. But a letter to the life insurance company from Clyde informed them Nita had died and identified Nelda as Mrs. H. J. L. Stark. No mention was made of the sons and Nelda received the money.

"Eleanor was quite a lady," said Mildred. "Everyone liked her and I'll always remember the looks we exchanged on those trips to Louisiana. It just never seemed right to see Nelda with Lutcher. Seemed to be common knowledge she was a lesbian, but Nelda had him fooled. Starting as far back as the day they buried Ruby when she was sitting in his lap as they drove to the cemetery."

"Excuse me, Mother. What did you say?" Mary Anne asked.

"Everyone knew Nelda was 'different'."

"No, no. The part about sitting in Mr. Stark's lap at the cemetery. How would you know that?"

"Your dad and I were in the car that followed the family. George and Eleanor were with us. If you just looked straight ahead it was no secret Nelda was sitting in his lap, running her hand through his hair and resting her head on his shoulder. Talk about moving in while the body was still warm, she didn't lose one moment."

A man's voice was heard as Mary Anne's husband entered the kitchen from the garage, announcing his arrival almost as a warning. Just in case the women wanted to change the subject before he joined them. His slender frame broke the six foot mark and his glasses framed a handsome face as Jeff Logan walked in, a boyish smile instantly injecting a warm feeling in the room's atmosphere.

"Ladies, I know you have lots to talk about, but you also have to eat. So I'm inviting you to dine with me this evening at a little Italian place said to have some of the best cuisine in Arkansas. Think you can be ready in 15 minutes?"

It was unanimous as each moved quickly to freshen up for dinner with dear friends. Instinctively, they knew Nelda's name would not be mentioned. No one wanted to spoil the evening.

CHAPTER 13

"A lie can travel halfway around the world
while the truth is still putting on its shoes."

—Mark Twain

Tracy Corley was next on the list. He knew all of Homer's children in his role as a junior high school counselor before taking a job in the Stark offices – "going over to the dark side" as Ramona often said.

When plans were in place to restore the W. H. Stark home adjacent to Nelda's offices, Tracy signed on as curator of the elegant Queen Anne style structure. Once it opened to the public, he could be found there early each morning and always had a pot of coffee ready when Homer stopped by to visit.

Rather short and round, there always seemed to be a huge grin on his face and a hug reserved especially for Homer and Becky's kids whenever they surprised him with a visit. He shared a love of antiques, flea markets and estate sales with Becky and they often called each other to compare notes or prices on items either might be interested in adding to their collections.

You could count on Tracy (still Mr. Corley to Rachel) to know something about everything going on in the Stark offices. When he learned Nelda was going to rid herself of Lutcher's gun collection and considering giving it away to one of the guards, it was Tracy who phoned Homer and advised him to pay a visit to Nelda. He did, and she gave him his father's guns. But today Rachel was interested in something far more explosive than rifles and shotguns as she called ahead to see if her friend was home.

Part of his salary package with Nelda included use of one of her rental homes for only $100 a month. Located next door to Eunice and across the street from Shangri La, it was less than 60 seconds by car or a relatively short walk from Homer's house. Rachel chose a combination to avoid having her car spotted at his home. She parked at the community center two blocks away and walked the rest of the way.

The loud doorbell shattered the silence and Rachel laughed quietly as she heard Mr. Corley coming to the door. He always seemed to bump into something and utter the same expression each time. The door opened and she was not disappointed. His smile, hug and enthusiasm warmed her heart.

"Rachel. Girl, it's good to see you. How are the boys?"

"Michael and Patrick are just fine – happy and healthy, and you are obviously feeling better, walking like nothing ever happened!" she said, referring to an illness that sidelined him several months earlier.

"Yes, ma'm. I'm doing great. We've got a lot to catch up on."

He ushered her into the kitchen area and offered her a Coke, pouring it into a Tweety bird collectible glass he used on special occasions, then took her on a tour of the living and dining areas, pointing out some of his latest discoveries. A cranberry vase, cut glass ice cream bowl, Roseville pottery, a stunning cobalt blue crystal bowl, miniature carnival glass punch set, tiny western figurines. He always had something new to show her. The whole house seemed to burst at the seams with hundreds of items he purchased over the years as part of one collection or another.

Conversation flowed from her job and her boys to his plans for a trip to his hometown of Gilmer in East Texas. Eventually each took a seat at the massive dining room table. Tracy at one end, Rachel at the other. They faced sideways and leaned forward in order to make eye contact since the table was always filled with some of the taller pieces he collected and blocked your view.

To someone visiting for the first time, it may have seemed like an odd arrangement. But it was normal for the two friends.

"Tell me how I can help. You know, I can't even imagine what stories you've heard," Tracy said with a definite twinkle in his eyes.

"Are you sure you don't mind, Mr. Corley? I would never want to put you in a bad situation. But I'd appreciate it if you could help me with some details – telling me some and confirming others."

"Don't worry about it. Ever since Nelda died, I've thought about retiring anyway."

Rachel glanced at her list and decided to start with Nelda. What were his impressions of her grandmother? What was she like? Could he tell her anything that would explain her actions?

He responded with stories of a woman who was eccentric and charming in some respects, mean-spirited and controlling in all others. Rachel could picture Nelda as each Dorothy Doughty porcelain bird, the largest collection in the United States, was carried by either her grandmother or Mr. Corley when the Stark Museum prepared to open in 1976.

"She wouldn't let anyone else touch them but us, " he said. "Don't recall how many trips we made from the Stark offices to the museum, but she was damn sure not going to let anyone else help – not even Eunice."

He continued with tales of Nelda's attempts to build the museum as she struggled with what was legal and what she preferred.

"You know, that woman was surely different," said Tracy. "One minute she focused on getting the museum built, the next she was complaining that she didn't want restrooms or benches anywhere in the place."

"The museum?"

"Yep. When the architects brought the floor plans over to the office, she gave them a fit about the public restrooms. Didn't want any in the building... said she didn't want people coming in off the street to use them.

"They finally convinced her the law required it in all public buildings, and I guess that was the problem. She didn't think of it as a public building, but her building. Thought if she was paying for it, she could build it any 'damn way' she wanted."

Mr. Corley said it even got worse a few weeks later when a more detailed plan showed benches placed throughout the museum viewing areas.

"She was still mad about the restrooms and here they come with seating for those visiting the museum. Nothing elaborate, just benches scattered about for those who wanted to sit down."

"Why was that a problem?" asked Rachel.

"I remember her exact words: 'I want people in and out… no reason to let them stay any longer than necessary,'" said Mr. Corley. "Eunice was the only one who could convince her to keep the benches, but Nelda made sure there weren't any comfortable seating areas anywhere in the place."

Rachel took a deep breath and started to ask another question. But she repeated herself, stuttered and seemed genuinely unsure if she should even ask. How could she bring up Nelda's lesbian lifestyle when it was almost common knowledge Mr. Corley went the same direction, so to speak.

"Go ahead, Rachel. There's nothing off limits between us."

"Well… you know Miss Nelda and Eunice were, uh.."

"Queer." He said the word without hesitation, catching her by surprise. "Honey, everyone around here knows that. Been like that for years, or at least as long as I can remember."

He continued with names of others – including himself – who worked with them, socialized with them, or did business with them. Prominent women in the community who led secret lives, partying at Nelda's Big Lake home or going to flea markets together. Plus a few men with money and others like him who were on the payroll. Even one of the security guards. Rachel knew about her grandmother and Eunice, but had no idea Orange was what Mr. Corley referred to as "the San Francisco of Texas."

He referenced the "Rainbow Bridge" and chuckled at the irony that it was renamed by conservative members of the community in 1958, long before "rainbow" came to be identified with homosexuals.

"We just had to be careful and keep to ourselves... in fact, through all the years I knew Nelda and Eunice, there was only once when they were caught... you know... kissing."

"Kissing?"

"Yeah, I was at the Stark House when a young man – a former student of mine – came to the side door, clearly upset, loosening his tie and all. I thought it was the heat, but soon found out he'd walked in on Nelda and Eunice.

"Said he was scheduled to interview with Nelda for a security job, but the receptionist sent him in without realizing what was going on... told me he was 'startled backwards' and wandered across the parking lot when he remembered I worked here. Once he settled down, I sent him on his way and reassured him nothing would happen... but didn't recommend scheduling any more interviews."

"Certainly hope not," said Rachel, smiling at the confused state of the job applicant.

"Queer, gay, lesbian, homosexual. Doesn't matter what you call us, we were just that way," added Mr. Corley. "Our generation simply didn't talk about it. Couldn't afford to come out of the closet. That's what they call it now, right? I mean, could you imagine that I'd ever gotten a job at the junior high? They would have called me lots of things besides Mr. Corley!"

Rachel looked at him and they both broke out laughing.

"Now what else do you want to know?" he asked.

Finally she was completely comfortable, thanks to his candor and ease with the subject, so Rachel asked about Eunice and Margaret Sadler's relationship. What exactly was going on there?

"I don't have to tell you what was going on, just that it's been at least 28 years because that's as long as I've lived next door to Eunice. Margaret's car was always in front of Eunice's house at 6:30 each morning—that is, until she retired a few years ago and started coming at 7.

"Nelda didn't like it one bit, even built the theater just so they didn't have an excuse to go to Houston for plays or whatever. And when they did go, for the opera or a special exhibit or something, Nelda always made them pack a lunch and sent her driver to escort them. She didn't want them stopping along the way and expected Eunice back at a certain hour.

"Guess you could say Nelda and Eunice were like a married couple who knew too much about each other's business to get a divorce. They seemed to be miserable a lot of the time, if you ask me."

Rachel took a sip of her now warm Coke and kind of wished it was something stronger. She had no idea Margaret had been in the picture so long or how unhappy her grandmother had been. Stories her parents shared with her were more recent, dating back only two or three years. Still she remembered how upset her father was the day he drove Eunice back from Houston when Nelda was in the hospital, only to find Margaret waiting on the front porch.

It seemed like a good time to ask what Mr. Corley knew about Ruby. Specifically, what he might have heard about her from Nelda or others in the office.

"Everyone used the same word to describe Ruby – sweet. Must not have been a mean bone in that woman's body, but Nelda saw that as a weakness. I always thought it a bit odd that you hardly ever heard anyone speak of her. Even Nelda rarely mentioned her name.

"One time she did tell me about a white mink coat that belonged to her sister. Seemed the coat was Ruby's favorite gift from Lutcher and wasn't to be worn by any other woman. It even stated that in her will; I saw it right there in black and white. But Nelda seemed to take special delight in wearing the coat after Ruby's death just to show no one could control her, not even from the grave."

He seemed less eager to discuss Ruby than the status of the gay population in Orange, but Rachel had a couple of questions left. She prefaced the next one by describing her trip to Jamestown, missing documents at the courthouse, news clippings about Ruby's marriage and death, and finally Jim Henderson's Tennessee story.

Tracy Corley didn't say a word. He just sat there in the mahogany arm chair with the wine-colored upholstery, head bowed and staring at the floor. His hands telegraphed to Rachel what he was about to say as he nervously rubbed them together, kind of like preparing for a big moment.

"You know, don't you?"

It was all he said as silence engulfed the room for what seemed like an eternity.

"Am I right, Mr. Corley? Everything points to her but the last thing I want to do is exhume another body."

Rachel hoped the older man could confirm her suspicions and he did. Ruby was Homer and Bill's mother.

"How did you figure this out – almost 80 years after he was born? There might have been clues, but so much was done at the time to bury the truth," he said, adding that Nelda would be so stunned the secret was discovered.

"It wasn't any one thing, just putting unrelated items together," said Rachel. She told him about the headline on Ruby's front page obituary saying she "died of a mysterious illness" only a year after her marriage to Lutcher. There it also stated she attended college in Tennessee.

"To think her father, a night watchman at Lutcher & Moore, could afford to send her to one of the most expensive and exclusive girls schools in the country just didn't make sense," said Rachel. "I remembered Jim Henderson's story that they picked up the boys in Tennessee and I called the college to ask about her. Told them I was writing a book about my family and just learned my grandmother attended their school.

"She registered for the fall semester, but didn't attend at all in the spring. I'm sure by then she couldn't conceal her pregnancy, so she moved in with one of my grandfather's close friends in Johnson City, Tennessee – a Mr. Graham he met through Rotary."

Mr. Corley was paying strict attention, following every point she made, as Rachel continued the story.

"Add that to Jamestown as the birthplace. Seemed strange to list a fictitious birthplace for 'adopted' children, plus the fact Ruby's will included a rather unusual passage referring to Homer and Bill. Not at all what a stepmother of only a year would have written. And a couple of years before she died, Nelda started telling me how much I looked like her. I didn't think much of it at the time since I'd no idea we might be blood relatives."

"Seems like lots of people knew Lutcher was the father, but very few suspected Ruby was the mother," added Tracy. "I think that's why Lutcher almost protected Nelda to a fault in the beginning."

He recounted how Nelda was kicked out of college in her freshman year, only to be reinstated with one phone call from Lutcher. Or how he let her serve as hospital administrator in Orange when time after time Nelda showed no compassion or patience in a profession built on both.

"But the strangest thing of all – I never understood why she posed as a nurse when all along the closest thing she had to medical experience was killing cats for a nickel each in the biology lab at college, or at least that's what she told me."

"There just had to be a connection, some reason a man that powerful looked the other way whenever she got in trouble," said Rachel. "Ruby was the only reason I could come up with."

They talked for twenty minutes or so longer, discussing Eunice's influence on Nelda and covering more routine topics like Fiestaware, carnival glass and Hummel figurines. The conversation came full circle and it was time for her to leave.

The pathway to the door wound around more of his treasures and Rachel hugged him goodbye before she walked in the dark past Eunice's house, down the driveway and around the corner to her car. Moments later she arrived at her parent's home and walked into the den where a rerun of *Gunsmoke* was the television show of choice. Homer turned down the volume, adjusted his pipe and glanced toward his oldest daughter.

"So, how did it go?"

"Well, Daddy. I've got good news and bad news."

"And that would be…"

"The good news is Ruby is your mother."

"That's fine with me," he replied, almost not surprised, and turned back toward the television. "She was a really sweet lady. So what's the bad news?"

"That would make Nelda your aunt."

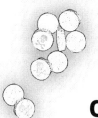

CHAPTER 14

*"Sometimes reality trumps
what you can make up."*

— *Scott Turow*

At 6'3" and 205 lbs., John Creswell was a hard worker who kept to himself yet remained keenly observant of what went on around him. He was a day laborer at the Dupont chemical plant when a 1947 strike forced him to look elsewhere for employment.

He found it at the Stark offices, where he worked in the maintenance and shop area, first as just an employee, then as the man in charge. After 52 years, 8 months on the Stark payroll, he retired shortly after Nelda's death. It was the end of an era, for he had become much more than a name on the payroll. Creswell was a confidante of both Lutcher and Nelda Stark. He listened to their problems, their victories, their dreams. He provided a safe place for them to vent. Above all, he could be trusted.

Homer admired the work ethic and skills of Cres, but the two men had never been particularly close. Cups of coffee, conversations about fishing and hunting, or a wave across the parking lot represented the most likely contact between the two. Yet they remained on friendly terms throughout the 50+ years they had known each other.

It was not unusual when Homer picked up the phone one October evening and called Cres to check on a statistic for Rachel. The two men hadn't talked since shortly after Nelda's funeral, but there had been no reason to trigger a phone call until now.

Creswell answered on the second ring, starting a conversation that on the surface appeared to be between two old friends who kept in touch frequently. They caught up on the last few months, talking about the grandchildren and Creswell's new home. A few moments were even spent talking about the Roslyn Ranch and any progress that might have been made to transfer it to Homer.

"The lawyers are in it now, Cres, so who knows how long it will take with them running the show. Rachel called me with a question about the pier at Big Lake. I told her you were the one with the answers."

"Sure, Homer. You know if I can help, I will. What does she want to know?"

"Do you remember how long that pier is, and when you rebuilt it?"

There was no hesitation on Creswell's part. "868 feet long, six feet wide, and we finished the work around 1970. It was after Hurricane Camille blew the place to pieces."

The answer prompted recollections of improvements made to the home and the 10 acres of waterfront property on Big Lake east of Lake Charles. Both men remembered months of drilling by barges that worked to restore the bulkhead and reinforce the shoreline damaged after suffering a direct hit from the powerful Category 4 hurricane.

"Yeah, the guys at Lutcher & Moore drew up the plans, but I rebuilt the pier and the house the way it should be done," laughed Creswell. "Miss Nelda didn't really care if the pier was that long, but it was one of the few grandfathered over there and once you made it shorter, you could never add to it."

So the pier was restored to its original length, almost three football fields long, and the width doubled from three to six feet. Allowing Nelda to ride her three-wheel bicycle up and down the pier, something she didn't do too often because she was afraid of water. Never learned to swim.

The phone call ended soon, but not before Creswell offered to visit again with Homer and Rachel – "There might be something I know that will help with her book."

With only minutes to kickoff for Monday Night Football, Homer made a quick call to Rachel to answer her question and mentioned Creswell offered to visit with her about the book. That was all the incentive she needed to convince her father to make arrangements for her to see Creswell.

Two days later, she drove with her parents to Creswell's home. It was only a few miles from Orange, just north of Interstate 10 but far enough away so that you didn't notice the traffic. The house itself was not only brand new, but the result of Creswell's own planning and supervision. He lived for years in a home on the Stark Ranch, a property of 150+ acres near the county airport. Now he had his own home and was justifiably proud.

A fence surrounded the property, but the first thing you noticed were the vibrant flowers and plants along the front and side of the home. Someone, probably Runie – Creswell's wife – spent a lot of time in the garden. The American flag on the mailbox, large mastiff dogs in the run at the end of the driveway, rocking chairs on the porch. It was just as Rachel imagined.

As Homer's Landcruiser turned into the driveway, they drove past the gate Creswell left open for his guests. Both he and Runie rose from their seats on the porch and walked toward the car. Hugs and greetings were the norm as they met, with Becky bringing some of her famous mayhaw jelly for the couple.

The tour of the property began outside, then moved into the home as sunlight pierced the pine trees lining the property behind the house. From the large family room with a vaulted ceiling to the three bedrooms and two baths, the house was immaculate and tastefully decorated. Family pictures scattered throughout the home allowed Rachel to see a side of Creswell she had never known. The gruff, silent man she had known from a distance for so long, appeared to be no more than a teddy bear who could be fiercely protective of his family and friends.

They ended up seated at the breakfast room table in the kitchen, drinking freshly made coffee and talking about plans for the coming week. Eventually, a pause in the conversation allowed Rachel an opening to ask a few questions as she glanced at suggestions on her notepad. This man knew so much about her grandparents that she wasn't sure where to begin.

Shangri La seemed an appropriate starting point.

"You know, very few people can imagine how much time and money went into putting those gardens together," Creswell began. "Why, your grandfather sent men all across the South to bring back azaleas, gardenias, camellias – the best they could find."

"Was there a certain nursery they used?' asked Rachel.

"Nursery? No, no...you don't understand. They would drive by plantation sites or through the best neighborhoods in towns and cities in Louisiana, South Carolina, Georgia, Alabama, Florida, Mississippi. Once they spotted a likely suspect, they'd call Mr. Stark and describe it to him. If he wanted to buy it, they just went to the door and made an offer. Don't recall anyone turning him down.

"Yes, sir. Money could buy anything. Paid over $1200 each for a lot of them, and that was 50 years ago. Those plants were so huge it took a couple of days to ball them, and then only one or two would fit on the flatbed trailer behind a truck.

"I recall an azalea from the Laurel Hill plantation that weighed 40,000 pounds or more... about 130 years old. A dozen or so had grown together over the years, I'd guess 45 by 65 feet in sheer size. Separated them into about 100 plants and used a second truck to get them here.

"Sometimes we had another truck meet drivers at the state line to remove one plant in order to meet weight requirements at those inspection stations, allowing the original truck to bring the second plant across. Had orders from Mr. Stark not to drive fast so the leaves wouldn't burn."

Once the trucks arrived in Orange, workers were instructed to follow sketches made before the plants were unearthed. That insured each was planted so the branches were pointed in the same direction as when they were first located.

"And planted probably isn't the best term to use, not when your dad was concerned."

"I know. He never dug a hole in Shangri La – that was always part of its beauty," said Homer. "You might say they were placed."

Between the two, they described how all plants – even the large ones weighing tons – were positioned on the ground and soil added around each in such a manner that it created the effect of gently rolling mounds as opposed to the level property so common near the bayou.

Other duties kept Creswell busy in Shangri La. One of his regular jobs was bringing a pickup truck load of live crawfish twice a week to start feeding aquatic birds Mr. Stark was trying to attract to the area.

"One thing was certain, you did it his way. Whatever that man said he wanted, that is exactly what we did. I'd pick up crawfish over in Louisiana, but couldn't return until late afternoon so I'd be driving west into the sun. That way the ice wouldn't melt as fast. And he was right about the crawfish attracting birds. Probably a thousand mallards and more than a hundred egrets showed up at the lake on a regular basis."

He told other stories, explaining the use of sawdust, peanut hulls and bales of hay to fill in the marsh and bring the land above grade along the perimeter of Shangri La. A trailer camp set up on part of the property during World War II. The houseboat that was moved from the Muskrat camp in the marsh only to eventually deteriorate and sink after years of neglect in Shangri La's lake near the hanging gardens. An "artist house" that was home in the early 1950's to Lorentz Kleiser, a remarkable artist known for his floral paintings. The bat house. Even how bricks from the streets of Dunkirk ended up in the courtyard area by the greenhouse.

"Byron Simmons came in the office out of breath and told Mr. Stark a ship came in for repairs with an interesting cargo. Seems it was used during the war to evacuate soldiers from Dunkirk who each carried bricks and stones aboard for ballast. Now they were going to dump them in the Gulf of Mexico before repairing the damage, but Mr. Stark wanted them. Didn't hesitate for a moment, sending trucks over with several of us to unload as many bricks as we could get our hands on."

Creswell was doing almost all of the talking, with the others paying close attention and occasionally adding a comment or two. Rachel asked about the Christmas display she remembered from her childhood.

What she recalled was the largest Christmas tree she had ever seen, surrounded by decorated images and sounds of holiday music echoing through the area. Cars from all over the county would be lined up along Park Avenue and 16th Street, with hundreds of people walking over to see the display through gates at the main entrance of Shangri La.

"Yes, sir. He'd ship a 65-foot tree from Oregon for us to have ready for that display the week before Christmas. Came in on a flatbed car and we'd have everything set up for its arrival."

He described a 10 inch steel pipe, 12 feet long that was used to secure the tree. Along with lighting the tree, neon figures were placed at the base: Christmas packages, Santa Claus, Mrs. Claus, a sleigh and reindeer, even an image of Trubbie, Mr. Stark's cocker spaniel. A sound system in the gate house added holiday classics with "White Christmas" and "Rudolph" the clear favorites.

"Why did he stop putting up the decorations?" asked Rachel.

"Not sure, but I think he just lost interest after he tried opening Shangri La to the public when the azaleas bloomed each spring. He worked hard and went to so much expense to create these beautiful gardens, but when he shared it with the public they simply didn't show any respect. They'd cut the flowers, throw trash on the grounds, chase the swans. Finally he thanked them for coming and locked the gates. Same time we quit ordering the Christmas tree."

As the subject changed to his experiences with Nelda, Creswell noted that although Mr. Stark was a pretty tough guy, "she had him beat all to hell." Both of them were known for wanting things done their way, and you stood a good chance of going home if you believed otherwise. But he liked her and blamed Eunice for turning her against Homer and Bill. "Miss B could be a nice lady, but she was pure Benckenstein and Mr. Stark said that family had been a leech for years."

"As for Mr. McKee, I know he was getting rich off all those mineral leases the Starks owned. Just got a call the other day from someone wanting to process a lease, but he wanted the name of someone besides McKee to contact. Said he wanted too much off the top."

A fresh pot of coffee replenished cups around the table as Rachel asked Creswell if he could describe how the copies, the hundreds of thousands of copies, were made during the previous lawsuit. She was told the machines were set up in his maintenance shop since it was one of the few places large enough for the job. What she did not know was how the process worked.

He set the scene, telling them how ten copy machines ran five days a week, eight hours a day for 6 1/2 weeks as copy after copy was made.

"We brought the documents from all over Orange. The Stark offices on Front Street, the Dr. Pepper building, the old Orange Investment Company building, the vault in the old bank building, the Stark Museum."

"What happened then?" asked Rachel. "How did they separate the documents from what could be copied and what was pulled?" She already knew from reviewing the boxes that Knox and Henderson, the noted Houston firm representing Nelda, pulled several documents, but had no idea when or where those decisions were made.

"Two lawyers did that," responded Creswell. "That guy, uh... Kevin Jordan, with Knox and Henderson, and Roy Wingate, Miss Nelda's attorney. They'd go through the papers and pull the ones they set aside and the ones they wanted us to burn."

Burn? Rachel looked up, but no one else around the table seemed startled by what he just said.

"Burn? What do you mean burn?" she quietly asked.

"You know. Burned. The lawyers told us to take the documents they wanted burned to the Stark Ranch. To go to the back edge next to the canal and stay until every piece of paper was ashes."

"How many papers and files are we talking about, Mr. Creswell? A couple of folders?"

"Oh, no. There was a pickup load each week. Even your grandfather's boat."

"Boat? You mean a picture or a model of a boat?" asked Homer.

"No. A 15-ft runabout. It was the only boat he owned that was still here and I really didn't want to burn it, but I knew she'd find out if I didn't. Miss Nelda said she didn't want anyone else to have it."

Rachel pictured lawyers going through these documents during the discovery phase of a lawsuit, casually selecting which ones to burn. As they sat at the table, Enron would soon make headlines with its shredding of documents, but the Stark lawyers were years ahead of them.

"Was anyone else there when you burned them?"

"James Sears and George Washington, but George is dead and James can't afford to say anything or he'll lose his job," said Creswell. He glanced at Runie and remembered they had discussed burning the documents at the house.

Creswell casually volunteered that it reminded him of when they burned the will.

"What? When was this?" asked Rachel.

"Right before Mr. Stark died – about two weeks if I remember correctly. Mr. McKee asked me to bring a five gallon metal bucket to the office. Seemed like a strange request, but I brought it to him and watched as he and Nelda went down under the landing in back of the office and set papers on fire in that bucket. For some reason I thought it was Mr. Stark's old will since George Kelly had just returned with a new one signed in the hospital."

Rachel remembered the memo in the boxes instructing Kelly to bring a new will to the hospital, plus a call from John McDonald, the bank president, describing Nelda and Clyde dancing around a small fire at the base of the outside stairwell. He thought it was the will, but had no way to prove it. Add what Mildred told them about Nelda holding Lutcher's hand, guiding him as he signed documents during the same time period, and all the pieces seemed to fit. She joined her parents and the Creswells in the living area as they said their goodbyes, then turned to ask Mr. Creswell if he would mind giving a statement about the documents being burned.

"Don't mind at all, but I'm not talking to the other side."

"No, it would be one of our lawyers just so we can document what you told us tonight. We'd really appreciate it."

Within hours, plans were in place to take Creswell's statement the following week. Patrick would arrive on Wednesday to go over events outlined to his mother and grandparents. If everything checked out, Byron Steele, Homer's attorney, would drive from his Houston office Thursday morning with a court reporter to take a sworn statement.

But things hit a snag as routine tests were scheduled for Creswell in the local hospital and he would be unable to meet them on Thursday. Byron could not make it on Wednesday and it was starting to look like another week would better suit everyone's schedule.

"Mom, I know you don't like it, but Byron can't be there Wednesday and the next time we can get everyone together is the following week."

"Patrick," said Rachel, hesitating before continuing. "Patrick, I know what everyone says, but I'm telling you we need to get his statement before something happens. You can just say I'm paranoid, but too many people have died, disappeared or been disabled for some strange reason or another. Remember how they turned Clemmie into a vegetable and used drugs to control my grandfather? Three people who died of food poisoning? Or the judge they put on the payroll? And God only knows where the technician is who was working on the DNA samples.

"If nothing else, just plan on coming here tomorrow to take his statement yourself. We'll get a court reporter and at least have something on record."

Patrick argued the point, explaining he was not even close to as experienced as Byron Steele and wouldn't want to leave something out.

"Experience isn't helping us if he can't show up. Email Byron, call his cell phone, do whatever you like and ask him what questions you need to cover. If we need to follow up later, fine. But at least get something now in case anything, God forbid, goes wrong at the hospital."

Patrick drove from Dallas the next morning. Shortly after two o'clock that afternoon, Homer took him out to Creswell's and they shot the breeze with the 85-year old man, covering the burning of documents as well as the growing deer population in Texas.

True to his word, Creswell was prepared to make an official statement* and Patrick was more than glad to take it. He returned with the court reporter after dinner that evening, spent less than an hour at the Creswell home, then promised to return early the next morning with a copy for his signature.

By 9:30 Thursday morning, Patrick began his return trip to Dallas. Information in his briefcase cast a new light on the Stark Foundation lawyers and their role years earlier.

*Excerpt from John Creswell's sworn statement (November 7, 2001) regarding documents burned during lawsuit filed in 1988 against Nelda Stark and the Stark Foundation:

Q. Was there a place during this prior litigation that they set up as a document kind of management center, where they made copies of documents?

A. Yes. That was in my maintenance shop.

Q. So, you were intimately familiar with the area that they used as this copy center?

A. Yes.

Q. You were there frequently and had personal knowledge of what was going on there?

A. Every day that that was going on, I was either there or in and out of there. But I reported for work there every day.

Q. And did you observe attorneys and staff members for these attorneys making copies of documents? Did you see them in there making copies of documents?

A. Yeah. Yeah.

Q. Were some of the documents, in fact, not copied, but left in some of the boxes?

A. Yes. Some of them were put back in the box –

Q. And they were never – I'm sorry.

A. – and not copied.

Q. Not copied. Do you have personal knowledge as to what was done with the documents that weren't copied?

A. Yeah. We brought them back to the office building and put them back in storage.

Q. So, you put all of them back in storage or were some of them disposed of in a different way?

A. I guess we just – we burned some. But I didn't know. I thought you were talking about those that were copied.

Q. No, I'm talking about the documents that were not copied.

A. Well those that were not copied, yes, we burned quite a few of those. And those that we didn't, that I wasn't told to burn, we hauled them back to the storage facilities that they came from.

Q. Okay. So, just to make sure I understand completely, the documents that were not copied you, in fact, took to a place and burned them. Is that correct?

A. All those that I was told to burn.

Q. Okay. Where did you take these documents to be burned?

A. At the lower end of the Stark Ranch, the very west end of it.

Q. Did you actually take the documents yourself and drive them out there and actually participate in the burning of the documents?

A. Yeah. We loaded – I was driving a company truck. We loaded them up in a company truck and I drove the truck out there.

Q. And you actually observed the documents being burned?

A. I stayed there until every one was burned.

Q. Did they tell you to stay and verify that the documents had been burned?

A. Yes. They told me to see to it that they were burned beyond recognition, just completely burned.

Q. And did you, in fact, kick around the ashes to make sure that there was no remnants of the documents?

A. Oh, yeah. I had to do that to protect myself. The wind could have blown them out and blown them away. So, no, I stayed there to see that they were completely burned.

Q. And you said that they told you to make sure the documents were burned completely. Are you talking about "they" meaning people from the Stark office?

A. Yeah.

Q. Was there a gentleman named Roy Wingate in this copy center?

A. He was involved in that. I don't know what title he had, but he was there nearly every day.

Q. And he was aware that you were taking documents to be burned?

A. Yeah, uh-huh.

Q. Was there also an attorney there named Kevin Jordan –

A. Yeah

Q. – that was involved in making these copies –

A. Uh-huh

Q. – and also involved in having the documents shipped, or taken out to be burned?

A. Uh-huh

Q. Is that a 'yes'?

A. Yes.

Q. Okay, I'm just making sure she gets it down right, that's all.

Now when you took the documents that you're talking about that were burned, this happened while that other lawsuit was ongoing. Is that correct?

A. I don't know how that copy work was, during, before.

Q. Well, it was during – when that copy center was –

A. It was done during the time that the copy center was activated.

Q. Okay. Well, then, I can tell you that it was – that the copy center was activated during the pendency of the prior lawsuit. So, is it your testimony that you took the documents to be burned while the copy center was operational?

A. Yes, uh- huh.

Q. Now, you just took the documents to the Stark Ranch to be burned. You didn't review them at all, did you?

A. No, I didn't look at them. The only thing that I saw, I saw a few building material tickets that probably I signed, and I don't even remember whether I found many of those or not. But I did remember seeing some of those go to the fire.

Q. Did you see any dates on any of the documents?

A. Yeah, we talked about the dates, going back into the 1920s.

Q. Okay, but you didn't, by any means, look through most of the documents. You didn't look through all the documents nor did you look through most of the documents?

A. No, I didn't look through but very few of them. I just picked them up and burned them as I got to them.

Q. I understand...

How many people were involved in actually going out there to burn the documents?

A. A man that worked under me, Earl Kelly – and he's dead now – and a man by the name of Joe LeBlanc...

Q. Mr. Creswell, based on what you observed, you had personal knowledge that the Foundation, Stark office, Nelda Stark instructed you to burn or destroy documents that were never copied and a part of the previous lawsuit. Is that correct?

A. Previous to this lawsuit?

Q. Well, I'm talking about the one when the copy center was in operation.

A. Oh. Yes.

Q. That's a 'yes'?

A. Yes.

Q. And that Roy Wingate knew full and well what was going on?

A. Uh-huh.

Q. Is that a 'yes'?

A. Yes.

Q. Okay. And Roy Wingate worked for Nelda Stark? He was her attorney?

A. I don't know. I don't think so.

Q. Oh, you don't think he worked for Nelda Stark?

A. Uh-huh. I think he worked for the law company they hired out of Houston. I don't know who they are.

Q. Okay. But she hired them?

A. Right.

Q. Based on your observance of what happened out at the Stark Ranch and your personal knowledge, is it clear to you that they did not want anyone to see the documents that they instructed you to burn, other than, obviously, you, that burned them?

A. Well, apparently they did not. They didn't want them seen by anyone...

CHAPTER 15

*"Repetition does not transform
a lie into the truth."*

— *Franklin D. Roosevelt*

As the alarm went off at 5:30 that August morning, Rachel had been up for hours. Probably most of the night, but she was too sleepy to recall what she was working on when she curled up on the living room couch, too tired to make the corner into the bedroom. It was a short-lived nap as she searched in the dark for the off switch to the alarm, finally locating it and thankful the noise was gone.

She reached for the faded pink chenille robe, the one her sons swore needed to be replaced, and struggled to put it on as she wandered into the kitchen. Coffee, orange juice, even a diet Coke. Something to drink should wake her up. It was good to be home.

With the morning paper in one hand, juice in the other, she went to the guest bedroom that doubled as her office. Her computer sat on a small table near the window, but boxes and documents were scattered throughout the room. On the bed, next to the chair, stacked by the doorway, across the floor. Even her dog, Travis, was asleep on a file folder near the window.

As she surveyed the disarray of the room, Rachel had to admit she made quite a mess during the night. Whatever was she looking for? There were no clues as she sat in front of the computer, touching a key to activate it from the sleep mode. As an image appeared on the monitor, she rubbed her eyes to make certain she wasn't hallucinating.

On the screen, listed first among a search she apparently entered before falling asleep, was an entry for Lutcher & Moore records. Not only an entry, but a significant one at that. It indicated the company's historical records were part of a collection now housed at Stephen F. Austin University in Nacogdoches – deep in the pine forests of East Texas.

When she searched the internet a couple of years earlier for information on the family-owned lumber company, there were only brief references to H. J. Lutcher, the family patriarch who acquired the vast holdings forming the basis of the Stark fortune. She was anxious to learn about this astute businessman, Lutcher Stark's grandfather, who moved from Pennsylvania to Texas after locating what he considered the best virgin timber stands in the country. Even more importantly, a key document in Nita's estate – a $400,000 note to Lutcher & Moore she allegedly signed ten days before her death – never surfaced, despite claims by Nelda and the Stark Foundation lawyers that it had just been misplaced.

Rachel never understood why Nita would borrow $400,000 from the lumber company when she was gravely ill, heavily medicated and certainly not in need of money. The woman was bedridden, lapsing in and out of a morphine-induced coma for the last several weeks, and there was no logical explanation why the wife of one of the richest men in the South would need a loan. And if she did borrow the money, where did it go during the 10 days between the date the note was issued and her death? It had been a major issue in the lawsuit regarding Nita's estate, for payment of her half of the community note virtually erased most of the assets identified in her inventory.

In spite of constant assurances from lawyers on both sides that the note was legitimate, the explanation was neither logical nor in keeping with what she knew of her grandmother. Yet less than one month after Nita died, her grandfather listed it in court documents as a liability. Surely he would not have deceived his own sons, the primary beneficiaries to her estate. Rachel just wanted to understand what the note was for, why it would be necessary. Perhaps the records in Nacogdoches would provide a reasonable explanation.

Without hesitation, she clicked on the link to the site. The home page came up immediately and gave the customary overview of the collection and its location within the university library. Documents were given to the Forestry Institute by Boise Southern after purchasing Lutcher & Moore in the early 70's, but it had taken more than 20 years to catalogue and include an internet presence. Just below the introductory paragraph was another link to the inventory, with a warning stating it was a large document and would require a significant amount of time to open.

If Rachel had anything, it was time. She flashed a grin and hit the appropriate key, then went to the kitchen in search of something to eat along with the juice. When she returned a few minutes later, there was a 41-page document on the screen detailing each of the boxes now housed in Nacogdoches. For the next couple of hours, she reviewed the listings, trying to determine what information she might find based on the general description of each box. Included were letters and personal correspondence, ledgers, shipping tables, reports on everything from turpentine to sulphur, insurance reports, accident claims, interoffice memorandums, telegrams, ordinances and proposals, audits. There seemed to be something about every phase of business interests involving Lutcher & Moore. More importantly, it listed many items identified with Lutcher & Moore Cypress – the Louisiana corporation noticeably absent from documents provided in the earlier lawsuit.

Once she printed the 41-page outline, Rachel placed a call to the university library to check on hours and days of operation. It was between summer sessions and the fall semester, but she hoped it was at least open on a reduced schedule. It was. Her call was transferred to the forestry institute to confirm the collection was available for review, then Rachel left that afternoon to be there when the library opened its doors Saturday morning at 10.

Although it was almost four hours by car from College Station to Nacogdoches, time passed quickly as Rachel took turns talking to herself and Travis, and calling family members to ask for possible details she might overlook at the library. The winding road cut through timber stands that were dramatically impressive, yet prompted sentimental thoughts at the same time. She wondered how her grandfather could inherit, correction steal, so much property that was in plain view, yet no one said a word. How much did it cost to buy their silence?

She checked in the motel, asked for directions to the campus, and drove the relatively short distance to try to locate the library before nightfall. A few wrong turns and Rachel was in the parking lot, staring at the rather library-like structure in front of her. While glad she found it, a nervous feeling gripped her stomach as she realized there was always the chance the note did indeed exist. Or not. Either way, she would have the answer tomorrow.

As she returned to the La Quinta parking lot, it was impossible to miss Ramona. Leaning against her white Mustang as she talked on a cell phone, probably to one of her kids. A tall, striking blonde dressed in black and hot pink, anyone would take a second look at her. She waved at Rachel as if to say "gotcha" upon surprising her big sister.

"Thought you might need reinforcements," she laughed, pocketing the cell phone and moving towards Rachel's car, pleased with herself for not mentioning her plans as they talked a couple of hours earlier.

"How did you know where I was staying?"

"It's Nacogdoches and there's a LaQuinta. As long as you have that dog, I know where to find you."

Yes, Travis was always with Rachel and they took him for a walk before settling in for the night. Conversations about the newly-discovered files brought Ramona up to date on what they would be looking for the next day, but neither seemed tired or sleepy.

"Rachel, have you seen Erin Brockavich?"

"Erin who?"

"Okay. You are just too wrapped up in this and need a break."

Ramona switched on the television and found the movie channel, keying in the code for the investigative movie featuring Julia Roberts. It was the perfect diversion as they laughed at moments that seemed to imitate events of the previous months. Soon both were fast asleep, with Travis in his usual place curled up next to Rachel.

Morning dawned and could not have come sooner. The sisters were anxious to leave for the library, even if it was more than an hour before it opened. A Shipley's donut shop was on the way, not a bad way to start the day. Two chocolate-filled donuts, an apple fritter and a cinnamon twist later, they had read the local paper, finished off two pints of milk and listened to three amusing little old ladies. Judging from their conversation, it was a weekly breakfast meeting, an opportunity for them to not only catch up with each other's lives, but do so dressed in their Sunday best. As interesting as the ladies were, the sisters left for the library and arrived just as the doors opened, made their way up the elevator to the second floor, and followed the signs to the forestry reading area.

A college student named Sara was in charge as they signed the guest register, indicating "family research" as the reason for being there. The young lady was quite friendly, explaining the procedures in reviewing the materials in the Lutcher & Moore collection as simply asking for one or two boxes at a time.

They sat at the table nearest the reception area, then requested boxes 39 and 62. Judging from the table of contents, they fit the time period when Nita died and they had to start somewhere. Ramona volunteered to make copies and came prepared with brightly colored post it notes and a notepad.

Eighteen boxes later, Rachel had reviewed hundreds of documents ranging from original telegrams to handwritten notes from Nita as she traveled with Lutcher. Ramona was organizing copies of the more important papers, but devoted the rest of her time to examining the documents. It was fascinating to see the personal notes mixed in with interoffice memos and shipping reports. A few postcards, correspondence between the Stark offices in Orange and their grandfather's hotel suite in New York City or Chicago, field notes from oil rigs, cash receipt and disbursement statements from Lutcher & Moore Cypress Lumber Company in Louisiana. It was a side of the family never seen before, painting a picture of Lutcher Stark as someone who spent little time in the office, preferring to travel the world as his father sent one message after another asking him to return to help with the family business.

A pink memorandum caught Rachel's eye when she saw Nita's name in the content. It was a rather innocuous message acknowledging a Pi Beta Phi note at the University of Texas held by Nita with instructions to deposit any payments to her Lutcher & Moore account. Interesting, if for no other reason than it seemed strange to mix the lumber business with an Austin sorority house.

Another memo questioned if Lutcher was ever going to call a Board meeting for Lutcher & Moore following his father's death. His response, neatly written in the margin, was typical Lutcher Stark: "I am the company. Why do I need a Board meeting?"

Next was correspondence with politicians regarding the Panama and Intracoastal canals. How amazing her family had such connections with the White House and Congress. A draft toward the bottom of the box yielded one of the more interesting documents – a plan carefully crafted to defeat the Internal Revenue Service's attempts to impose estate taxes. It was hard to believe their grandfather created such a paper for review as he and his staff departed by train to plead their case to the Dallas IRS office. The fact they included tickets to the Texas game for each of the commissioners did not go unnoticed.

Four o'clock. Only an hour remained before the library closed for the weekend and Rachel wasn't certain which box to look in next. As she moved her finger down the table of contents, it became obvious. The ledgers. All the ledgers from the 1930s and 1940s were neatly listed at the end of the directory.

After six hours with Sara, the two sisters were now on a first name basis and Sara was more than willing to allow them to review four ledgers at a time. She went back to the reference area and returned with 1938, 1939, 1940 and 1941.

"Are you auditors?" Sara asked as the requests shifted from boxes to the more official ledgers. Ramona shook her head at the question, trying not to laugh.

"Not by a long shot, but we're flattered you think so," Rachel responded. "We're having a hard enough time with the boxes and thought these might at least be easier to follow."

As Sara returned to the front desk, Rachel opened the 1938 ledger as Ramona followed every movement. Yes, it was definitely a ledger. An exquisite one at that. The attention to detail in the opening statement, the errorless typing of column after column of figures, the onionskin paper that simply added an historic touch to a otherwise routine document. Plus the binding with gold lettering on the spine. She turned the pages and tried to determine in what manner a note would have been listed more than 60 years earlier. There were sections for Notes Receivable and Accounts Receivable. To be safe, she examined both and noticed the Pi Beta Phi note in Nita's name. That, plus notes for the W. H. Stark Estate, the Miriam M. Stark Estate and the Frances Ann Lutcher Estate.

The sight of those notes was rather startling, for it was obviously not unusual for her grandfather to issue notes on estates. Lutcher appeared to have a habit of leaving them open as executor. But had Nita signed a note before her death? Would it appear on the same elegant pages in the 1939 ledger?

Rachel closed the 1938 records, then carefully moved the next one in front of her, almost afraid to open it. Ramona returned from the copy machine and was anxious to learn if they might be on the verge of something significant as the 1939 ledger was opened. There they found some of the identical notes from the year before, for slightly different amounts. Nothing but the Pi Beta Phi note was in Nita's name. As she turned the pages, thinking it might have been out of order, Rachel examined each of them hoping the note would not appear. She looked around the room to see if anyone else could tell how excited she was. Sara was talking to another student and the only other persons in the room — two middle age ladies searching another section — had no interest in what the sisters did or did not discover.

The 1940 ledger was scrutinized next, just in case the note was not entered in a timely manner with the death of Nita and extenuating circumstances. A review of that year found no note in Nita's name, not even the one for Pi Beta Phi. It had disappeared.

1941 was next as time was running out. Rachel reviewed the now familiar sections, this time finding the note to Pi Beta Phi resurfacing with Lutcher Stark as the lienholder, not Nita. No mention of Nita, there or anywhere else in the ledger.

With only 15 minutes remaining before closing time, Rachel marked the pages she wanted copied and asked Sara for 1945. There wasn't time to look at other years, but this should confirm whether or not the alleged note was paid off in 1945 like the attorneys said. As she turned to the Notes Receivable page, once again Rachel found no note in Nita's name. A new entry, however, was dated January 2, 1945. An unsecured note for $400,000 in the name of Lutcher Stark. Her eyes followed the entry across the double page, stopping at the column with the notation "$215,217 paid 12-15-45, balance $184,783."

It was exactly the same amount deducted from Nita's estate when Bill and Homer signed the inventory on that date. An inventory prepared by the same reputable Houston firm responsible for the Lutcher & Moore ledgers now in front of her. Rachel spent a few moments quickly turning the pages to find stocks, bonds, real estate transferred from Nita's estate on that same day in December 1945 to satisfy the note. A note that Lutcher entered into while married to Nelda, not Nita. It was like turning the pages of an Agatha Christie novel, with all the facts pointing in one direction.

Waves of emotion rolled over Rachel as she began to realize her grandfather created a fraudulent note to cheat his own sons out of their inheritance. While the same auditing firm made no mention of the note Nita signed in the Lutcher & Moore records, it was the highlight of the estate inventory copy she had at home – one prepared by the same auditors. An inventory that contained prefatory remarks explaining that Nita's estate wasn't worth much, especially because of the indebtedness created by the Lutcher & Moore note.

All suspicions were confirmed in the official records of the Lutcher & Moore Lumber Company, even though it seemed at times almost hopeless that they would ever locate them. She closed the ledger and started to return it to Sara before gathering their materials, only to have Ramona suggest a look at the 1946 ledger.

There was no logical reason to go one year after the payment from Nita's estate was made. Nothing was left to take, but Ramona, fresh from a divorce that gave her every reason to suspect anything and anyone, insisted. They exchanged the 1945 ledger for 1946, then brought it back to the table, handling it as if it were fragile. As expected, they found no notes or accounts receivable remotely connected to Nita. Missing, however, was any entry at all reflecting the balance Lutcher owed on the $400,000 note. Somehow the entire "$184,783" balance disappeared from the books.

The sisters were not even surprised at this point – after all, Lutcher Stark said it best – he was the company.

CHAPTER 16

"It depends on what the meaning of 'is' is."
— *Bill Clinton*

Richard Dyke. Slip 'n fall attorney by trade. Egotistical liar by nature. At least, that was the opinion held by several who crossed his path.

After more than two years of dealing with him, reviewing correspondence, studying briefs, and observing his courtroom antics, Rachel was convinced this man was the perfect example of why lawyers should be on the endangered species list.

One of the attorneys for the Stark Foundation/Estate, Richard Dyke positioned himself as defender of all that was right in the world and constantly looked for opportunities to manipulate the facts. Even when his "facts" were disputed by clear evidence, the judges seemed attentive only to what he wanted them to hear. The Texas Attorney General's office, a party to the suit due to the Foundation's interest in the Estate, also seemed to go along with whatever he said and totally ignored contradictory information furnished by the Stark family.

Rachel watched from her seat on the second row as he swooped into the courtroom with his assistant and stacked binders, books, briefcases, and other items critical to his appearance on the table set aside for the plaintiffs. Yes, the Stark Foundation was the plaintiff, having sued her uncle's family six months after Nelda died. Two years later, after avoiding any discovery at every turn, filing false information with the courts and continuing to operate the Foundation in a manner that violated the law, they were here to argue their motion.

"You don't like Buzz, do you?" asked Randy, knowing he would hit a nerve with Rachel.

She glared at her cousin but said nothing, yet a smile signaled she enjoyed hearing the nickname they had assigned to the attorney who reminded them of a buzzard, staying alive by living off the misfortune of others.

Randy hadn't really expected an answer. At the same moment, voices of Billy Clyde Cavanaugh and Kevin Isern, attorneys for the Bill Stark family, could be heard as they entered the courtroom.

The two lawyers, Billy Clyde from Louisiana and Kevin from Amarillo, were exact opposites of Richard Dyke. Honest, personable and anxious to correct wrongs of the past, they were well prepared for the day's battle.

They went straight to work organizing their materials before visiting with Byron Steele and Bob Garner, Homer's attorneys there to observe, and Patrick Nugent, doubling as attorney and interested grandson of Homer. It remained a mystery why only half of the family had been sued by the Estate/Foundation, but was comparable to the tactics used years earlier by Nelda's lawyers to draw Homer's family into the 1988 lawsuit.

Something about Richard Dyke was simply irritating to Rachel. From the first moment Walter Riedel used his name to explain why Homer's family could not retrieve personal possessions stored by Nelda prior to her death, Rachel suspected he was gearing up for an ego trip. "Nothing could be distributed until each item was appraised," according to the attorney's email. Homer's books and toys, the Ford pickup he received as a gift from his parents, even photographs and personal items of Nita apparently were considered part of Nelda's estate. Rachel couldn't understand what right the Estate had to items that belonged to her dad. Or why they would even want them.

Her fears were confirmed when she went to the first court hearing for her aunt's family in Louisiana. Closing her eyes, she could picture the scene as she arrived a few minutes late and slipped into the rear of the courtroom.

"Your honor, these people are just after another bite of the apple," he was telling the judge. "They filed a lawsuit in 1988 and we gave them everything we had. Every document they requested, hundreds of thousands of them. And here they are again, asking for more money even after signing a release and receiving $2.5 million just to go away."

The words startled Rachel when she first heard them. But the hearing apparently was not going well and she was trying to understand Dyke's explanation as to why subpoenas issued for Eunice and Walter could simply be ignored. Neither was present and, according to Richard Dyke, did not plan to be. Somehow laws did not apply to those with money and power.

It was at that moment she decided she neither liked or trusted Richard Dyke. These people? Bite of the apple? It would become his calling card, one used by other attorneys for the Foundation as they conveniently left out facts and painted a picture that was not true. From the beginning, they had portrayed the Stark family as vultures, implying they simply wanted money or property that belonged to Lutcher and Nelda Stark.

The truth was Homer and Bill's families never wanted anything that belonged to Lutcher or Nelda. They simply wanted Nita's possessions that her will showed she clearly intended for her two sons to inherit. Nothing more. The problem arose when extensive research showed much of Nita's wealth, inherited from her parents and acquired during the marriage to Lutcher, was included in both Lutcher and Nelda's estates. Not accidentally, but by design.

Dyke's statements about the documents were lies, and he knew it. They had not produced everything, only a lot of duplicate forms, receipts and ledgers that had little to do with Nita Stark. So much was missing, but the sheer mention of 400,000 documents made almost anyone think they had done their duty. He also conveniently left out that some of the documents produced had been altered, while others misrepresented the financial status and assets of Nita. It was part of a legal maneuver used to overwhelm the opposition with sheer volume of information, a tactic designed to not only give the perception you are complying with the law, but make it almost impossible to review that much material. She wondered to herself if this technique was actually taught in law school or just acquired after passing the bar.

As for the "apple," Rachel preferred to think of it more as an orchard. One originally owned by Nita and Lutcher during their 28 years of marriage, a union that had no premarital arrangement, no separation of property reflected in any documents, and clearly the intent to share based on their actions and correspondence with the Internal Revenue Service. Documents in the now infamous boxes showed Lutcher and Nita were aware during the marriage of the community property and forced heirship laws of Louisiana. Laws that equally divided the couple's assets between them, regardless of how they were acquired, and required assets to be divided between children upon the death of a parent, even if they weren't mentioned in the will.

"He just didn't plan for Nita to leave everything to the boys."

"What? What did you say?" asked Randy.

"Oh, I'm sorry. I'm just thinking out loud," said Rachel. "How do you think they can possibly get around burning all those documents during discovery?"

"Who knows. These people come up with the strangest explanations. What worries me is that the judges seem to bless what they say, even if it doesn't make sense and is easy to disprove."

Both were referring to the brief filed by Kevin just weeks ago, one that included Creswell's startling affidavit describing efforts by the Foundation attorneys to destroy truckloads of files during the discovery phase of the original lawsuit. The timing was even more interesting since Enron's demise became public just after Creswell's statement was filed. Surely the judge read the papers and watched television.

"Destroying documents in anticipation of a lawsuit, and especially during discovery, was illegal in Houston," she told Randy. "Do you think the law applies in Orange County?"

"Sorry, I forgot for a moment who we're dealing with," said Rachel, answering her own question. "Remember the letter we found from the Houston firm doing some work for

Granddaddy in the 1950s? Saying they didn't know what was going on here, but the last time they checked, Orange was in the same state as Houston."

"Kind of makes you wonder, though…about lawyers," said Randy.

"What do you mean?"

"Well, have you ever noticed that if someone testifies in court they have to swear to tell the truth… swear on a Bible and the whole thing?"

"So what's your point?" countered Rachel.

"Why don't lawyers have to tell the truth? Richard Dyke says things that aren't true all the time – not sure if it's because he's stupid or just knows he can get away with it – but even when it's pointed out by Kevin or Billy Clyde that he is saying things that aren't true…"

"Lying."

"Right, lying… even then the judge seems to look the other way. Seems to me that if anyone should be telling the truth in a courtroom it should be the damn lawyers."

"Got to admit, I didn't realize lawyers weren't required – or apparently even expected – to tell the truth until watching these guys in action," said Rachel. "And thinking back, it seems the Foundation's lawyers from before did the same thing. Which I think is kind of illegal."

"Kind of?" came Randy's response. "Remember when we asked Kevin and Byron?"

The two remembered posing that question to their lawyers as it became increasingly obvious that the Foundation attorneys made statements in court and in papers filed with the Court that were either not true or factually inaccurate. Plus it appeared they were participating in fraudulent activity of their clients by helping to cover it up.

"And when a lawyer realizes his clients are involved in fraud, they are required to advise the client they must resign if the fraudulent activity persists, right?" asked Rachel.

"That's what they told us, but don't hold your breath. These people think they are above the law. Guess the Foundation's deep pockets are too much temptation."

Moments later, Judge Donovan entered the courtroom and the circus was indeed back in town. Richard Dyke made sure of it, fumbling with different exhibits and trying repeatedly to get the overhead projector to work.

Eventually he was reciting his case. Not in some dramatic manner that might conjure up comparisons to well known lawyers, but really reciting it. Reading each page with only occasional emphasis at one point or another. Slowly reviewing each of the points made by the Stark family lawyers.

"Burning documents, that's what they said we did," he told the judge, referring to Creswell's statement. "Well, so what? We burn documents, shred documents, whatever…all the time…all as part of our document retention program. There's nothing unusual about that, your honor."

It seemed ludicrous to Rachel that the argument was even being made. Selectively sorting documents during a lawsuit and then having them burned at the back of a ranch next to a canal seemed a stretch for document retention, even in Texas. Plus the fact there was no record of anything they burned and no evidence of the document retention program.

And then Richard couldn't resist taking a shot at Creswell, the longtime employee of Lutcher and Nelda Stark who had been perhaps the most loyal and trusted: "You know, what we have here is the word of an 85-year old man who may not remember things quite the way they happened. He may just be confused about the facts."

Exactly at what age did people become disposable to Richard Dyke? Rachel looked behind her at 93-year old Eunice – executor of both Nelda and Lutcher Stark's estates – and turned to face the judge, a 78-year old man who suffered a stroke a year earlier. Were they okay in Richard's opinion just because they agreed with him?

Richard Dyke went on for almost an hour, citing one case or another to support a point he was trying to make. Eventually he addressed the issue of the Roslyn Ranch and its acquisition by Nelda.

"Your honor, I find it appalling that we are even questioning Nelda Stark's claim on the Roslyn Ranch. She was certainly entitled to compensation for serving as executor of an estate worth hundreds of millions of dollars, and it was her right to choose that property as payment for her years of service in handling Lutcher Stark's estate."

It was hard for Rachel to continue listening to this man. She recalled times in previous months he simply lied, not only in conversations and in court, but even putting it in writing. Months after Nelda's death, Homer hired a lawyer for the first time in his life to pursue ownership of the ranch as promised him by Nelda. It began as a friendly exchange between Byron Steele and the Stark Estate, with a letter from Richard Dyke in December 2000 expressing their intent to prepare a settlement offer to include the ranch. He said they just needed a little time to take care of estate matters prior to the end of the year.

Anticipating transfer of the ranch to Homer, Patrick initiated planning for a family limited partnership to manage the property. No one heard anything more until a second letter arrived six weeks later. Bad news from Richard Dyke. His lengthy explanation cited several reasons they could not give Homer the property, with heavy emphasis on refusal of the Attorney General to approve the transfer of property left to the Foundation.

Various examples listed in the letter looked familiar to Rachel, so familiar she checked them against a document given to Foundation Board members during a special workshop in the Spring of 2000. The same cases, the same arguments which were now quoted by Richard Dyke as new information were included in the presentation he made to the Board. It was neither new nor relevant, but he used that argument.

She especially didn't understand why the Attorney General's office thought it was okay for Nelda to take the ranch in 1965, but objected if she gave it to Homer two years before she died. But their attorney was front and center, supposedly paying attention on behalf of the public interest.

Richard Dyke mumbled a few more words, then closed his presentation and took a seat as Kevin took his turn. He did not require an overhead projector, nor a podium. It would prove to be a masterful presentation, complete with impressive factual information to dispute Richard Dyke's arguments. For the first time in an hour, the truth would see daylight.

The courtroom was quiet as Kevin methodically countered the arguments made by Richard Dyke. Burning documents was illegal during discovery, at least in the rest of the country. He quoted numerous cases stipulating that when documents are destroyed during a lawsuit, it is assumed they would have benefited the other party – in this case, the Stark family. The Enron debacle in neighboring Harris County provided plenty of ammunition.

Secondly, Nelda Stark illegally took control of the Roslyn Ranch property. With the approval of those involved in the conspiracy of silence set in motion years earlier. The judge, the lawyers, even the Attorney General's office.

"She had no authority to take property without payment to the Estate, and no compensation as executor was permitted in Lutcher Stark's will," Kevin said. "In fact, his will specifically stipulated that Nelda was to receive no compensation for serving as executor of his will."

With that, he placed an enlargement of a page from the will, with the paragraph stating that fact highlighted in bright yellow, on an easel facing the judge. Making it absolutely clear Richard Dyke misrepresented the truth by presenting the same page earlier, without including the highlighted section.

"Nelda Stark not only stole the property from the Estate she was sworn to administer according to law, but by doing so she stole from the Foundation she served as Chairman of the Board and CEO.

"If you will note in our pleadings, your honor, no deed was ever issued to Nelda Stark for this property. Instead, more than 10 years after Mr. Stark's death, a correction deed for water rights for the ranch property was filed, leading one to believe she already held title to that property. She did not."

As Kevin moved to another point, Rachel closely watched Jim Barringer, the attorney from Austin representing the Attorney General's office. Perhaps now he would understand that property was misdirected from the Foundation by the same people responsible for its operations.

Sounds of books hitting the floor attracted the attention of almost everyone in the courtroom as Richard Dyke was nervously going through items on his table, almost desperately looking for information to contradict the points being made by Kevin. His face moved left and right as if at a tennis match, bringing a smile to Rachel's face as he tried to pull a response together for his closing remarks.

Kevin stopped for a moment and walked over to help pick up the books that had fallen from the table, smiling as he set a couple on the corner of his opponent's table. Then he launched into his remarks without missing a beat, backing each of his points with case law.

It was Richard Dyke's turn to add his final argument. With two books open to specific pages and a ruffled appearance, he made his way to the center of the courtroom. There he once again brought up the ranch, Creswell's poor memory, previous actions in Texas or Louisiana courtrooms, the release and the Lutcher & Moore records he briefly acknowledged in his opening statement.

With discovery of the Lutcher & Moore records in a university library, the Stark family felt they finally learned the truth about the alleged note signed by Nita. It simply did not exist, never had, despite arguments presented by Nelda's attorneys in both the 1988 lawsuit and the current one.

Richard Dyke said he, too, visited the university library and reviewed the documents. Yet his findings were quite different as he suggested the dozens of copies furnished in Kevin's brief were simply incomplete and misleading. Plus they had

been available during the previous lawsuit and now "these people simply wanted another bite at the apple because they didn't
even bother to examine public records."

Quite pleased with his performance, Richard Dyke trium-
phantly returned to his seat. Kevin just smiled, then stood and
selected a few documents to refer to in his remarks. He hoped
the Lutcher & Moore records would be brought up, and was
confident Richard Dyke would do just that.

"Your honor." Kevin started to speak, then took a moment
to shake his head in amazement at the opportunity before him.
When first told of the lumber company records located in Nacogdoches almost two years earlier, Kevin was careful to explain
they could not be used since they were available to the family
during the initial lawsuit. But when Rachel explained the materials were not available to the public until after the case was
settled in 1991, it was a new ballgame.

"Sir, words fail me on occasions such as this. I am simply in
awe of Mr. Dyke's allegations that I would present false information to bolster a case when the statute of limitations covering those documents had expired."

"If Mr. Dyke had visited with the librarian when he was in
Nacogdoches, perhaps he would have learned the documents
were not catalogued and made available to the public until
1992 at the earliest, more than a year after the case ended. A
timeline supports our contention that this new evidence was
not available to us, nor was mention of it provided during discovery by Mr. Dyke's clients even though they were aware of
its location.

"Not only does this new evidence from the original Lutcher
& Moore records support my clients' argument that fraud has

been a player in this case since 1939, but representatives of the Foundation and Estate have continued to conceal that fact by actions as recently as those witnessed today.

"Yes, they represent a non-profit organization. But that does not give them the right to confiscate assets of another individual's estate for their own purposes. Whether you use the Bill of Rights, the Ten Commandments or the Constitution of the United States of America as your basis, none of them endorses stealing property from one family to support the greed and power habits of others.

"Your honor, we stand on the merits of our case, the truth and the laws of the State of Texas."

With that, Kevin took a seat and Richard Dyke, stunned for a moment by this turn of events, began arguing that he should be allowed to present a second closing argument. It was a circus indeed as he begged for five minutes of additional rebuttal, a most unusual request that was actually granted by the judge.

Finally, after three to four minutes of nothing of substance from Richard Dyke, the hearing was concluded. Rachel and Randy stayed behind as Walter, Eunice, Roy and several members of the Foundation staff who had been given the afternoon off to attend the hearing filed from the courtroom. The cousins exchanged a few words with friends, then left to wait for Patrick in the rear parking lot of the courthouse.

"It's almost like a parade," said Randy, laughing at the more interesting people who exited the building.

Rachel had to agree, watching Jim Barringer from the Attorney General's staff struggling to remove his tie, sling his coat over his arm and waddle down the sidewalk to his car. She wondered if he even stayed awake during these hearings. He always seemed sleepy.

Next was Eunice and a couple of longtime Stark employees who made numerous trips throughout the afternoon to bring her M&M's from the candy dispenser next to the gumball machine in the hallway. The sugar jolt was probably necessary to give the appearance she was alert.

The judge, carrying a box of documents to his car, seemed irritated as he walked across the parking lot. Probably not too happy the hearing lasted so long, since he hated the drive back to Houston in late afternoon traffic. Being a visiting judge had not proven that glamorous.

Kevin, Billy Clyde and Patrick were laughing as they rounded the corner at the bottom of the courthouse stairs.

"What's so funny?" asked Randy.

"You know that bailiff in the courtroom, sitting up against the wall on the side of the bench?" asked Kevin.

"Yeah, he actually seemed to be paying attention."

"Well, Billy Clyde and I were trying to get our things together and leave when he just came up and offered to help. Nice guy, didn't say much, but as we loaded everything on the cart he leaned over and said 'If I ever need a lawyer, expect a call from me. You guys were great'."

It had been a good day in court. Finally.

CHAPTER 17

"Do not consider it proof just because it is written in books, for a liar who will deceive with his tongue will not hesitate to do the same with his pen."
— *Malmonides*

The room was quiet. Even rain hitting windows of the 14th floor conference room had stopped. Ominous clouds in every direction gave one the feeling it was merely a break in the storm stalled over Houston. Lightly tapping her fingers on the rosewood table, Rachel broke the silence and patiently waited for the lawyers to say something, to respond to papers filed regarding the release her family signed to end the 1988 lawsuit.

It was not a new subject, but they seemed to be hearing the story for the first time. How often did she have to tell them what happened? Why didn't they just take notes? Did they not believe what she put in front of them?

Byron Steele and Bob Garner carefully reviewed the release supposedly signed by the Homer Stark family, then glanced at the papers Rachel had shown them – each carefully stored in a vinyl sleeve and marked as you might expect a courtroom exhibit to be identified. Patrick sat to his mother's left, drinking a Coke and occasionally making note of something or another on a yellow legal pad. A smile crossed his face as he glanced at the two experienced lawyers who seemed puzzled by the turn of events.

"Can we start from the beginning?" asked Byron.

"Again?" Rachel shook her head and looked at the ceiling, not sure why they wanted her to repeat the story.

"We know you've told us before...on several occasions... and again today, but we need to hear it one more time," said Bob, trying to sound apologetic after almost four hours reviewing the rather unusual situation.

"Come on, Mom. We'll record everything this time so you won't have to repeat it," said Patrick, enjoying the moment as he knew the story would remain the same as the first time she told them three years earlier.

At the center of attention was the release, one that was now an issue in a Louisiana courtroom where the billion dollar Stark Foundation was squaring off against the families of both Homer and Bill Stark. The case had gone before a judge in 2001, with a decision made to allow discovery by the families with attorneys for both sides in agreement. Patrick recalled the meeting between attorneys to iron out the details, only to learn soon after that the Foundation hired a second firm and filed a motion to recuse the judge. Almost magically, the first judge disappeared and it would be 20 months before a second, then third judge finally sat before them.

The hearing held no surprises. Lawyers for each side presented their arguments as the judge appeared to listen, but in the final moments one of the Foundation lawyers made what the families thought were the same exaggerated, and in most cases, erroneous statements that were introduced in Texas courtrooms on the other side of the Sabine River.

"Both families signed a release in the first case, your honor, and they are included in our exhibit for your review," said Jack Singleton, a short, red headed member of the bar who Rachel found almost as obnoxious as Richard Dyke. He reminded her of a chubby Tom Sawyer character in a suit.

Quickly she sent a note to Alan Clark, a Louisiana attorney hired by her family, reminding him that no release signed by the Homer Stark family had been introduced in either state. He reviewed the files at the table, then waited for the first opportunity to question the validity of opposing counsel's statement.

"Judge, with regard to Mr. Singleton's comment regarding a release from the Homer Stark family being filed in any courtroom – in Louisiana or Texas – I believe the record will show he is mistaken. Not only has no one filed a release supposedly signed by my clients, but they have interrogatories, sworn and notarized statements, from Homer Stark clearly denying that the release they presented was a true and correct copy of the one he signed. Furthermore, they have never questioned the veracity of his response."

"Mr. Singleton?," the judge said, turning to the opposite side of the aisle. "Is there or is there not a release from the Homer Stark family filed with this court?"

Almost like a two-minute drill, the Foundation delegation huddled with their legal team to decide what signal to call. Several in the group talked at the same time, indicating a degree of confusion among the usually confident group. Silence followed and Mr. Singleton stood to deliver the news. Apparently there was no release filed from Homer Stark's family.

"But we have a copy and will take care of that within the next few days," he added, again apologizing for the confusion.

"You have 10 days to file the release," Judge Gray said, continuing as he turned to the Stark family attorneys. "And Mr. Clark, your clients will then have 10 days to examine the release and file a response. Is that clear to both sides?"

It was. Knowing her father clearly denied the authenticity of the release presented years earlier and that the Foundation lawyers never questioned his response, Rachel was curious to see what they would produce.

Exactly 10 days later, Jack Singleton filed the same release Homer refuted when they presented it the first time. Now it was Rachel's turn to formally tell the story no one bothered to ask, and she was looking forward to putting the facts on record.

Patrick called his mother to give her a brief idea of what to include in the affidavit, stressing the importance of providing a factual outline with no reason to include detail that could be added in court. From his vantage point as a family member, he knew from the beginning about questions surrounding the alleged release when it was attached three years earlier as "Exhibit A" for Homer's interrogatories.

"Make them work for the truth," he said, reminding her of their tendency to create excuses or hide behind the Foundation whenever their version of the facts was questioned. Rachel promised to email a draft of her response by Sunday, allowing him more than a week to format the final version.

Just the bare minimum. No details about events surrounding the final version of the release signed by the Homer Stark family. It had been almost 10 years since they signed on the dotted line, ending the legal battle to determine the fate of so many items that were not included in Nita's inventory. Documents produced by the Foundation clearly showed real estate and lease properties owned by Lutcher Stark were actually held by his Texas corporations and protected as separate property. The Southwestern art collection was purchased after his marriage to Nita. The Colorado ranch and other items were gifts or bequests to Lutcher Stark.

On the surface, it appeared Homer's children were mistaken about additional claims of Nita's estate. Yet they were anything but comfortable with the language of the release presented to them for endorsement. Questions raised with their attorney always ended with his assurance "they can't do that" or "it's not legal" or "you can't sign away fraud in the future." But they were still included and caused heated conversations about signing the document.

In a stroke of brevity, Rachel prepared a one-page affidavit based on Patrick's instructions. The typical comments about age, sound mind, personal knowledge, and address were followed by "just the facts" as the next paragraph explained it was not the release the family signed since Rachel was the last person to sign and initialed each page. The document showed no initials. Additionally, she pointed out how it was different in content and wording. Both Eunice Benckenstein and Clyde McKee were specifically listed in the revised version. Neither was named in the release produced by Jack Singleton.

Her final paragraph explained changes made to exclude Nelda individually since she had been dismissed from the suit; any references to future fraud or omission; protection for the attorneys; the phrase "forced heirship"; and several other words, phrases or sentences inconsistent with the facts.

The one-page document was forwarded to Alan and filed the first week of May with the Court, well within the 10-day time period set by Judge Gray. No one was certain how long it would take him to rule, but there was hope he would come to a decision that summer.

Ten weeks slipped by without any news. To Rachel, it meant the judge might be seriously reviewing the case and the outcome may not be predetermined this time. She was wrong.

One of the large manila envelopes that seemed to scream lawyer was in her mailbox one Friday afternoon in July. The return address showed it was from Alan, but she didn't have a good feeling about its contents. If it was good news, he would have called.

She leaned against the kitchen counter and opened the package, reading the brief cover letter explaining the attachment was another affidavit filed by Jack Singleton. No other explanation of what was to come. As she turned the page, it was unclear how he could simply file something more than two months after the judge began reviewing the case.

The answer was obvious when she realized the affidavit was from Lawrence Watson, one of the lead Knox and Henderson attorneys in the 1988 case. Bigtime lawyers seem to get special treatment and here he was filing a response that to her knowledge was not even allowed. What could he possibly say that had any relevance to the release? As an attorney for Nelda Stark, he never attended any meetings of the family with their attorney and she doubted Maxwell Shaw would have shared the details about the necessity for producing a second release to sign.

But there it was. Several pages of his firm's role in developing the release, working with Shaw, problems posed in obtaining the Homer Stark family signatures. So what was the point? Rachel couldn't grasp the purpose of the affidavit, unless it was simply to confuse a new judge and use the name recognition of Watson's firm to influence his decision.

She moved into the living room, now reading the affidavit for the second time when the ringing of the phone broke her concentration. A glance at the caller ID showed it was Alan calling from Lake Charles, possibly the only person she was interested in talking to at that point.

"Alan, hard to believe you're still in the office this late on Friday afternoon."

He laughed and countered with a remark about the long hours that come with a law degree, then came right to the point.

"Did you get the package I sent?"

"Yeah, I was actually reading it for the second time when you called. What in the world does it mean? I can't figure out what it's got to do with the second release we signed – and how can they file something so late?"

"I knew you'd ask me about that," said Alan. "The judge let them file it, and that's his prerogative. But I haven't figured out myself how it helps their case. His affidavit doesn't lay a glove on you. Nothing he said contradicts what you stated. In fact, it almost supports your statement."

"So is this when we get to tell the whole truth?" asked Rachel, knowing Alan already had the full set of notes made years earlier and was familiar with details omitted the first time around.

They talked for a few minutes, with Alan promising to notify the judge they would be filing a response and Rachel agreeing to forward a second affidavit to Alan early the following week.

"Then what happened?" asked Byron Steele, making one final entry on the note pad before glancing up as Rachel recounted events surrounding the release.

"I guess I got mad."

Byron grinned, almost as if he expected the response from this woman who spent years discovering new documents for the case and reviewing thousands of papers produced the first time around. She had a right to be mad, considering the conspiracy and fraud uncovered in the process.

"Okay, you were mad. That's certainly understandable, but what did you do next?"

"Honestly? I just sat there in the dark that night trying to figure out the best way to make our case. I knew what happened, but the only way I could actually prove it meant I had to find the first release – the one they said we signed. So I left the next morning for Ramona's house in Dallas."

"Tell us everything about what you found. How you found it. Where it was," said Byron.

Over the next hour, she told them a story they had heard before. Explaining the meetings and conversations between Maxwell Shaw, Ramona and Rachel regarding the final months of the original case. How neither sister wanted to settle, but agreed to do so only after negotiating changes in the release they were expected to sign. They wanted nothing unusual, just to clarify some issues that were in keeping with what Shaw was telling them privately.

The confrontation came in late December 1990 – between Christmas and New Year's, as Shaw arrived at Love Field in Dallas on his private jet with the release to be signed by Rachel and Ramona. He was personally carrying the only original of the document from one city to another to gather the Homer Stark family signatures. Earlier that day, he was in Toledo, Ohio for Rebel to sign. Now he was at a private terminal at Love Field, presumably minutes away from acquiring signatures that had proven the most difficult to gain.

"There were five of us in the room when we met," said Rachel. "An attorney friend of Shaw's from Dallas apparently met him at the private terminal. I don't remember his name…but he was dressed in a western cut jacket and said very little, never sat down. Just stood slightly behind Shaw, who was seated to Ramona's left. I was to her right and Jed Nau, an attorney for Ramona's husband, was there to make certain everything went smoothly. He sat opposite Ramona, next to Shaw."

"I think we've got the picture, Rachel," said Bob Garner. "You don't have to be that specific."

Rachel disagreed. She took a moment to share her opinion and convince them it was important to understand the setting and the mood in the room.

"Ramona was the last to arrive, dressed in dark leggings, hot pink shorts, and purple jacket, with a backpack slung across a shoulder. It was freezing outside, but she had been working out and came straight to the terminal. "

The scene she described next began with Shaw producing the document, almost theatrically presenting it as he pulled it from his briefcase and placed it squarely in front of Ramona.

"He gave her a pen to sign the release, but she wanted to read it first. Ramona's really good about sizing up people and she didn't trust Shaw. I think she wanted to make certain he made the changes we discussed."

"And did he?" asked Byron.

"Nope. She got past the first couple of pages, then balked. Asked him why it did not include changes about waiving the rights of her heirs. Ramona was adamant about that from the beginning."

Rachel described how Shaw kept assuring Ramona it wasn't necessary, and the whole time Jed Nau just sat there. Even though he was there to protect the interests of her children, he said nothing to ease her mind and it became obvious Ramona was upset as she signed the release.

"So she did sign it?" asked Byron.

"Yeah, but I felt bad because she started to cry and I told her she didn't have to sign if she didn't want to. Mr. Shaw told her the same thing and she pointed out she had already signed. I told her to mark through her signature, and she did – several times."

"Then what happened?" asked Bob Garner, the only one in the room who had not heard the full story on previous occasions.

"Well, Mr. Shaw's face turned red. Don't think I've seen anyone get that mad that fast. But he pushed away from the table, stood up, picked up the release and slowly tore it in half. Then he let it drop to the table – all the while staring directly at Ramona.

"Then, not to be outdone, Ramona stood up, picked up the two halves of the release, and tore those in half. She didn't lose eye contact with Shaw either. The release was scattered across the table in pieces and he stormed out of the room with his friend in tow. She left a minute or so later."

Following that meeting, Rachel explained it took two months to come up with a revised release acceptable to Homer's family. Changes she noted in the first affidavit submitted in Louisiana were incorporated in the second release and it was circulated for signatures in late February.

"I was the last one to sign and checked to make certain the changes were there," said Rachel. "I also initialed each page, thinking I was supposed to since I just had a will drawn up the week before and was told then to initial each page of that document. Then it was sent overnight to Mr. Shaw's office. "

"Everyone signed?" asked Byron.

"Not Ramona. She would never sign anything for Shaw after that meeting at the airport. He said he would take care of it, but I didn't realize that meant her signature from another document would be attached to a copy of the original release they destroyed."

It had been an intriguing story, certainly a confrontation that would long be remembered for the reactions of two strong-willed individuals. But it was still the family's word against the Stark Foundation attorneys.

"We are still back at square one," said Bob. "It's almost impossible to prove this happened. You signed a release and Homer received part of the settlement funds."

"We have never denied signing a release," said Rachel. "We just didn't sign that one. All we asked was for the language of the release to reflect what we were told wasn't legal anyway. If you can't sign away rights to fraud in the future, why include it? And if the forced heirship law covers all properties you are forfeiting – and there was no list provided – why would we sign it?"

"Besides, it isn't just our word against theirs," she added, motioning to the torn documents in the vinyl covers.

Byron and Bob turned their attention back to the rather remarkable remnants of the December 1990 release, neatly placed inside the vinyl sleeves. Rachel always said they existed; she just couldn't find them.

"Ramona took some when she left that meeting at the airport, kind of shoving them in her backpack after Shaw left the room. He didn't notice she had taken any, and I wasn't certain she still had them after all these years. Not until the Foundation refused to honor Nelda's gift of the ranch to my dad and we were forced to go to court. I called Ramona after the interrogatories were sent to our dad and she swore she still had the papers she took more than 10 years earlier."

After receiving the affidavit submitted by Watson regarding the release, Rachel called Ramona about the pieces she took with her that night.

"She was positive she had them, she just didn't know exactly where they were," said Rachel. "So I drove to Dallas the next morning to help her find them. I never doubted her, I just hoped she hadn't misplaced them when she moved to her new house."

"You know, I have to ask," said Byron. "Where did you find them?"

"Well, it wasn't easy because Ramona keeps records of everything. But we went through a lot of binders and finally narrowed it down to a few that didn't contain family photos, design ideas or background information on different projects. That's when she discovered the ziplock bags with the pieces inside, tucked into one of the larger binders with other papers related to the case."

"And?" asked Byron.

"Then we went to Kinko's and copied them, making sure she put the original in a safe deposit box on the way home in case you wanted to have them authenticated."

Silence took over the room as the attorneys weighed what they had just heard... and seen. It would certainly be intriguing to file Rachel's second affidavit, along with copies of the original release. Even though Ramona had not taken all of the pieces, she did have those that clearly showed her signature marked out, Rebel's signature and that of the notary public in Ohio, plus sections of the document with signatures of her aunt and cousins.

"One more thing," said Rachel, pausing to make a point. "My aunt's family signed only one release and these pieces clearly show it was destroyed by Shaw two weeks later. Who falsified the release on record for my cousins? And aren't the Foundation and its lawyers guilty of knowingly filing a false document with the Court?"

"So, I'm sending the affidavit to Alan to file, right?" asked Patrick, taking his cue from expressions around the table.

"Absolutely," said Byron. "Judge Gray should find it very interesting."

CHAPTER 18

"Word on the street is that the Foundation's biggest fear is if a lawsuit ever went to court, the IRS would be on the sidelines watching every move."

— *Anonymous*

"Tell me about the foundation."

They had been at it for close to six hours the following day, except for occasional breaks, and now Byron Steele wanted to focus attention on the Stark Foundation. The conference room reflected the long hours of discussion. Empty coffee cups and soft drink cans, candy wrappers, discarded styrofoam boxes that had contained lunch and dinner, and an open box of donuts leftover from breakfast dominated the credenza against the south wall. Notepads seemed scattered across the massive rosewood table, but the five persons who had been there all day knew there was a method to the placement of each.

"Where should I start?" asked Rachel.

"Your choice. All I really know is what I've read about them in the papers," said Byron.

"That's the problem. No one really knows much about the Foundation, only what they want you to know. And when they want you to know it."

"Humor me. Give me some specific examples of what you mean."

"Well, for starters, they don't follow the law. In fact, they have done everything they can to misrepresent what they do – and have for years, almost since it began in 1961."

Starting with the Articles of Incorporation, Rachel passed out copies for each attorney to follow along. Kind of like "show and tell" for adults. She gave each a yellow highlighter, asking them to mark the purposes of the non-profit Stark Foundation as identified on the first page of the document: "...exclusively for public charitable, religious and educational purposes."

"Now if you read the rest of that paragraph it notes that 'no part of its earnings or property shall ever inure to the benefit of any private individual'. Take a moment to review it – pretty brief, actually – and then I'll give you the rest of the story."

Only three pages in length, it was a quick read.

"So what is so strange about the Articles of Incorporation? They look pretty standard to me," asked Bob Garner.

"They do, don't they?" agreed Rachel. "But that's what they want you to think. When it comes to this Foundation, you might as well check your conscience at the door when you swear to abide by the law."

Before they could comment, she distributed a prepared packet of materials clearly marked with colored tabs indicating topics such as Grant and Charitable Activity Summary and Application; Self Dealing/990-PF; Cost Analysis of Charitable

Operations; H. J. Lutcher Stark's Will/Inventory; Donor's Intent; Texas Attorney General's Office.

Asking them to turn to the section regarding her grandfather's will, she proceeded to unveil the basis of her allegations.

"First, it is clear he is leaving half of his estate to Nelda, the other half to the Foundation. But it also specifically says that all antiques, art and jewelry from his separate estate go directly to the Foundation – with the sole exception of items in their private residence. Secondly, it clearly states no compensation will be paid Nelda for serving as executor of his Estate."

No one said anything. By now they knew Rachel would explain her comments without any help from them. She opened a large file box and gave each a three-ring binder with two sections, one with a lengthy inventory of Foundation assets dated 1988 and the second with memos and documentation reflecting the division of the Estate.

"What you will find is that the Foundation did not receive anywhere close to half of his separate estate and certainly did not acquire all of his art, antiques and jewelry. Simply cross check an item from his inventory with one of the 11,326 items on the Foundation inventory."

She used a small painting by Rembrandt's best student, Gerrit Dou, as an example. Although Nita purchased it in 1927 in Europe, it was listed in Lutcher's inventory but not in Nita's. Supporting her claim was not only the receipt in Nita's name, but shipping instructions from the Frankfurt firm of J. & S. Goldschmidt.

"The fact it wasn't even listed in her estate is another issue, but it was one of many discrepancies that's easy to prove. Just look at the acquisition date of many of the properties in the Foundation inventory that were 'given' by Nelda. They weren't hers to give, but separate property of Lutcher's. Everything from cars to paintings to umbrellas to porcelain and everything in between – almost all in the antiques and art categories mentioned in his will."

She directed them to memos and documentation that proved her point. Calculations with backup sheets to show there had been anything but an even division of property between the widow and the Foundation she controlled. Included were several pages of jewelry sold by Nelda in the 1980s – all of it traced back to Lutcher's mother or grandmother. An Alexandrite brooch sold for $120,000; diamond necklaces, bracelets and pins brought tens of thousands of dollars; pearl necklaces, gold watches and rings with diamonds, sapphires or rubies bringing top dollar. All of it acquired by Lutcher prior to his marriage to Nelda. All of it bequeathed to the Foundation. Yet none of it listed in the inventory.

"What makes it even more interesting is that the jewelry actually belonged to Nita, not Lutcher," said Rachel, noting a letter from Lutcher to the IRS that the jewelry pieces were gifts to his wife from his mother.

"We'll need some time to review this," Byron said, obviously a little surprised by the amount of detail before him.

"I know, but let me give you something more to think about."

Turning to the Self Dealing section, they found numerous papers filed in Orange County where Nelda either sold or gave herself properties from her husband's estate.

"It might be okay to do this in some circumstances," said Rachel, 'but she gave herself properties such as the Colorado ranch for serving as executor – a direct violation of the will – and in other documents she sells property to herself for less than the appraised value. Regardless of which method she used to transfer the properties, they defrauded the Foundation which she served as Chair."

"A word of caution, Rachel," said Bob Garner. "You can't just make these allegations without some kind of credible evidence. Remember she might have been the Foundation Chair, but she couldn't make decisions without approval of the Board."

"Mr. Garner, the Board was on Nelda's payroll. Of the six other members, four were employees, a fifth handled all her insurance, and my dad wasn't even invited to most of the meetings.

"No one was going to vote against her, and the records show no one ever did. For almost 40 years, no one crossed her. They even had minutes of meetings that were never held, but when my dad shared his concerns with Rose Ann Reeser, the Attorney General's representative, she waited almost two years before writing a letter accusing him of conflict of interest and he was removed from the Board."

"What about the appraisals? How do you know they were low?"

Using the Big Lake property in Louisiana as an example, Rachel explained it was listed at $75,000 in the estate inventory but sold to Nelda for $58,000 in 1967.

"Hardly grand larceny. Who knows what kind of shape it was actually in," said Byron.

"Nelda knew," said Rachel. "If you'll turn to the documents following that transaction – the ones directly after the ranch – you'll have a better idea of what I'm talking about."

There they found details of the rebuilding of the Big Lake property after a hurricane destroyed most of the pier and caused major damage in 1968 to the lakefront home.

"After Camille hit the year after she 'bought' Big Lake, Nelda used Lutcher & Moore monies to pay for the repairs and improvements. Almost $300,000 that should have come from her pocket was funneled through the lumber company accounts, which she also controlled after Lutcher's death. The bottom line is she was stealing from the Foundation and apparently with the Attorney General's permission."

"Are all these documents examples of other transactions like this?" asked Byron.

"Pretty much. There's even a resolution included from the Foundation, signed by Clyde and Eunice, 'giving mineral interests' to Nelda since the Foundation 'didn't need them anymore.' Self dealing was just a way of life with these people."

At first glance the foundation tax returns seemed okay on the surface, but Rachel urged them to check documents showing art that should have been on the Foundation inventory did not appear until after Nelda's death, plus a rare book collection of Miriam Stark's was given by Nelda to the Foundation in exchange for a tax writeoff.

She reminded them that half of the furnishings and art now in the W. H. Stark home was originally given by Nita and Lutcher in 1937, but divided between Nelda and Lutcher when the gift was rescinded in 1953.

"Nelda treated it as community property, even though the half she claimed rightly belonged to Homer and Bill through Nita's estate. She knew it, Eunice and Clyde knew it – they just failed to inform anyone else. Even the Internal Revenue

Service might have been interested in why there was no estate tax paid when the 'gift' didn't make it to UT."

Next was an exchange of letters between Clyde McKee and Nelda's Louisiana attorneys regarding Homer and Bill's rights under the forced heirship provision. When Clyde was told the two sons indeed had rights to their father's property, he countered with a letter stating at the time of Lutcher Stark's death he only owned about $40,000 in land. Conveniently missing was the property that would bring in millions in the Boise Southern purchase.

There was a unanimous, albeit informal, vote to take a ten-minute break, then return to spend at least another hour before heading home. Garner broke for the elevator to squeeze another cigarette in downstairs. Patrick checked in at home, but Byron seemed more interested in reading some of the documents they had not yet covered.

As Rachel returned to the room, Byron motioned for her to join him at the end of the table as he scrutinized documents in the binder.

"Where did you get these?" he asked.

"These documents?"

"Yeah, how long have you known about them?"

"Kind of depends on which ones you are talking about. Some were given to my brother when he was named to the Board in 1998, others were located in Nacogdoches a couple of years ago, and a few were actually produced during the 1988 lawsuit. What does it matter?"

He explained the four-year statute of limitations on fraud, noting that the clock started running once you had reason to believe fraud was being committed. If the papers were produced in 1988, the statute of limitations had expired.

"Actually," began Rachel, "that is not entirely true. Even though the documents were produced some years ago, the perception when you read them is there is no fraud. Everything is just fine. They supplied names, dates, descriptions, appraised value, donor – just about everything you would want to know about each item in the inventory.

"It was not until other documents were discovered years later that contradicted what they furnished — not until then did we realize they had forged or falsified thousands of pages. Maybe not originally to mislead us, but definitely to deceive someone."

She followed her accusation with one example after another, each neatly filed in that section of the binder, with a running commentary on the relationship with other items or events. For many documents produced by the Stark Foundation in 1988, Rachel countered with public records from Louisiana, memos and accounting sheets from Stephen F. Austin, copies of company minutes kept by former associates of the Brown family, correspondence from the Secretary of State's office, and sworn statements from friends, employees and business partners now more likely to talk with Nelda six feet under.

"So you're telling me none of these documents would fall under the statute of limitations?" asked Byron.

"No, I can't say that's true about all of them."

"About how many of them would you say were inaccurate... misleading...fraudulent?"

Rachel cocked her head to the left, squinting her eyes as she gave serious thought to the question, and concentrated on coming up with an accurate response.

"Maybe 90 percent?"

"Ninety percent?" Byron repeated her response, possibly thinking he misunderstood her.

"Somewhere around there. Although it could be higher if we went through all the boxes again. When you think about all the items they said were true, but weren't, it covers an awful lot of information, years and documents. To be honest, about the only thing I know they were truthful about were the receipts for the rat poison and phenobarbital – and I think that was an oversight on their part."

What began as a conversation between the two had attracted the attention of Bob, J. R. and Patrick, who listened in as the litany of examples was rattled off by Rachel.

Byron seemed puzzled. "So let me get this straight. You are telling us that the Foundation operates outside the law while the Texas Attorney General's office looks the other way. "

"Not exactly. I'm saying that Nelda Stark and the Foundation Board knowingly violated federal regulations for decades while representatives of the Texas Attorney General's office – acting, of course, on his behalf – have chosen to protect the Foundation. That's not what I call looking the other way. They are part of the problem.

"The first Attorney General involved in this case was later convicted of bribery, not really giving me a feeling of integrity and credibility for that office," she added.

"Bottom line is that Nelda Stark was the executor of Lutcher Stark's will, a primary beneficiary of his will, and CEO of the Stark Foundation – the residuary beneficiary. She did whatever she liked, the Foundation Board – again composed of employees who reported to her – rubber stamped her wishes, and there was no one to object as she was protected by the illusion that she was operating a charitable foundation."

Fresh from his tobacco infusion, Garner raised his 6'4" frame as he stood to throw his questions into the mix. An accomplished trial lawyer, he wanted to make certain Rachel had the material to back up her charges.

"Okay. We're in the courtroom and good ole boy Richard Dyke is starting to cross examine you. Are you ready?" asked Garner.

"I believe the better question would be is Richard Dyke ready," she responded.

Garner grinned as he turned away from Rachel. He was new to the case but learning quickly that she rarely said anything that could not be substantiated. He composed his next question and turned to face her as he delivered.

"What has the Foundation done to make you think it is above the law?"

She smiled, signaling he had asked an easy question.

"The key function of the Stark Foundation's Directors is to establish policy by selecting from the purposes set forth in the foundation's Articles of Incorporation and Bylaws – goals that are in line with the express wishes of the donor and resources available to the Foundation.

"From day one, Nelda Stark's intent has been to give the minimum amount required by law – even when she was giving it to her own projects, a fact even Walter Riedel admitted in his partial deposition."

"The museum, of course, was specifically mentioned in the Articles of Incorporation and Lutcher Stark's will. However, construction and remodeling of the Lutcher Theater not only diverted millions from the original purposes of the Foundation, it does not fall within the 'donor's intent' clause. As a member of that Board, you also are aware most of the funding provided by the Foundation has actually gone to subsidize their own projects..."

Garner couldn't help but laugh and motioned for her to stop.

"My God, do you mean Richard Dyke is also on the Board – at the same time he's representing them?"

Byron confirmed it. "Unless he's doing it for free, I'd say he's got a problem," said Garner. "Are these people crazy?"*

"No, they just think they're bulletproof," said Rachel. "And wouldn't you if you thought the Attorney General was asleep at the wheel?"

Garner started to make excuses for the Attorney General, noting that he probably had no idea what was being filed in Orange County or presented in the courtroom. Midway through his response, he saw Byron, J. R. and Patrick shaking their heads in unison.

"Okay, maybe there is a link," Garner said. "But you have to have information that clearly shows the violations you are talking about."

"I know. I've been telling you for months. Look at the section in the binder titled 'Grant and Charitable Activity Summary' and you'll see what I'm talking about."

As they turned to the papers, they found a cost analysis of the Foundation operations for the three years preceding Nelda's death, with notations and sources clearly identified across the bottom of the chart. Following that document was a year-by-year summary since the Foundation was created in 1961.

Looking at the bottom line, it seemed she was correct. From 1961 to 1999, 67% of the monies had gone to support "Direct Activities," another name for the museum, theater and W. H. Stark home. Plus add 21% in total grants, with most of that going to support the same direct activities, and another 12% for administrative costs and you had a foundation that was giving very little to the outside world. If they were required to give six percent, they tried to give not a penny more. Most of it to themselves.

Following a pause to absorb the information, Garner raised a question concerning the cost analysis.

"Rachel, not that I would doubt you, but are you certain about these figures? I thought the museum and theater were already paid for, so why would you have these multimillion dollar operating expenses?"

He singled out the average annual costs: $2.9 million for the museum and $2.1 million for the theater. Why were they so high?

"The museum costs are driven up since they include acquisition costs of new art, at least one million dollars a year. The theater is undergoing extensive remodeling even though it was less than 10 years old."

Patrick commented on the numbers showing cost per person to operate the museum, noting that 5400 visitors resulted in average costs of $521 each.

"Seems kind of high to me," he said. "For that kind of money, you could fly all the fifth graders in Orange, their teachers and chaperones to Washington, D. C., pay their hotel and meals, and let them see some big-time museums."

Sad but true, the Foundation showed no interest in using their monies to set up a significant scholarship fund for local students or improve the quality of life in a town that desperately needed the help. Nelda Stark held the town hostage economically for almost 40 years, tearing down most of the downtown area, razing historical homes, refusing to sell property even though she was the largest landowner in the county.

"They do what they want with no regard for the Articles of Incorporation, the bylaws, Lutcher's will or donor's intent," said Patrick. "Not much of a charity, more like their own private stash they can use tax free without regard for any guidelines they should be following."

"Exactly, and that is easily proved," said Rachel. She began checking off examples, pointing out the number of grants given to outside groups and that some had connections with interests of the directors rather than the donor, showing grant applications from various years and how the 'areas of interest' varied from one to the next, or critiquing examples of straying from the intent of her grandfather.

"They have simply done whatever they wanted to with no regard for obeying the law," she said. "Adding a comma here, a new topic there, or basically making it up as they went along. There was no one watching over their shoulder. The Attorney General's office appears to be on their team."

As she stopped to catch her breath, Byron asked Rachel for clarification regarding donor's intent. How did she know they violated it?

"Two reasons. First, we knew what my grandfather's interests were – almost anyone could determine that by what he supported when he was alive. And secondly, the Foundation was limited by the three areas listed in the Articles of Incorporation, a document he created.

"For example, public education, religious and charitable activities would not cover medical research, private education or building a theater, a resort hotel, economic development or a tourist attraction. Nor would he have set up any scholarship fund with the University Interscholastic League, not with his history with that organization. It would have been one of the last places he donated dollars. He would have certainly supported scholarship programs in Southeast Texas, charitable projects, education improvements, summer camps, music programs designed to challenge students, underwriting repairs and maintenance of the First Presbyterian Church.

"They were specifically not to provide grants for operational expenses or endowments, but did it anyway – often to organizations with a tie to trustees of the Stark Foundation or their attorneys."

Garner stopped her for a moment, seeking clarification on what she just said.

"You mean self dealing?"

"You could say that," she responded. "One director is on several other boards that received millions from the Stark Foundation for buildings, salaries, you name it – totally outside their grant guidelines disallowing monies for bricks and mortar. A wife of one of their lawyers runs a non-profit that's on the grant list, and the list goes on and on."

"So Walter's just continuing the same mode of operation they followed when Nelda was alive – disregarding what they are supposed to fund, even selling off the family's art collection that's supposed to be exhibited in the museum?" asked Garner.

"Actually, he's probably more obvious than Nelda. She was low profile and avoided publicity, but Walter and ole Richard Dyke seem to seek it out," Rachel added, pointing out that since Nelda died, the Foundation actually sold art from the Stark Collection that was to be housed in the Stark Museum – even giving some of it away. Plus the Foundation had probably spent at least $50 million to "bring Shangri La back to its former glory," a move she found upsetting on several fronts. Plus it is an ongoing drain on funds that could be better used for scholarships, education-related needs, and charitable purposes.

At one time in his life, Lutcher Stark had indeed enjoyed what was formerly known as the Fifteenth Street Farm. During his marriage to Nita, they acquired the land – including the old city swimming pool location, spent years developing the property, even allowing an artist to reside within its fenced borders. After Nita's death, he continued his passion for stunning floral displays that brought great pleasure to him as he developed a private retreat that even Walt Disney wanted to use for a movie. The answer was "No" to Disney, for Lutcher still remembered his failed experiment at opening the gardens to the public. His love for Shangri La turned to depression in the years prior to his death as it became a holding pen, a prison cell, for the wealthiest man in town.

When Lutcher died, Nelda kept the property, a move that surprised the family since she never cared for it. In fact, she did little more than have the grass mowed and even turned the water off – an action that resulted in most of the original plants succumbing to the hot, humid temperatures.

"Now they say they're bringing it back the way Lutcher Stark would have liked. But using Nelda's money. Whichever way you look at it, neither indicated any interest in developing Shangri La as a tourist attraction," said Rachel, adding that both Lutcher and Nelda are probably spinning in their caskets in light of what was being done.

"So why would the Foundation do that?" asked Byron. "Why don't they just sell the property and pocket the money?"

"Probably because if they sell it, they'd have to do a title search – a rarity for them anyway. But if they did a title search, Homer and Bill would own Nita's interest. That would just open a huge laundry list of other properties they have transferred or sold in the past that would raise the same questions. It's just harder to get by with it now than it was years ago. Besides, this way they have a new 'direct activity' that allows them to keep most of the money earmarked for distribution. They control the monies, it gives them a feeling of importance, and who knows if they receive any financial rewards."

She waited for a moment, but the questions ended. They were looking through some of the documents in the notebook, weighing the consequences of what they had learned. Apparently, the Stark Foundation was not only operating illegally, but appeared to breach everyday expectations of morality and ethics, not to mention the expectations that those who presume to serve the public good assume a larger public trust.

"People place their faith in foundations just because there is an expectation they abide by laws that govern them," said Rachel. "Even at Princeton University, there's a lawsuit where a donor's family filed suit because they aren't abiding by donor's intent. Somehow people seem to think they can spend restricted funds on anything they like, rather than what it was specifically designed to support.

"Directors of the Stark Foundation have clearly decided to ignore the intent of its donors. They have operated in darkness behind the thick walls of the old First National Bank building for decades, knowingly diverting property and monies not only from my dad and uncle, but avoiding estate taxes by undervaluing assets and hiding behind the tax exempt status of the Foundation. How many years have they pretended to be generous, when all along they were giving the bare minimum and mostly to themselves? Why are they so afraid to acknowledge that they hold assets that don't belong to them?

"If you ask me, they are really no better than your typical con artist, just with a lot of money to play with. My question is how many lives do they have to damage – how many laws do they need to break before they are held to the same standards as everyone else?"

Bylaws posted on the Stark Foundation website as recently as November 2009 showed directors were not to receive compensation. Those bylaws were written and adopted in 1962, sending the clear message directors were not to be paid for service to the Stark Foundation. However, bylaws "amended and restated" in 2005 – the year after one of the Foundation attorneys was appointed to the Board – reflect that each director was not only being paid, but received a 73% increase in salary the following year. Salaries for a five-hour work week went from $15,001 in 2005 to $26,000 per director in 2006 – the equivalent of $208,000 for a 40-hour work week or $100 hour. At the same time, the decision was made in 2005 that directors who served at least nine years would receive their salary for life when they left the Board.

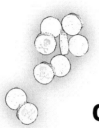

CHAPTER 19

*"All that is necessary for the triumph of evil
is for good men to do nothing."*
— Edmund Burke

There was something exhilarating yet calming about the beach. Especially on a perfect sunny day in early April, the surf pounding the sand and familiar sounds of seagulls and pelicans circling above. It was as if nature was having a conversation with the Gulf breezes.

Walking barefoot along the shore at Holly Beach, Rachel felt comfortable and relaxed away from the mountain of boxes and stacks of documents that seemed to occupy every waking moment the last several years.

At the suggestion of her kids, she was taking a break to truly do nothing in a setting where technology of any kind was difficult to find. It was the third day since her arrival and she had adjusted to the slower pace, taking life easy in the small beach community she visited as a child.

Nothing much had changed. It was like going back to a time long past when people valued others, trust was more than an entry in the dictionary, and wealth was measured by friends rather than dollars. Her idealistic nature had taken a hit as she tired of all the lies that had been told even before she was born.

Family values. At the end of the day, that's what it was all about. The problem was the values her grandfather taught his sons were not the ones he lived. Or at least it was looking more and more like that each time she opened a file, questioned oldtimers, or read his correspondence. It was the latter that was often the toughest to handle. There was Lutcher Stark's unique signature on documents meant to actually hide or perhaps even steal property from her father and uncle. Inventory forms, audit reports, ledgers, memos and letters. Regardless of the format, the end result was consistent. Beneath the lies was the truth, but those who benefited wouldn't admit it and the rest chose not to believe it. To do so would upset the balance of power in Orange.

Lutcher Stark, a man she had admired since childhood, was not quite the legend created in her mind. Stories about helping the local schools or the University of Texas, subsidizing bands or providing scholarship monies or medical treatment for those who needed help. All the tales Homer recounted of his father's good deeds predated Nelda. The fond memories he shared were true, but his children had not realized everything ended with the marriage to Nelda. It was possible even Homer failed to understand.

Rachel's opinion of her grandfather's business skills also changed. Reams of papers and notes and telegrams discovered in Nacogdoches had enlightened her about his expertise and work ethic. It was H. J. Lutcher, not his namesake, whose vision created a timber empire and had the foresight to build a fortune around it. With the help of his wife, Frances Ann – affectionately called the "Angel of Mercy" by the people of Orange, the couple not only built a church and contributed heavily to public schools, but constructed a fine hospital primarily to make certain the men in their mills would have proper care in a dangerous occupation. Together they made a difference in people's lives. Not because it was expected, but it was the right thing to do. Both realized with wealth came responsibility.

Yet her grandfather seemed to focus on collecting art, traveling, and his "jobs" as a University of Texas Regent and Rotary Club officer. He was a man accustomed to getting his way. Inheriting a fortune, as opposed to working for it, was the difference between Lutcher Stark's work ethic and that of W. H. Stark and H. J. Lutcher.

When Nelda entered the picture, it seemed to slowly transform him. Sooner or later, the only trips were to Colorado and for weeks rather than months. The man who traveled the world in his previous life remained in his hometown, living in a house with his in-laws not much larger than the garage of his other home. He dropped support of the Bengal Guards, rescinded the University of Texas gift, and seemed unusually dismayed and depressed. Shortly after he married Nelda, friends noticed the changes – even the way he sat in the car. Instead of sitting up straight behind the wheel, he was slouched in the back seat so that you only saw the top of his hat.

Leona, a family servant who never understood the control Nelda held over Lutcher, recalled a meeting in Galveston when Nelda was diagnosed with breast cancer in the 1950s. "Not much we can do for her," the doctor told Mr. Stark, who turned to Leona as the doctor left the room, lighting a cigarette as he stared out the window. Even years later, she remembered clearly his exact words: "Well, Lee, it looks like we get to live again."

But Nelda beat all the odds, despite the abysmal cancer survival rate. "She was just pure meanness, sure as I'm standing here," Leona offered as an explanation of the medical miracle.

Sounds of a small boat just off the Louisiana coast caught Rachel's attention, a reminder of her grandfather's casual approach to work. Business associates recalled meetings in the Stark offices on Front Street, which backed up to the Sabine River. They told her it was not unusual for board meetings to be well into the agenda when the sound of Lutcher's speedboat could be heard over the discussion. He'd always approach at full speed, then cut the throttle back just as he neared the dock. It made the damndest noise and signaled the heir apparent would be with them shortly. Sure enough, within minutes he'd enter the room with no explanation, no word of apology for being late. Not even to his father.

Slouching in a faded green aluminum chair on the front porch of the weathered cabin, Rachel was perfectly comfortable with the view of a brilliant orange and red sunset slowly disappearing beyond the water's edge. The change in scenery and pace had done wonders for her attitude. Walks along the beach each morning and evening, coupled with hours in the middle of the day to relax with a good book, had awakened a mindset almost lost in the years of research.

Yes, life was good. Even Travis adapted to the change in lifestyle with new territory to explore, birds to chase and remarkable treats from Thibodeaux's grocery to sample before curling up for an extended nap.

Time had given Rachel a great gift: the pleasure of reading a romantic novel or enjoying a glass of wine with no feelings of guilt if she didn't spend every spare moment tying loose ends together. Darkness brought a spectacular show in the heavens as stars outshone any she had ever before seen. It was almost mesmerizing, possibly because of the wine, and brought a peaceful feeling in what some might consider the middle of nowhere.

"Can you believe that full moon?" she said to no one in particular, although Travis lifted his head to see who had joined them. Raising her glass to the heavens as if making a toast, Rachel began a series of comments and questions for the grandmother she never knew.

"Miss Nita, I just want you to know we finally figured it out. You must have been wondering what took so long, but Granddaddy had a hell of a plan. Attorneys, judges, bookkeepers. Never seen anything quite like it. If we hadn't found the second set of books, I guess we'd still believe you died without much to your name.

"By the way, it's important you know how much you were loved. Not only people who knew you well, but grandchildren you never met. That's the biggest disappointment to me – that you didn't live long enough to even know one of us. Or to see what fine young men you raised. Daddy and Uncle Bill would have made you proud. When World War II broke out, they didn't try to get out of the draft like Granddaddy did in the first war – they enlisted and fought in the Pacific. Daddy as a gunner's mate in the Navy and Uncle Bill as a torpedo pilot in the Marines."

Rachel laughed quietly at the thought she had occasionally wondered if her grandfather actually started World War II, kind of like a diversion to keep his sons out of the country so he could transfer deeds, stocks and other assets while they fought for his freedom. Lutcher Stark was a powerful man, but she doubted the war could be blamed on him. Yet he certainly knew how to take advantage of a situation.

"Oh, another thing, Miss Nita. We just can't figure out what Granddaddy was thinking when he married Nelda. I know she acted like a nurse, hospital administrator, technician, or whatever else she claimed to be. But did he know her degree was in education, not biology? That black bag she carried around all the time was just for show, at least according to her college records. Seems like a stretch to make an education major a nurse in all those press releases. Almost think he couldn't have known or he'd never have left you or Ruby in her care.

"And all that art she supposedly collected on those trips through New Mexico on the way to the ranch? Leona said Miss Nelda and Miss Eunice always stayed behind at the hotel. Granddaddy would take Leona with him to shop at the galleries, but Nelda and Eunice didn't have any interest in leaving the room."

Rachel paused for a moment, smiling as she recalled what Homer referred to as "the night the gun should have gone off." Looking toward the heavens, she told Nita about the late night phone call Nelda made to Homer, frantically pleading for him to come take Lutcher's gun.

"'He's gonna kill me, Homer. Please come over and take it away from him.' That's what she said to Daddy, Miss Nita. And you know how Daddy is…went right over and convinced him to put the gun away. Of course, in hindsight, he should have stayed in bed and let Granddaddy take care of the situation himself. Could have solved a lot of problems that night."

The wine was kicking in as Rachel decided to retire for the evening and continue her conversation another day. But as she opened the screen door, she turned back and looked up to share one more moment with Nita.

"Remember that little painting with the dog you bought in Frankfurt – in 1927, I believe. Somehow all those paintings you and Granddaddy bought ended up in Nelda's inventory. The lawyers said they were 'lost', but you and I know better. Anyway – that little painting you liked so much just sold for $4.7 million at Christie's in New York City – a nice return on your investment, although the Foundation thinks they are entitled to your half. We still haven't been able to locate the Rembrandts you and Miriam bought on the same trip, but they probably aren't scheduled to be 'found' yet. Sweet dreams."

As morning dawned on Day 4, the cool breeze off the Gulf was envigorating but Rachel decided to sleep a little later than usual and pulled the sheets and blanket over her head in an effort to darken the room. Thibodeaux's prediction of overcast skies and possible showers appeared correct as she heard the light sounds of rain dancing on the metal roof. Perfect. She loved sleeping in on rainy days.

"Rachel, are you there?" came a voice as she woke to some-one knocking. Glancing at the clock she squinted to see it was half past nine and grabbed her robe to answer the door. It was Thibodeaux with freshly made beignets protected by his umbrella.

"Sorry to bother you, but we were a little worried when we didn't see you out and about this morning. Can't be too careful with all that's going on."

"How nice to know you're watching out for me," said Rachel, realizing the conversations they shared the last few days already had him on the same wavelength as her family, friends, and attorneys who had seen the email from the Foundation's attorney warning her that to show up at the next hearing would be at her own peril. Combined with the list of persons who had died of food poisoning, some mysterious illness or simply disappeared, everyone was on edge.

"I'm fine, just sleeping a little later than usual...but I don't think anyone knows where I am except for my family, and they certainly won't tell."

She thanked him again for his trouble, promising to come by later that day. As he returned home with his slightly bent red umbrella visible most of the way, Rachel couldn't resist the warm beignets and poured a glass of milk. It was the perfect breakfast on a rainy morning. The only thing better would be eating on the porch and taking advantage of the view, a move she made without hesitation.

Funny how the sight of waves breaking on the shore seemed peaceful, while a lone jogger in the distance was undisturbed by the inclement weather. Holly Beach remained a small water-front community composed of aging cabins that had seen more than their share of hurricanes pound the low lying areas along the coast. Costly storms plus shallow muddy waters of the Gulf had limited growth, a situation the locals seemed to like just fine. Holly Beach truly was the ideal place to disappear.

Rachel dressed and straightened the cabin before making a quick trip to her car. A box, one she affectionately called her Magic Box, was taken from the back seat and placed squarely in the center of a table in the small kitchen area. It was unmistakably red, not the usual white or brown color of the other dozens of boxes scattered throughout her house. Inside were several expanding files, each clearly labeled with a black marker noting the general content.

She was familiar with each document and its relative importance to the case against the Foundation. Collectively, they detailed the illegal and fraudulent actions she believed had been taken by Lutcher Stark, Nelda Stark, Eunice Benckenstein, Clyde McKee, Walter Riedel, their lawyers and a cast of characters who assisted the lot in concealing what she thought might be one of the biggest fraud cases one might imagine, even in Texas. What began as an interest in family history took a dramatic turn along the way, opening doors to a lifestyle and decisions that were carefully draped in darkness for almost a century.

Closing her eyes, Rachel tried to picture 1939. Nita died in the midst of Lutcher's most powerful days. Rich beyond measure, he lost the love of his life. Perhaps even more importantly to him, he was at risk of losing half the fortune he carefully acquired through luck, timing, and power. Unlike wills of his grandmother, father and mother, naming him the executor and primary beneficiary, Nita named their twin sons as her only heirs. Lutcher would receive only her Montgomery Ward stock and wedding ring, but he would serve as executor and guardian, roles that set in motion a clandestine sequence of events as he used all the money and power at his disposal to funnel assets from her estate to his control. Actions that went into overdrive when he married Nelda. It was a scheme driven by greed that became a tale of betrayal so unthinkable that any allegations of wrongdoing were immediately dismissed.

Opening the red box, Rachel first selected the folder marked boldly with a large question mark across the front. These were the more interesting pieces to the puzzle. A few simply documented unusual behavior or actions. Each contributed to the overall understanding of how assets of an estate could be so manipulated that attorneys, judges, notaries and employees at several levels effectively made them disappear. Inside were news clippings, letters, photos, a telegram, handwritten notes, even an affidavit from a convicted murderer who delivered cocaine to Nelda's home.

First in the file was an 8" x 10" black and white photograph of the Bengal Guards practicing in the old band hall at Orange High School. It was one of dozens Nelda gave Becky in 1998 when she cleaned out shelves in a remote part of the Stark offices. Neatly arranged in black leather-bound albums, the pictures were wonderful reminders of happy days. Rachel recalled the first time her mother showed them to her, with a story for each image and calling off names of almost every girl pictured. Midway through the second album, Becky turned to the group shot of the Bengal Guards rehearsing in the gym. As she pointed out some of the girls in the picture, Rachel couldn't help but notice images hanging on the walls – high on the walls of the gymnasium.

"Mother, what are those – those pictures on the wall?"

"Oh, your grandparents would hang part of their art collection in the gym. Sometimes Mr. Stark would rotate new ones in, but I think those are Remingtons and Duntons. Miss Nita always said he hung everything high, but you needed to so they weren't hit during the basketball games."

Her mother continued to the next page, and the one after that, each with the same scene from a different angle that would allow a glimpse of another painting on a different part of a wall.

While it was a trip down memory lane for Becky, her daughter knew it was much more. It showed the Stark Foundation, Nelda and their attorneys lied during the 1988 lawsuit, misrepresenting the art as separate property of Lutcher purchased after his marriage to Nita. Yet here it was, hanging on the gym walls as the 1937 and 1938 Bengal Guards practiced below.

Several pages clipped together held an assortment of details: a memo directing George Kelly to bring the new will to the hospital just two weeks before Lutcher Stark's death; another putting a judge on the payroll in exchange for looking the other way when Lutcher destroyed his father's latest will and went with an earlier one; a "game plan" for defrauding the Internal Revenue Service; a letter from a Louisiana judge explaining his signature on a document would have no more authority regarding the twins than that of the janitor (but he signed it anyway).

Next was a title opinion issued by Brad Duggan, an Orange attorney who certainly was familiar with the Stark family since Homer and Bill's kids attended school with Brad's sons. Somehow he simply "forgot" to mention Lutcher's marriage to Nita or his two sons when he drafted the opinion needed to sell Owens Illinois some of the Stark lands for its new plant.

A short stack of transactions – all of them presumably illegal –were examples of many more that showed gifts of Foundation property to Eunice and Nelda, or sales of some at bargain prices far below appraised value. Another illustrated the manner in which Nelda used her authority as executor of Lutcher's estate to improperly distribute his assets.

As Rachel stared at one in particular, the Roslyn Ranch property in Colorado, she remembered why her opinion of the justice system had taken a nosedive over the last several years. There, for example, was a document awarding Nelda the ranch as compensation for serving as executor. Signed by the judge and filed in Orange County, perhaps one of the most corrupt legal entities in Texas. Did the judge even look at the document? Did he not check the will to see that it exclusively precluded Nelda from any compensation as executor? Or did he look at it and just ignore the wishes of the deceased?

And the Texas Attorney General's office, the department charged with overseeing charitable foundations, took no action when it was called to their attention that she had cheated the Foundation out of that and other properties. Even last week, Rachel had spoken with the head of the Charitable Trust Division with regard to mismanagement of Foundation monies. Once the woman realized the call concerned the Stark Foundation, her attitude was decidedly different... more defensive, saying there were more than 50,000 charitable foundations in Texas and "we can't keep up with all of them."

While Rachel considered the options, there below the ranch transaction was the letter from the DNA firm. All that stress to exhume her grandfather's body ended with no real surprises. The drug test came back within two weeks as inconclusive, kind of what they expected based on the deterioration of the sample. But the man assigned to run the DNA test had simply disappeared a week after telling them he should have the results shortly. His office had no forwarding information regarding address, phone, city, state. Nothing at all. Eight months later they notified the family the sample was found in a paper sack in a cabinet. So much for chain of custody and any reliable results.

A faded news clipping from 1937 said it all. Mr. and Mrs. Lutcher Stark had presented the University of Texas a $5 million gift, one representing the exquisite art, antiques and rare books collection of Miriam Stark. It was a spectacular acquisition for the Austin campus, but one that was never delivered. Instead, Lutcher Stark rescinded the gift in 1953 according to a second news clipping attached to the first.

Change of heart? Pocketbook was more like it, thought Rachel, recalling correspondence that her grandfather had already decided in the mid-1940s to keep the items for himself. Nita's half of the gift was never distributed to her sons, but taken by Nelda.

Near the back of the folder was another photo, this one of Homer's Model T pickup truck, a gift on his 16th birthday. It had been stored for decades in the old Dr. Pepper building in Orange, first by his father and then by Nelda. After Nelda's death, he inquired about moving his truck and the Hupmobile that belonged to his mother – an engagement gift from

Lutcher – but was told they no longer belonged to him. They were listed on the Foundation inventory, a move that Richard Dyke claimed made it impossible to return to him according to some law he misrepresented. It was a hurtful thing to do to Homer and she kept the photo to remind her what a lying bastard he truly was.

Returning to the cabin after lunch and a leisurely walk, Rachel decided to look at a few other items in her Magic Box. There was the Lutcher & Moore file with minutes and audits that painted a rather extraordinary way of doing business. Orange Cameron Land Company documents were among those that included the most obvious infraction against Nita's estate, detailing 167,320 acres in Louisiana – land and mineral rights – in one transaction alone that was omitted from her inventory.

The green file folders were reserved for tax matters, and had grown substantially over recent years. Only one was in the red box, with supportive documentation safely stored in the event anything happened to Rachel, accidentally or otherwise. She glanced through the tax information that was neatly typed and summarized by year. One set related to Lutcher Stark's dealings, another for the Foundation. In the folder was one of her favorite items – the 1938 tax return for Nita and Lutcher. Although Nita's tax returns had been pulled by the Knox and Henderson attorneys, this one was overlooked as it was attached to tax appeal papers filed contesting a $208 payment to the IRS. What it clearly showed was worth much more than the extra taxes: Nita and Lutcher's income was treated as community, regardless of the source. A letter from Lutcher to the IRS was attached to the return confirming the community income.

Next to the tax information was a file on mineral rights, or what Rachel called the invisible assets. Over the years, Nelda sold most of the real estate, timber and jewelry, and reinvented the art. But the mineral rights, so much more difficult and time consuming to trace, remained under her control. Royalty checks totaling millions would roll into her offices, yet they represented wealth that wasn't visible to the public. Titles had never changed and made it easier for her to simply extend the life of the fraud over most of the 20th Century.

At the front of the box was the Shangri La file. Relatively minor in value compared to other assets, it was personal. For here in this virtual paradise, Lutcher spent his last years as a prisoner of his own wife. While he languished behind locked gates in his garden, his most trusted employees looked the other way as Nelda took over. When he died, she took Shangri La. Not because she wanted to, but she had to. Or at least that was Rachel's opinion. To sell it might have involved a title search, plus she didn't want to upset Homer or Bill. Even after her death, there was reluctance to chance a sale and the Foundation decided to make it a new project, pouring tens of millions of dollars to supposedly restore it to the so-called glory days. Yet they went down a different path, while the profit from the sale of the property and savings from money invested could have been put to better use for the community. Not to mention the value of that 252 acre tract was removed from the tax rolls when transferred to the Foundation

Holly Beach renewed Rachel's interest in having a life outside courtrooms, libraries and conference rooms. But to get there, she also knew the importance of setting the family history straight and, somewhere along the way, resolving issues that seemed as obvious to her as they were imaginary to the Stark Foundation and its attorneys. The end seemed in sight and Rachel understood it was now time to focus on a plan with the best shot at some form of justice.

It took only a few minutes to review the table of content pages attached to remaining files that represented a snapshot of the sheer volume of documents safely stored in multiple locations. What it all came down to were choices. Here in this box was the sum total of Lutcher Stark's choices. They had consumed him, transformed him, and ultimately revealed him for what he became. Ditto for Nelda, Eunice, Clyde, Walter, and all the others who traded conscience for power and money.

"When people we trust the most not only lie to us, but deceive us in a most unimaginable way, what do you do?"

Rachel couldn't recall who had posed that question to her, but she knew the answer. Her father and uncle had chosen to believe what they were told, disregarding a conspiracy of controlled corporations, professionals and even the justice system that participated in the Big Lie.

As for how Nelda exerted such control over her grandfather, the only answer seemed to be blackmail and possibly an addiction to drugs only she could provide. She had motive, access and priceless information to keep him in line. Living with Ruby while she worked 20+ years in the Stark offices provided details of business transactions, dealings with the government, and an impressive listing of assets. While it was nothing more than dinner conversation to Ruby, Nelda took notes and developed a plan to win over the richest man in town and his substantial holdings. She often described her sister as weak, overlooking the financial support Ruby provided for Nelda's college education or the efforts made on her behalf to assist her with employment when she graduated.

Had Ruby simply gotten in the way? Probably, at least based on Ruby's comments when Nelda came in to give her a shot. "Sister, you're not fooling me. I know you're trying to kill me." It was an uncomfortable thought for Rachel, picturing Ruby's happiness at being married to Lutcher only to die prematurely in the "care" of her younger sister.

Moving to the porch, Rachel stared for the longest time at nothing in particular while reflecting on everything examined earlier that day. How could her family have been so stupid? So naïve? So totally out of touch with what was happening right in front of them? Laughter from Thibodeaux's interrupted her train of thought, but also prompted her to make the short walk to ask his opinion.

"You wanna know what I think?" said the elderly man with the bright blue eyes and wide grin, hesitating before he continued. "They didn't see it coming, didn't have any reason to suspect their dad would do such a thing. Especially when he gave them no reason to think otherwise.

"There were lots of signs, especially after he married Nelda."

Thibodeaux smiled, then shook his head.

"Signs are everywhere – remember that," he cautioned. "But if you have nothing to fear, you don't really waste your time looking. And when you trust someone – like Homer and Bill trusted Lutcher – you don't expect betrayal."

As Rachel absorbed his words, Thibodeaux proceeded with an example.

"Take birds and dogs. They pay attention to signs. Their lives depend on it."

The leap from her grandfather to the birds was too great to follow, a fact easily communicated by Rachel's puzzled expression.

"Birds and dogs?"

"Yep, you know – like when the weather's getting ready to change. If you look outside and notice the birds are gone and the dogs are acting spooky, you'd best be right behind them because I guarantee a big storm, even a hurricane, is on the way. They don't need a barometer to know what is about to happen."

"And my dad and Uncle Bill?"

"They couldn't be expected to believe Lutcher would betray them, not after spending their entire life being cared for and loved by the man. He was everything to them. Anyone who saw father and sons together, listened to Lutcher talk about how proud he was of 'his boys'...wasn't any reason to think the worst."

"But...", he added, pausing to gather his thoughts. "But no one had ever seen anything like Nelda. Best we can figure Lutcher thought he knew her, being Miss Ruby's sister and all, but she was the enemy instead."

He repeated stories handed down by his father and uncles, plus a few oldtimers like Jimmy Monceis and Carl Jennings. Each followed the same pattern, describing two completely different people – Lutcher Stark before Nelda, Lutcher Stark after Nelda.

"Night and day, I tell you. It was like his soul disappeared and someone we didn't know or like took over his body. No place on earth that man would rather be than right here, hunting and fishing or talking about it. That all ended with her, slowly at first but eventually he stopped coming at all."

Daybreak came and it was time for Rachel to go home and put her decision into action. She replaced each file in her Magic Box and carried it out to the car. As she returned to the cabin for her suitcase and a sack with leftover grocery items and dog food, Thibodeaux called her name.

"Rachel, you leaving?"

"Got to get home," she said, walking over to the gentle giant of a man who had been so kind to her. "Don't think I'll ever forget your stories, or the food. And I always enjoy Holly Beach. Not another place like it in the world."

"You got that right," he said with a laugh, leaning his fishing pole against her car to give her a hug. "Next time you're here, I'll take you fishing – just like the old days."

"That I would love," she said. "But first I need to do a little fishing of my own."

"Let me know if you land the big one," he said with a wink. "It's out there, you just need the right bait. Somehow I think you've got that covered."

CHAPTER 20

*"When there is no justice, the rich win
and the poor become tired of hearing people lie."*
— **Frank Galvin in The Verdict**

Mark Twain once said that the truth is a fragile thing, but a lie, well told, can live forever. A lie, well financed, was alive and well in Texas.

They had established a game plan for corruption: bring in a high powered legal team; manipulate the data to make certain key documents disappear or delay producing them for years; attack the opposition; intimidate witnesses; see that key players were kept quiet, discredited or eliminated. Declare victory. And deny, deny, deny.

Timing had been on their side for more than 70 years. With power and greed in spades, Nelda, Eunice and Clyde operated below the radar, above the law and without conscience. Now Walter followed suit.

It was another court hearing, this time in Texas. Same cast of characters for the Stark Foundation/Estate: Walter, no doubt in his dual capacity as executor and CEO of the Foundation; the lawyers, Richard Dyke, Craig Spencer and their staff, plus a representative of the Texas Attorney General's office; and the usual suspects who attended to show support.

Weeks earlier, Rachel held no great expectations for this hearing. She was convinced it would follow the same pattern as those that came before it. Whatever was decided in her family's favor would be altered days later, the result of a late filing or some other such document that the Foundation lawyers would create to continue the illusion that Homer's family had no rights to his mother's estate.

Money – lots of money – brought them to this day. Her father had inherited a legacy of lies and broken promises that reached the Texas Attorney General's office. Homer and his brother were victims of a vast conspiracy created by a small inner circle of friends and family. Cloaked in secrecy and hidden from public view through the façade of a private foundation, the clandestine dealings of a triangle of thieves had escaped justice for decades.

It seemed strange that the "other side" just never got it. Nelda didn't get it, Eunice didn't get it, Clyde and now Walter didn't get it. To Homer, it was all about character and doing the right thing. He was a man who valued friendship, practiced fairness and was loyal to a fault. And his heart wouldn't let his mind believe his father would deceive him.

Now that he knew the truth, it still wasn't about money to Homer. Sure, he'd like some of the wealth willed to him 65 years ago by his mother, but there was so much good that could be done with the rest. So much that could make a difference for the people, especially the children, in Orange. All he wanted was the family ranch, his personal belongings that had been stored for him, and an active voice in the Foundation. But

Walter and his gang were so consumed with greed that they couldn't imagine he was serious.

Instead, the Stark lawyers lied, misrepresented their intentions and abused the law for more than 60 years to avoid justice. From a sole practitioner in a small town to a nationally respected firm in Houston, each was aware of the stakes, not to mention the legal fees that could be generated on an hourly basis. And each continued to represent the Foundation after becoming aware of the ongoing fraud – a somewhat illegal act in most jurisdictions.

For the first time in four years, construction at the Orange County Courthouse ended and the hearing was set in the regular courtroom. It was much larger than smaller versions they had seen previously and gave one the impression it was truly a place where justice was administered. Possibly a result of the impressive wood paneling and rows of the finest yellow long leaf pine you could afford. Suitable for a town at the hub of the lumber industry. The low murmur of ceiling fans mounted high above them kept the room comfortable in spite of the warm temperatures.

"It's like a scene from Perry Mason," Rebel told sisters Ramona and Rachel as they recalled the popular television show of their youth.

"Too bad Perry Mason doesn't practice here," replied Ramona, glancing around the room to get a better idea of the setting.

They hesitated a moment before walking down the center aisle to the front row, directly behind Byron Steele, John Scott and J. R. Metcalf, the lawyers who believed in them from the beginning. Joining them moments later was Alan Clark, a Louisiana attorney who had worked with them and simply wanted to see if justice would finally see daylight.

It was the first hearing for Ramona and Rebel to attend. Both lived out of state and decided this was the one they didn't want to miss. It also was the third hearing in four years to be held the week of Homer's birthday. Somehow no one thought it was happenstance, but just another way to wear Homer down. He was 81, turning 82 the next day.

Seated in the third row, behind the Foundation attorneys, were Walter and members of the Stark Foundation Board – each with the confident appearance that spoke volumes about the issues at hand. They had no plans to lose control of the Stark fortune and hired a legal team that seemed to operate on money as opposed to ethics. Eunice and Roy stayed behind at the office, along with other employees who were typically there for show.

Somehow they didn't think today's hearing was any different from all those that came before. Richard Dyke assured them it was just one more attempt to take "another bite of the apple." He wasn't even certain what the hearing was for, only that Byron Steele wanted to file a motion regarding settlement of the claims.

How impossible, Richard Dyke thought to himself, smiling as he recalled the initial settlement letter three years earlier that he withdrew six weeks later. It had been a shining moment for him, at least in the eyes of his clients. He had lied and gotten away with it, or at least as long as no one was looking. And since he controlled the local media, and the courts would not allow discovery or testimony, it was his time in the spotlight with financial rewards beyond his dreams.

Glancing around the courtroom, he grew more confident when he realized Homer, Becky and Jake stayed home. Rachel was there, with two of her friends, but no one could elicit the sympathy of the judge like Homer. The whole town seemed so fond of Lutcher Stark's son that it was always better if Homer was not present.

It was exactly 12:47, thirteen minutes until the hearing was scheduled to begin. Richard Dyke stepped back to visit with Walter, reassuring him it would be brief and painless. Then he made a quick call to the pro shop to confirm his 2:30 tee time at Sunset Grove. As a well-dressed, distinguished man entered the courtroom, followed by a television camera crew, Richard motioned to Walter, who immediately grinned as he saw the group and left his seat to greet them.

"Who is that?" asked Rebel. Ramona turned and immediately recognized the newcomer as a television anchorman from the Dallas-Fort Worth area where she lived.

"Charlie Haldeman," she responded. "Probably the best known television personality in the Metroplex, and I have no idea what he is doing here."

"Bet he's the television producer who's been working with the Foundation," said Rachel. "We heard someone was talking to Walter about a feature on private foundations for a statewide program, so he must be the one."

Indeed, Walter was obviously thrilled to have Charlie and his crew in the courtroom. It also seemed crystal clear that this was not their first meeting as Richard Dyke and others from the Stark Foundation Board welcomed him.

"But why would Walter want them in the courtroom? Why would he want to take a chance on what happens?" asked

Rebel, who immediately answered her own question. "Sorry, sometimes I forget they seem to know exactly what is going to happen as if they wrote a script."

Moments later the sisters were joined by Ida Marie, her three children and their spouses. They had lived through every hearing in both states, only to find months later that the laws they sought shelter behind apparently did not apply if the other side had more money. Perhaps today would be different, but no one was placing any bets.

Rachel smiled as her son Patrick and another young man in his mid 30's arrived and took a seat near the rear of the courtroom, across from the massive cypress doors that marked the entry. John Edgerly looked just like an attorney, except for the small lapel pin that set him apart. They met several times in the last few months, and each occasion brought her closer to fully appreciating the behind-the-scenes work he had undertaken for her family.

Sheer luck introduced her to John a year earlier as he was seated at her table during a charity luncheon in College Station. Bright and well mannered, he provided a wealth of information.

A few minutes later, you could hear the unmistakable voice of Leon Parish as he entered the courtroom. Just behind him was Adolph Hryhorchuk, Tom Kelly, Jesse B. Gunstream, James Pruter, and several others whose faces were familiar. Homer's friends had shown up even though they weren't certain themselves what made this hearing different from those that came before. Only that they were asked to be there.

For once, the playing field seemed level. It was encouraging to see the family side of the aisle outnumber the paid following. Only the judge was missing.

As the final moments crept by, Rachel turned to catch Patrick's attention. Not a problem, as he and John were sitting comfortably in the back, eyes focused on the players up front as Patrick acknowledged his mother with a wink and a smile.

"All Rise, the Honorable Frank Donovan, presiding judge for the 260th District Court."

Expected, yet unexpected, the bailiff's announcement echoed through the chambers.

Judge Donovan entered in the traditional black robe and took his seat, allowing others to be seated as the hearing began. From the first moment, it was obvious he was not happy to be there. As a visiting judge, he drove from Houston to oversee the Stark case and had better plans for late April than presiding over another hearing that was predetermined.

"Gentlemen, I hope we can make this brief and to the point. It is my understanding that Mr. Steele has filed a motion requesting approval of a negotiated settlement to resolve these issues once and for all... What say you, Mr. Dyke?"

True to form, Richard Dyke adopted the "talk first, think later" form of legal expertise.

"Why, your Honor, once again the Stark family is grasping at straws. Talks of settlement, much less one that has been agreed upon, are totally fabricated and should be dealt with harshly by the Court.

"It is not only totally absurd to make that claim, but unethical behavior on the part of my colleagues to claim such a resolution to this case when we have not discussed any such options for more than two years. They haven't even been allowed to take discovery, much less negotiate with us."

He was on a roll, and the judge was allowing him to continue – possibly thinking at some point Byron Steele would object.

But Byron Steele, a distinguished and successful Houston attorney who had been treated with no respect in Orange County courtrooms, entered no objections. He just let Richard Dyke talk and ramble on about the injustices that had been dealt Walter and the Foundation Board as they suffered through these nuisance suits.

Eventually he realized no one cared how long he spoke and sat down, thinking he had once again mesmerized the Court.

"Mr. Steele, what do you have to say for yourself regarding this motion and Mr. Dyke's obvious objections to even being here under somewhat extraordinary circumstances?" asked Judge Donovan.

Before Byron could stand to address the question, the Judge continued on with his comments, strange even in his own courtroom. He provided a condensed version of the legal maneuverings of the Stark Foundation/Estate, in each instance siding with Richard Dyke and his legal team. Apparently, the Judge never had shown any inclination to even hear what the Stark family had to say, much less allow them the opportunity to prove their claims.

For more than 15 minutes, Judge Donovan spoke and Richard Dyke was silently applauding each word – almost too embarrassed to glance at Byron Steele. But he did, and noticed Byron was taking it all in stride. Just waiting for his turn to speak.

Finally, the Judge allowed Byron to address the issue.

"Your Honor, it was not my intention to mislead the Court regarding this hearing, nor was it my intention to allow Mr. Dyke and his clients the proverbial 'heads up' on this issue, but our settlement was not with the Stark Foundation…"

A cell phone ring interrupted Steele's comments and all eyes focused on Walter Riedel as he took the call and tried to act apologetic to Judge Donovan who was not pleased with the interruption. Signs throughout the courthouse sent a clear message that cell phones should not be in use when court is in session, but Walter had a habit of doing what he liked and Rachel had counted on it. Cameras were rolling as the action unfolded.

Distress and panic set in immediately, almost too quickly for Walter to comprehend what was happening as he heard Steele's next comments…

"…due to inequities and obvious corruption that has penetrated the legal system in Orange County for decades, if not a century, my clients have negotiated a settlement with the Internal Revenue Service. Our motion is to dismiss the case based on these developments."

Walter's immediate reaction was to get to the Foundation office less than a mile away, but he was too late. Treasury agents posted in the courthouse hallway greeted him with their badges before reading him his rights. Two others entered the courtroom and did the same to Richard Dyke. Obstruction of justice and conspiracy apply to lawyers as well, and there was no statute of limitation for ongoing fraud.

Rachel, Ramona and Rebel were picturing the scene their father should be witnessing.

As part of the settlement, John Edgerly – the head of the criminal investigation arm of the IRS –promised Homer a front row seat at the Stark offices as they were officially notified of the problems facing them.

Parked next to the W. H. Stark historic home, Homer did indeed have a front row seat from the passenger side of his Toyota. Together with Becky and Jake, who was trying to keep a straight face long enough to record the confrontation on tape, he witnessed a scene his family thought was all but impossible a few weeks earlier. Those who brought the family to their knees, ruined so many lives, and brought economic development of Orange to a halt, finally lost.

It happened just as John Edgerly described to Homer six days earlier. Totally by surprise to avoid any more shredding or burning of documents. No more opportunities to cover for each other. Even a camera crew on the scene to record every second.

Nope. This time the United States government was in charge and had more than enough evidence to put these people behind bars. They just wanted more to add to the thousands of documents that had been carefully screened, organized and filed over the last six months.

Roy Wingate came out first, clasping his chest like he was having a heart attack despite the handcuffs. For years he escaped depositions and hearings due to so-called health issues, only to be seen at the country club or one of several locations he frequented in town.

Next was Eunice. She wasn't handcuffed. At 96 years of age, she was no threat to run but it did Homer good to see the woman who carefully crafted the whole macabre scheme assisted into the back seat of a patrol car. If the devil did indeed have a wife, he guessed Eunice might have won out over Nelda. Or perhaps Eunice was the devil herself.

Other employees drifted out, obviously shaken by the turn of events, and were escorted by agents who would spend hours "debriefing" them on what really happened behind those marble walls and the massive vault that held so many secrets.

Finally came the boxes, tens of thousands of records that had been withheld for years would finally see daylight. So many it would take six men the next two days to secure them and transfer them to a Ryder truck for the trip to Washington, D.C.

Locks were put on the Foundation offices, the Stark museum, the Lutcher Theater and the W. H. Stark home. After more than 70 years, the Stark family could only imagine the celebration heaven was hosting.

Picture H. J. Lutcher and his wife, Frances Ann, in total charge of the gathering. Lutcher and Nita, W. H. and Miriam, Bill, Ruby, Clemmie, Mademoiselle, Sonny Boy, Murray, Julia, Leona – all finally enjoying a victory over Nelda and Eunice. Especially since those two had reservations for eternity in much warmer climates. Perhaps a place called Neldaville, since God wouldn't want them and the Devil wouldn't want the competition.

For the survivors, Homer's smile and presence lit up the room as his family met at Sunset Grove for a celebratory drink and birthday cake. He arrived to find each of his seven grandchildren, their spouses and eight great-grandchildren. They had flown in, driven in, and one even took the train. Just to share this moment as a family.

News of his victory spread effortlessly throughout Orange and old friends and classmates joined the party as tears of joy flowed with the champagne.

Coach Hryhorchuk and those who shared the moment in the courtroom were retelling the scene for all who would listen and laughing loudly whenever Richard Dyke's arrogant comments were mentioned.

It was an impressive gathering of "old Orange." Bengal Guards from the 1930s and 1940s, the Red Hat Club, classmates of Homer and Becky's, former employees of Nelda, and the lawyers and treasury agents who remained steadfast.

Just as the party reached its peak, Ramona and Rebel were startled to see Charlie and his camera crew enter the clubhouse. Even more surprised when Rachel went straight to him and gave him a big hug.

"You were wonderful. I don't know how we can ever thank you."

"Thank me? My dear, you have given me the story of my career and we can hardly wait to put it together," said Charlie. "We've already got a straight news story going out nationally tonight that should be quite a conversation piece for your neighbors."

She took him over to her sisters, introducing Charlie as her friend of almost 20 years – one she had kept in touch with since she moved from Dallas. Not that she didn't trust the IRS, but one thing Rachel learned from years of researching her family was to have a safety net, something to fall back on just in case things were not as they seemed. The perfect solution seemed to be adding a camera crew to the mix to shadow the IRS as they investigated a large claim against a taxpayer. She knew firsthand Walter and the Foundation had the money and the power to alter fate, so she wanted to make certain John Edgerly's efforts could not be canceled by someone higher up the chain of command.

"Mr. Stark, it has been an honor and a privilege to work with you. Your trust was well placed and I know you will be pleased with the results."

With those words, John Edgerly fondly hugged the smiling 82-year old man and bid farewell, promising to keep him apprised of the outcome in the weeks to come.

As he left the clubhouse, the agent took a moment to survey the sheer beauty of Sunset Grove – thinking how remarkable to find such a place in a tiny Southeast Texas town. He walked the 50 yards or so to the midpoint of the bridge spanning the lake at the 18th green, pausing to reflect on the history of this unsuspecting town that was finally back on course.

While Charlie would lead with national coverage of today's events, tomorrow's news would announce details of the settlement. In return for an abundance of records and knowledge provided by the Stark family, Homer would receive the 10% recovery fee of $100 million. True to his nature and consistent with his request for years, Homer only wanted the Colorado ranch and the personal possessions that had been kept from him for most of his life. His attorneys would be paid and the remainder would be held in trust by a new Stark Foundation to provide educational scholarships for children in Southeast Texas and Southwest Louisiana.

No Benckensteins, McKees or Riedels need apply.

"That's the most bizarre story I've ever heard."

Rachel laughed at the comment from Sam and Laura Barton, the 40ish couple seated next to her when they boarded the plane three hours earlier in Dallas. What began as a simple observation – "Looks like you are bringing lots of work with you – whatever do you do?," prompted Rachel to tell the story of Lutcher Stark, the subject of her latest book.

"Is all of that really true?"asked Sam, seeming a bit worn out from the recital of facts.

"Everything but the last chapter. Legally, it was over. Without the money to challenge the Foundation in court, it became too stressful for my dad. Honest and fair, he was an easy target for those who aren't. And as long as we couldn't get a little objectivity from the bench, our lawyers thought it hopeless to continue.

"Publishing a book seemed about the only way to tell our side of the story without going broke or relying on the wheels of justice in Orange County. So we made the ending more like a dream sequence – creating a picture of the way we thought it should be."

Laura spoke up and asked Rachel if she ever figured out what would possess her grandfather to marry, or more importantly stay married, to someone like Nelda.

"You know, my dad always thought it had something to do with taxes. Told me stories about how much my grandfather complained about the tax rates and figured Nelda and Eunice discovered exactly what he was doing and pulled the blackmail card."

Rachel said she didn't think much of that theory until she recently discovered a tax table from the 1940s that was in the bottom of one of the boxes.

"That made me a believer," she told them.

"What do you mean by that?" asked Sam.

"Guess I've always assumed that tax rates on the wealthiest Americans back then were pretty much in the neighborhood they've been in the last 20-30 years – 38 to 50 percent – maybe even lower because of the Depression and the long road to recovery," said Rachel. "And although I'm not a fan of big government, I couldn't imagine anyone not paying taxes. But the chart changed my mind."

Rachel asked her new friends if they had any idea what the tax rate was in the late 30s and 40s.

They hesitated and admitted they had no idea. 25 percent? 60 percent?

"Actually, the rate was high for everyone, from 20 percent on incomes from 0 to $2,000– no tax credits back then, up to 91 percent on incomes over $200,000," Rachel explained.

"91 percent? Are you certain?" asked Sam.

She pulled out a copy of the tax table and pointed to the highest bracket. It plainly stated taxes on $200,000 would be $156,820 plus 91% of any amount over that figure.

The Bartons stared at the table in disbelief and commented that they didn't see how anyone accumulated wealth – at any level – with rates that high.

"Somehow I doubt that my grandfather was alone in evading taxes. Daddy thought all along that was the secret to how Nelda gained control of the Stark fortune – sheer blackmail with lots of drugs as a safety net in case Lutcher thought of cutting her loose."

"Amazing. Simply amazing," said Laura.

"It is, isn't it?" Rachel said. "I think he was trying to preserve as much wealth as possible – legally or not. Understating values, manipulating assets, and total control of the estates of his grandmother, parents and Nita."

The pilot's voice interrupted them, announcing their approach and current weather conditions in the nation's capital.

Historic monuments and impressive governmental buildings were easily recognizable as American Flight 8513 made its approach to Dulles International. The Lincoln Memorial caught her eye and she looked west to locate her final destination, prompting a smile and a quick glance at her watch. Less than two hours until her appointment.

After the Stark Foundation/Estate pursued legal fees of more than $1 million from her aunt and father, she decided it was time to turn them in. Enough was enough. The Foundation once again showed it could manipulate the justice system with unlimited funds, influence the Texas Attorney General's office and leave the Stark family behind as victims once more.

Even her father found it difficult to accept the continued coverup and lies preached by the Foundation and their attorneys. From information posted on the website and statements in the paper to museum publications and the script for the Shangri La tours, everything they touched seemed to reflect a different version of the truth. Certainly Lutcher Stark was turning over in his grave at decisions being made in his name. And it was a sure bet that even Nelda would not be happy with the actions they had taken since her death. If only she could get a pass from hell to make one last appearance at the next Board meeting and scare them all to death.

Holding that thought, Rachel smiled as the plane taxied to the gate and thanked the Bartons for their interest, promising to send them a copy of her book. She removed a box and carryon bag from the overhead storage bin, grabbed her briefcase from under the seat, and followed the crowd as passengers exited into the busy terminal. She bypassed baggage claim and headed straight for a taxi, gave the driver a Maryland address and settled in for the short trip in the DC metropolitan area as she transferred a large envelope from her briefcase to the box. Keys to the storage areas holding documentation supporting her claims, plus the location of each, would soon be out of her hands.

Nothing was said as the driver kept to himself and Rachel's thoughts focused on the meeting initiated several weeks earlier. She followed instructions on the website, contacted the main office, and was surprised to learn during the call that the young man on the other end of the phone was from Beaumont, only 22 miles west of Orange. Familiar with the power of the Stark name and Foundation, he suggested she "might be in grave danger" and instructed her on how to proceed.

Here she was, taking that step and glad to be handing over the "magic box" to someone with the authority and expertise, not to mention a full staff of attorneys, forensic accountants and investigators who could more than go head to head with the Foundation group.

The cab driver finally spoke, letting her know the fare as he pulled over in front of the building complex. Modern, fairly new and impressive in size, the three nine-story buildings formed a campus setting that accommodated 1.2 million square feet of office space and 4500 employees.

A quick look around provided an opportunity to savor the moment before she started up the steps to the main entrance, walked through the automatic doors and passed through security to the elevators. As she stepped out on the seventh floor and took a left turn, a young man approached her as she entered through the glass doors of the office.

"Rachel, glad to finally meet you. I'm John Edgerly. Welcome to the Criminal Investigation Unit, United States Internal Revenue Service."

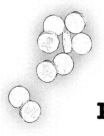

POSTSCRIPT

Every family has a story. And every town seems to hold a secret close to its heart, one that is quietly understood but seldom mentioned except in whispers or behind closed doors. *If the Devil Had a Wife* is the story of the Stark family in Orange, Texas – our family. What you have read is factual and represents opinions expressed by our family members, friends and total strangers who shared information, firsthand observations, and memories that we felt obligated to put in writing.

Our father, Homer Stark, was hesitant as we started exploring our family history. But he and our mother, Becky Havens Stark, encouraged us to seek the truth. They were, as you might expect, the source of stories and information that would have been lost forever without their eyewitness accounts. Even after their deaths – Mother in December 2006 and Daddy in March 2008 – we discovered a collection of tapes recorded years earlier by our father that provided even more details of the relationship – or lack thereof – between Lutcher and Nelda.

Central to the story are Nelda Stark and Eunice Benckenstein – a pair of women who systematically planned the demise of not only Lutcher Stark, but that of his sons – Homer and Bill. It was a cold, calculated takeover that no one really understood until it was complete. Even the government seemed unaware of the layers of fraud, deceit, and manipulation designed to create a sense of rule by law where none existed.

Over the years, the truth has been buried in lies or simply replaced by falsehoods that are repeated often enough to be treated as fact. It starts with one lie, one exaggeration, or one omission of fact – and grows from there. Each time it is endorsed by a public figure, an attorney, a judge, the media or someone who should know better, it seems even more credible.

For example, the Stark Museum of Art has always presented its collection as one selected primarily by H. J. Lutcher Stark and his wife, Nelda. That is a lie. What they fail to mention is the existence of his first wife, Nita, whose romance and marriage to Lutcher Stark has been reduced to not even a footnote.

While Nelda was certainly married to Lutcher Stark when he acquired some pieces of the collection, she had no interest in art other than having her name listed as an owner. She and Eunice chose to stay behind in the hotel room as Lutcher visited art galleries in Texas, New Mexico and Colorado without them. Her primary focus was money – and converting his assets to money as quickly as possible once he died.

Perhaps the most surprising comments from the tapes discovered in 2008 were in reference to Nelda and Eunice, especially since Homer rarely, if ever, said an unkind word about anyone. His opinion of them appears below in his own words:

"These two were the most vicious people I'd ever seen in my life, bar none. And if they had it in for you, there's nothing they wouldn't do to get you in a lot of trouble. Nelda was the hatchet man and Eunice played the 'nice' card, but it was Eunice who ran the show.

"...they had some kind of peculiar hold on him (Lutcher Stark) and then Nelda started taking over the Stark office. Old people started disappearing and new ones were put in – all on the side of Nelda and Eunice.

"Dad was more or less pushed off to the side. And I could tell as years went by there was something wrong because he was a very healthy man. In all the years I lived with him, I could never remember Dad going to the hospital for anything. I can hardly remember him ever being sick.*

"But all of a sudden he was being made a recluse. You could hardly get to see him. He would go straight from the office to Miss Eunice's house** and no one was allowed to see him.

"...Nelda always wanted money, power, and the hell with anyone else. And the same in spades for Miss Eunice Benckenstein. Everything revolved around those two women.

"What attracted him to Miss Nelda, I'll never understand. She's mean, she's vicious, and she's ugly as hell. Everything his life revolved around she didn't like... After he married her, everything he wanted to do, had to do and loved to do was taken away. And that's fact, not fiction."

All the mystery surrounding Nelda was lifted as we learned of her two-pronged approach: blackmail to gain control, medication to keep control. All with the help of Eunice, Clyde, and others who made a profitable living by keeping a secret. When Homer finally learned of the reasons behind Nelda's control of his father, he simply shook his head and tears filled his eyes. The man he considered the greatest father who ever lived had died an agonizing death.

*Lutcher Stark's interest in good health is underscored by the creation of the H. J. Lutcher Stark Center for Physical Culture and Sports at the University of Texas at Austin. It is scheduled to open in 2010.

**_Lutcher and Nelda Stark went to Eunice's house for dinner every evening. An extension of their home phone was installed at Eunice's in order for Nelda to answer the phone regardless of whether they were home or at Eunice's. No one can recall Lutcher Stark ever answering his home phone after his marriage to Nelda. She controlled all access._

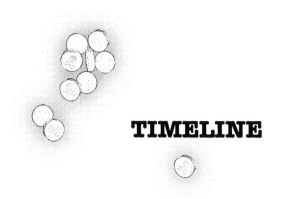

TIMELINE

1877 Henry Jacob Lutcher and his wife, Frances Ann Lutcher, move to Texas/Louisiana area after obtaining large land grants and purchase of additional acreage in both states. Mr. Lutcher and his partner, G. Bedell Moore, relocate their business interests from Pennsylvania to create the Lutcher & Moore Lumber Company headquartered in Orange, TX, and the Lutcher & Moore Cypress Lumber Company based in Lutcher, LA.

1881 Miriam Melissa Lutcher (oldest of two daughters) marries W. H. Stark.

1888 Carrie Luna Lutcher (youngest daughter) marries Dr. Edgar W. Brown.

1911 H. J. Lutcher Stark (only surviving child of Miriam and W. H. Stark) marries Nita Hill in Austin.

1912 Death of Henry Jacob Lutcher in Cincinnatti, Ohio sanitarium. Frances Ann Lutcher named executor of estate, which leaves property to wife and two daughters.

1924   Death of Frances Ann Lutcher in New York City. Will names H. J. Lutcher Stark as executor. Will includes bequests of $1 million to each daughter, with remainder of property to H. J. Lutcher Stark.

1936   Death of W. H. Stark in October. Co-executors are wife Miriam and son H. J. Lutcher Stark, but Lutcher Stark files as sole executor. Will stipulates property divided equally between wife and son.

Six weeks later, Miriam Stark dies unexpectedly at home after visit from Nelda Childers. Miriam's will names Lutcher Stark as executor and beneficiary.

1939   Death of Nita Hill Stark while in the care of Nelda Childers. Will names husband Lutcher Stark as executor and guardian of two sons (Homer and Bill). Estate left to sons, with husband receiving only Montgomery Ward stock and wedding ring. Lutcher Stark files court documents reflecting a debt owed by Nita's estate of almost $400,000 to Lutcher and Moore Lumber Company that is dated 10 days prior to her death.

1941   H. J. Lutcher Stark marries Ruby Childers.

1942   Homer and Bill, sons of Nita and Lutcher Stark, enlist in Navy and Marines and leave for action in World War II.

1942   Ruby Childers Stark dies while in the care of her sister, Nelda Childers.

1943   C. W. Benckenstein marries Eunice Robinson in October. H. J. Lutcher Stark marries Nelda Childers in December. (Benckenstein's first wife died suddenly in 1942;

he died in 1946 from complications from toe surgery following an illness of several months.)

1945   Bill returns from WWII in September; Homer in December. Assets of the Nita Stark Estate (as identified by H. J. Lutcher Stark) are distributed in part to her sons on December 15. Most of Nita's estate is transferred to the Lutcher & Moore Lumber Company in payment for note supposedly signed by Nita 10 days prior to her death.

1956   Sale of significant Louisiana lands (acquired during marriage to Nita Hill) to John Mecom and The Largo Company by Nelda and Lutcher Stark. Proceeds divided between Lutcher Stark and his third wife, Nelda Stark.

1961   Creation of Nelda C. and H. J. Lutcher Stark Foundation to provide funding for an art museum and support of public education, religious and charitable organizations.

1965   Lutcher Stark dies at John Sealy Hospital in Galveston. Nelda named executor of his estate which is estimated at $10 million. Each son is granted $1 million and the remainder is to be divided equally between Nelda Stark and the Stark Foundation, which she serves as CEO.

1971   Sale of additional Louisiana and Texas properties by Nelda Stark to Boise Southern with no title search. Estimates of proceeds range from $120 million to $300 million.

1979   Bill Stark dies in Houston hospital following cancer treatment and a private visit from Nelda Stark.

1988 Lawsuit filed on behalf of Bill Stark heirs alleging fraud in administration of Nita Hill Stark estate.

1989 Nelda Stark and her attorneys encourage Homer Stark to join lawsuit or his children will receive nothing. He refuses to take part in any legal action against his father, but agrees to the lawyers' suggestion to transfer his interest in his mother's estate to his four children.

1990 Homer Stark's four children become parties to the lawsuit in June as suggested by Nelda Stark's attorneys.

Bill Stark family signs settlement agreement in December after documentation produced by Stark Foundation and Nelda Stark reflects most of Lutcher Stark's wealth was separate property, not community. Lawyers receive $2.4 million; each family to receive approximately $1.3 million.

In trying to obtain signatures of Homer Stark family, the attorney destroys the document.

1991 Homer Stark family signs revised agreement on February 27. In March, Homer Stark is removed from the Stark Foundation Board for alleged "conflict of interest" cited by Texas Attorney General's Office with regard to the lawsuit in which he did not participate.

1998 Nelda Stark gives the Roslyn Ranch property in Colorado to Homer Stark along with money necessary to maintain it. She instructs Walter Riedel, an employee in her offices, to take care of the transfer of title and set up a bank account for Homer's use.

1999   Nelda Stark dies December 13. Executors of her estate are Walter Riedel, Eunice Benckenstein and Roy Wingate, with the bulk of her holdings left to the Stark Foundation.

2000   Walter Riedel is contacted to determine how the ranch will be transferred to Homer Stark since he failed to take care of the transfer prior to Nelda's death.

Several discussions and inquiries are made of the Foundation and NCS Estate with regard to allegations of fraud in the 1988 lawsuit that surface after the death of Nelda Stark.

In July, the Stark Foundation files against the Bill Stark family requesting that the earlier release (Dec. 1990) be upheld. (Attorneys representing the Foundation file the suit with knowledge they are bankruptcy creditors of a Stark family member, which is a violation of federal law.)

2001   Homer Stark sues Nelda Stark Estate, requesting the ranch property promised by Nelda, plus compensation for being removed from the Foundation Board under false pretenses. (Walter Riedel admitted there never was a meeting to remove him.)

2003   In January, the Nita Hill Stark Estate is opened in Louisiana and representatives of the Bill and Homer Stark families are named co-executors.

2004   Bill Stark family ordered to pay more than $600,000 in attorney fees, despite evidence challenging that amount.

Faced with almost $500,000 in legal fees submitted by the Estate with regard to his initial claim to enforce the ranch gift from Nelda Stark, Homer Stark signs a settlement agreement which waives the fees and includes an option for him to purchase the Colorado property. In return, he waives any rights he may have to his mother and father's estates.

2005   In April, Foundation files motion for hearing on Nita Stark estate in Louisiana.

In May, Foundation attorneys notify Homer Stark and one of his daughters that they are in violation of the 2004 agreement he signed because Nita's estate had been reopened almost two years prior to the agreement signed by Homer Stark. Although Homer and his daughter were told to attend the Louisiana hearing would be "at their own peril," Homer's daughter attended the hearing and the judge ruled she could serve as executor. Homer (who suffered a stroke in January 2004) remained at home and Foundation attorneys sought contempt charges against him. The judge ruled against them. In testimony under oath, the Foundation attorney who sent the "at their own peril" email stated Homer and his family violated the agreement with the Louisiana action, even though she had knowledge Homer transferred in 1989 his interest in the estates of his parents to his children. Those assignments had not been revoked, plus none of his children signed the 2004 agreement.

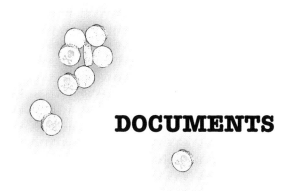

DOCUMENTS

$\mathbf{S}$amples of documents referenced in *If the Devil Had a Wife* appear on the following pages. A brief description of each is printed below in the order in which they are shown.

- **Drug store receipts** showing purchase of phenobarbital and other medications in 1955 and 1965. An incomplete list of receipts provided by the Stark Foundation show items purchased during 57 months from 1949 to 1965 included the purchase of 8,350 tablets (3,950 phenobarbital and 4,400 PBZ). In 1965, receipts through mid-June (when Lutcher Stark left for John Sealy Hospital in Galveston) show delivery of 37 prescriptions. From that point on, no phenobarbital, PBZ, prescriptions or other medications were delivered for the remainder of the year. Receipts reflect only purchases of items such as candy, cigarettes and Woolite from August through December. (2)
- **Tax table** attached to 1945 tax return
- **Pieces of torn release** document
- **Letter from Asst. Attorney General Rose Ann Reeser, Chief of the Charitable Trust Division,** suggesting Homer Stark be removed from the Stark

Foundation Board. Handwritten note is by Homer Stark. (2)

- **False minutes and resolution** regarding a Stark Foundation meeting that never was held.

- Document reflecting **sale of Nelda Stark's "community half" of Nita Stark's Hupmobile and Homer Stark's Model T roadster** to the Estate of Lutcher Stark.

- **Memo placing Judge V. H. Stark** (Lutcher Stark's uncle) **on the payroll**.

- Document filed naming **Nelda Stark as "sole heir"** to Lutcher Stark's estate in Louisiana, conveniently omitting the Stark Foundation and his sons' right to forced heirship properties.

- **Kinney affidavit** reflecting actions taken to hide items/information from Homer and Bill Stark.

- **Receipt from Goldschmidt's** for paintings purchased by Nita Stark. Note still life painting with small dog by Gerard Dou on list with note indicating NCS (Nelda Childers Stark) had taken it.

- List of **paintings by Dunton which hung in the band hall** of Orange High School in the 1930s.

- **Entry in Christies catalog** for May 2005 sale of painting purchased in 1927 by Nita Stark. It sold for $4.7 million.

- List of **deaccessioned art included in Stark Foundation income tax return** (990-PF) for 2005. Apparently the Gerard Dou painting was not included as the total sales is less than the price paid for that specific painting.

- Letter in 1960 to probate Frances Ann Lutcher Estate in Colorado, 36 years after her death in 1924. Includes note that property must be shown to have been Mrs. Lutcher's, yet does not mention fact the homestead (550 acres where the lake and cabins are located) was actually sold to Nita and Lutcher Stark in 1932.
- Letter from Provident Savings regarding stock they felt should be issued to Homer and Bill Stark as Nita Stark's heirs.
- Foundation income and expenses for 1965, the year Lutcher Stark died. Note differences in income before and after his death, including forecasts for 1966 and 1967. Also, expenses for Roslyn Ranch in Colorado are billed to the Stark Foundation.
- Memo reflecting division of community income from Mecom sale. Property was acquired during marriage of Nita and Lutcher Stark, yet Nelda Stark took the proceeds that should have been directed to Nita Stark's heirs, Homer and Bill Stark.
- Partial list of Frances Ann Lutcher's jewelry sold by Nelda Stark in the 1980s.
- 2007 tax return information from Stark Foundation (2008 information not filed as of November 2009): (1) Compensation for directors, highly paid employees, etc. as reported to the IRS; (2) Detailed information on fees paid directors; and (3) expenditures for Foundation projects.
- Letter from Clyde McKee stating Lutcher Stark died in 1965 with only $40,950 in property located in the State of Louisiana. (2)

FRANK MILLS

ORANGE, TEXAS, _____ June 19__

Name _H. J. S Stark_

Address _PO Box 201 - City_.

BOUGHT OF

SERVICE DRUG COMPANY
212 FIFTH STREET
PRESCRIPTION DRUGGISTS
DIAL 8-3508
TRUSSES AND BELTS

DATE	MEMORIAL	CHARGES		CREDITS
8	unicaps	3	11	
"	6 Raleighs 140 6 Sano 250	35	70	
13	Dr C W Henderson			
"	R1348971 R1252794	2	75	
16	R1312935 (C W Henderson)	12	50	
	R1312919 R1312970	2	75	
17	R1360960 (Sally Bozzano)	2	50	
19	R1313078	2	50	
21	R1313169	2	50	
21	6 Kleenex 210 2 aspirin 150	3	60	
24	R1313381 Sally Bozzano	2	50	
26	Spordie Zipps Fluid 1 Doz	2	55	
27	R1363450 Sally Bozzano	2	50	
27	500 Phenbarb 1/4 gr		75	
	100 PBz 1 mg	3	50	
28	amytal 120 amytal 75	1	95	
29	R1313566 Sally Bozzano	2	50	
		84	16	

Printed figures above show amount paid or charged

≈15 9639S −025.29 • CH

YOUR DRUGGIST
Nelson's Drug Store
PHONE TU 3-3543 ● 1608 W. PARK AVE.

ORANGE, TEXAS. 1 - 15 - 1955

SOLD TO Mrs. Welda Slark

ADDRESS House

Clerk	Amt. Rec'd.		Account Forwarded	
	42942			5 50
	6 Cn. Raleigh			18 00
100	Phenobarbital ½gr			75
100	Phenobarbital 1gr			1 00
				25 25
		TAX		04
	ACCOUNTS ARE DUE AND PAYABLE BY 10th OF MONTH	TOTAL		25 29

TAX COMPUTATION INSTRUCTIONS FOR TAXPAYERS NOT USING THE TAX TABLE ON PAGE 2 OF FORM 1040

Surtax Table

From the following table figure your surtax on the surtax net income on line 5, page 4, of the return:

If the surtax net income is:	The surtax is:
Not over $2,000	20% of the surtax net income.
Over $2,000 but not over $4,000	$400, plus 22% of excess over $2,000.
Over $4,000 but not over $6,000	$840, plus 26% of excess over $4,000.
Over $6,000 but not over $8,000	$1,360, plus 30% of excess over $6,000.
Over $8,000 but not over $10,000	$1,960, plus 34% of excess over $8,000.
Over $10,000 but not over $12,000	$2,640, plus 38% of excess over $10,000.
Over $12,000 but not over $14,000	$3,400, plus 43% of excess over $12,000.
Over $14,000 but not over $16,000	$4,260, plus 47% of excess over $14,000.
Over $16,000 but not over $18,000	$5,200, plus 50% of excess over $16,000.
Over $18,000 but not over $20,000	$6,200, plus 53% of excess over $18,000.
Over $20,000 but not over $22,000	$7,260, plus 56% of excess over $20,000.
Over $22,000 but not over $26,000	$8,380, plus 59% of excess over $22,000.
Over $26,000 but not over $32,000	$10,740, plus 62% of excess over $26,000.
Over $32,000 but not over $38,000	$14,460, plus 65% of excess over $32,000.
Over $38,000 but not over $44,000	$18,360, plus 69% of excess over $38,000.
Over $44,000 but not over $50,000	$22,500, plus 72% of excess over $44,000.
Over $50,000 but not over $60,000	$26,820, plus 75% of excess over $50,000.
Over $60,000 but not over $70,000	$34,320, plus 78% of excess over $60,000.
Over $70,000 but not over $80,000	$42,120, plus 81% of excess over $70,000.
Over $80,000 but not over $90,000	$50,220, plus 84% of excess over $80,000.
Over $90,000 but not over $100,000	$58,620, plus 87% of excess over $90,000.
Over $100,000 but not over $150,000	$67,320, plus 89% of excess over $100,000.
Over $150,000 but not over $200,000	$111,820, plus 90% of excess over $150,000.
Over $200,000	$156,820, plus 91% of excess over $200,000.

Adjustment on Line 7, Page 4, for Partially Tax-exempt Interest

standard deduction, enter on line 7 the same figure as appears
' ' ' ' ' .... allowance for any portion

Items that may be subtracted in line 7 are (a) interest on
$5,000 of United States savings bonds (at cost) and Treasury bonds (at face
' ' ' ' 1041, (b) interest on obligations of instru

Rebecca Celia Tweet Havens Stark
_____

_____
Ramona Elizabeth Stark
Individually and as Trustee of and/or
Beneficiary of the Homer B. H. Stark
1989 Trust

_____
Rebecca Nita Stark Nugent, Individually
and as Trustee of the Homer B. H. Stark
1989 Trust

Henry Jacob Lu____
and ___

ISU acting ___
___y and as
___cutrix of the Estate of
_tark, II, Deceased

_____
m Henry Stark, III

_____
_andall Hill Stark

_____
Linda Marie Stark Barras

_____
Homer B. H. Stark, Individually and as
Beneficiary of the Homer B. H. Stark

STATE OF TEXAS   §

COUNTY OF Jefferson   §

    Before me, the undersigned a_

Marie Stark, Individually and as Independe_

Deceased, who being by me duly sworn, _

Release, and that she has executed the R_

STARLA FOUST
Notary Public
STATE OF TEXAS
My Comm. Exp 11-09-92

STATE OF TEXAS   §

COUNTY OF Jefferson   §

    Before me, the undersig_

William Henry Stark, III, who being

authority, on this day personally appeared

    as Trustee of the Homer B. H. Stark 1989

ted that he has read and understands this

ease for the consideration stated therein.

_____
Notary Public

JOYCE A. ___
Notary Public, State of Ohio
My Commission Expires March 19, 1991

FRANK MILLS

Office of the Attorney General
State of Texas

DAN MORALES
ATTORNEY GENERAL

The Board of Trustees
Nelda C. and H.J. Lutcher Stark Foundation
P.O. Drawer 909
Orange, Texas 77630

March 5, 1991

Dear Trustees:

I congratulate you on the successful conclusion to the suit brought against Mrs. Stark and the Foundation by members of the Stark family. It is unfortunate that the Foundation was forced to devote such a large amount of time and resources to defending against the Plaintiffs' claims, but I feel that you and your attorneys did an excellent job protecting the assets of the Foundation. Despite the difficult circumstances, I have enjoyed the opportunity to become acquainted with you and with the Foundation's work and I hope to continue our cooperative working relationship now that the litigation has ended.

Now it is time to concentrate again on the real work of the Foundation. You have asked whether I believe that it is appropriate for Mr. Homer Stark to remain as a member of the board of trustees of the Foundation. I do not believe that Mr. Stark should continue to serve as a trustee.

As you know, the Attorney General has the responsibility to protect the public interest in charitable trusts such as the Foundation. Likewise, the trustees of a public charity have certain fiduciary duties to that charity. Among the trustees' duties are the duty to exercise due care over the use of the charity's assets and the duty of loyalty to the charity. The duty of loyalty includes each trustee's obligation to act for the good of the charity without regard to his own personal interests. If a trustee cannot fulfill these basic duties, he should resign from the board and if he does not, it is the duty of the remaining trustees to remove him to protect the integrity of the charity.

By taking a role directly adverse to the interests of the Foundation in the recently concluded litigation, Mr. Stark has placed his personal interests above those of the Foundation. In fact, Mr. Stark has asserted his own and his family's interest against the interest of the Foundation and through the suit sought

512/463-2100   P.O. BOX 12548   AUSTIN, TEXAS 78711-2548

to transfer Foundation assets to his own benefit. This action is a direct breach of his duty of loyalty to the Foundation. An individual who would sue the Foundation for personal gain demonstrates that he cannot fulfill his duty of loyalty and should not continue to function as a trustee. Therefore, I believe that it is the duty of the remaining trustees to request Mr. Stark's resignation and if he refuses to resign, to remove him as a trustee as provided by the Foundation's by-laws.

The Foundation trustees share with the Attorney General the duty to ensure that the Foundation and its trustees operate within the law and in compliance with their duties. If the law is broken or duties breached, the trustees must correct the situation. I am confident that the trustees understand the serious conflict of interest in which Mr. Stark has placed himself and hope that he will see fit to resign his position on the Board. If he does not, I strongly advise the remaining trustees to exercise their own duty to protect the Foundation by removing Mr. Stark from the Board.

Please let me know as soon as possible what action the trustees have taken or intend to take on this matter.

Sincerely,

Rose Ann Reeser
Assistant Attorney General
Chief, Charitable Trust Section
P.O. Box 12548
Austin, Texas 78711
(512) 463-2018

Note: On every press release concerning this suit — it was always plainly stated that I did not join in the suit!

FRANK MILLS

Pursuant to call of the Chairman of the Board of Trustees and notice duly given, the Board of Trustees of the Nelda C. and H. J. Lutcher Stark Foundation (the "Stark Foundation"), a Texas non-profit corporation, met in a special meeting at 2 p.m. on March 12, 1991. Eunice R. Benckenstein, Vice-Chairman of the Stark Foundation, acted as Chairman, and Mr. Clyde V. McKee, Secretary-Treasurer of the Corporation, acted as Secretary of the meeting. Present at the meeting were Eunice R. Benckenstein, Clyde V. McKee, Jr., Sidney H. Phillips, William H. Butler, and Walter G. Riedel. Absent from the meeting were Nelda C. Stark, John Sargent, and Homer B. H. Stark.

Eunice R. Benckenstein, acting as Chairman, called the meeting to order and stated that the only order of business was the consideration of the removal of Homer B. H. Stark as a trustee of the Stark Foundation. At the request of Homer B. H. Stark, Eunice R. Benckenstein read to the Board of Trustees a letter dated March 11, 1991 from Homer B. H. Stark. The letter was filed in the permanent records of the Stark Foundation. A copy of the letter is attached to these minutes. After the letter was read, Clyde V. McKee, Jr. moved for the adoption of a resolution removing Homer B. H. Stark as a trustee. The motion was seconded by Walter G. Riedel. Thereupon, the motion having been duly made and seconded, the following resolution was unanimously adopted:

RESOLUTION

RESOLVED, that, effective March 12, 1991, Homer B. H. Stark, be and he is hereby removed as a trustee of the Nelda C. and H. J. Lutcher Stark Foundation because of conflicts of interest in connection with litigation filed against the Stark Foundation.

There being no further business, the meeting was adjourned.

Clyde V. McKee
Clyde V. McKee, Jr.
Secretary

APPROVED:

Eunice R. Benckenstein
Eunice R. Benckenstein
Acting Chairman

L0271/0064/02IC13

BILL OF SALE

THE STATE OF TEXAS, (
              :   KNOW ALL MEN BY THESE PRESENTS:

COUNTY OF ORANGE. (

     That I, NELDA C. STARK, of the City of Orange, County of Orange, State of Texas, for and in consideration of the sum of One Thousand, Eight Hundred Six and 50/100 ($1,806.50) Dollars to me in hand paid by the ESTATE OF H. J. LUTCHER STARK, DECEASED, the receipt of which is hereby acknowledged, have BARGAINED, SOLD AND DELIVERED and by these presents do BARGAIN, SELL AND DELIVER unto the ESTATE OF H. J. LUTCHER STARK, DECEASED, all of my one half interest in and to the following automobiles and trucks situated in the County of Orange, State of Texas, described as follows:

Automobiles and trucks

Year	Make and Model	Serial Numbers
1965	Ford Econoline 1/2 ton pickup	E10JH666207
1955	Chevrolet Bel-air Coupe	0170593F55D
1962	Willys Jeep	54178-12009
1961	Ford Econoline 1/2 ton pickup	E10SH152958
1950	Crosley Super Sport Coupe	VC 20182
		Motor No. 110997
1909	Hupmobile Roadster	5813
1922	Ford Motel "T" Roadster	6620548
1937	Ford 1-1/2 ton winch truck	BB183361365
1962	Ford 1-1/2 ton pickup	F10CD300687
1957	Chevrolet 2-ton winch truck	B57K104970
1960	Ford 1/2 ton pickup	F10COD14373
	Cushman Truckster	026023

     And I do hereby bind myself, my heirs, executors, administrators and assigns to forever WARRANT AND DEFEND the title to the said property unto the ESTATE OF H. J. LUTCHER STARK, DECEASED, its successors and assigns, against every person whomsoever lawfully claiming, or to claim the same, or any part thereof.

     WITNESS MY HAND at Orange, Texas, this 20 day of

September , A.D. 196 5 .

Nelda C. Stark

FRANK MILLS

DATE   October 13, 1936

TO   D. A. Pruter

FROM   W. B. Simmons

You will recall at the conference held in the office of H. J. L. Stark at the time of the opening of the Will (October 12, 1936), Mr. H. J. L. Stark instructed me to see Judge V. H. Stark.

This is to advise that I have seen Judge Stark and the arrangements as outlined at the conference were explained to him, and I told him that Lutcher appreciated his attitude and he was being put on the pay roll and would be asked to handle legal matters from time to time and for this service he was to be paid $100.00 per month, office rent free where he is now located, and a telephone.

Judge Stark expressed his appreciation, said that he was glad to help out in any way possible and would welcome the opportunity to be of assistance at any and all times.

This is to be paid by W. H. Stark Estate.

ANCILLARY SUCCESSION : 14TH JUDICIAL DISTRICT COURT

OF NO. _15405_ : PARISH OF CALCASIEU

H.J. LUTCHER STARK : STATE OF LOUISIANA

JUDGMENT OF POSSESSION

Considering the petition for possession and
annexed documents, affidavits and in particular, the
last will and testament of H.J. Lutcher Stark, the
concurrence and waiver of the Attorney for the Inheritance Tax Collector, the law and the evidence being
in favor thereof:

IT IS THEREFORE ORDERED, ADJUDGED AND DECREED
that petitioner, NELDA C. STARK, be and she is hereby
recognized as the sole heir and legatee herein, and
that as such, she is hereby placed in possession
and full ownership of the following described property,
to-wit:

CALCASIEU PARISH:

1. An undivided 1/6 of 1/48 (1/288) mineral
   interest in and to:

   North Half of Northwest Quarter (N 1/2 of
   NW 1/4) of Section Four (4), Township Ten
   (10) South, Range Nine (9) West

2. An undivided 1/6 of 1/48 (1/288) mineral
   interest in and to:

   North half of Northeast Quarter (N 1/2 of
   NE 1/4) of Section Five (5), Township Ten
   (10) South, Range Nine (9) West

3. An undivided 1/6 of 1/48 (1/288) mineral
   interest in and to:

   South Half of North Half (S 1/2 of N 1/2)
   and North Half of Southeast Quarter (N 1/2
   of SE 1/4) of Section Nine (9), Township
   Ten (10) South, Range Nine (9) West

FRANK MILLS

STATE OF TEXAS

COUNTY OF ORANGE

AFFIDAVIT

BEFORE ME, the undersigned authority, on this date personally appeared **CHARLES M. KINNEY**, resident of Orange, Texas, currently residing at 4700 Tejas Parkway, Orange, Texas, who, after first being duly sworn, stated the following:

1.

Beginning in 1981 I was a security guard for the Nelda C. and H. J. Lutcher Stark Foundation and/or The Stark Museum and/or Nelda Stark, individually and during the course of my employment I had knowledge of the whereabouts of evidence in the case entitled *Ida Marie Stark, et al v. Nelda Childers Stark, et al*, docket number D880162-C filed in Orange, Texas.

2.

During the pendency of that case, i.e., *Ida Marie Stark, et al v. Nelda Childers Stark, et al*, docket number D880162-C the Nelda C. and H. J. Lutcher Stark Foundation and/or The Stark Museum, Nelda Stark, Walter Riddle, Sid Phillips, and Clyde McKee individually and/or in conspiracy together intentionally withheld evidence and deprived plaintiffs from obtaining evidence which had been requested by plaintiffs and ordered by the court to be turned over to plaintiffs.

3.

The evidence was withheld by the the Nelda C. and H. J. Lutcher Stark Foundation and/or The Stark Museum, Nelda Stark, Walter Riddle, Sid Phillips, and Clyde McKee by moving it to various locations throughout the county and was never turned over to plaintiffs.

4.

The evidence that was withheld consisted of inventory information and/or computer files and/or other computer information which contained an inventory of assets and/or property in the possession of the Nelda C. and H. J. Lutcher Stark Foundation and/or The Stark Museum and/or Nelda Stark, individually and an inventory of the date each asset and/or property was acquired and from whom it was acquired.

[signature]
CHARLES M. KINNEY

SWORN TO AND SUBSCRIBED, before me, Notary Public, on this _13_ day of

January , 2000, at _ORANGE_, Texas.

[signature]
NOTARY PUBLIC

340

TELEPHON ANT HANSA 114.
TELEGRAMM-ADRESSE:
ANTIK FRANKFURTMAIN.
BANK-KONTO:
DEUTSCHE BANK
DRESDNER BANK
FILIALE FRANKFURT.

New York City,
~~FRANKFURT~~ December 7,1927.
Kaiserstraße 15.

J. & S. GOLDSCHMIDT
Antiquitäten · Alte Gemälde.

RECHNUNG Mrs. H. J. Lutcher Stark

Orange, Texas.

#31- Work IV	✓	Painting lady with parrot in window, behind her a man, a carpet lying over the window			
		by - Gaspard Netcher			
		Heidelberg 1639- The Hague 1684			
		with certificate Dr. Binder			
acquired by Bill Stark from Nita Hill Stark Estate		Small painting peasants feast in landscape before inn, monogramed			
		by David Teniers, the younger			
		Antwerp 1610 - Brussels 1696			
#2- Nelda C.Stark	/ ✓	Small painting resting dog with still life signed by Gerard Dou, Leyden 1613-1675 (July 13 - 131)			
		See Dr. Hofstede de Groot and Smith's Catalogue.			
#4- nc	✓	Small painting chariot on hill with peasants By Jan van Goyen,Leyden 1596-The Hague 1665			

LIST OF PAINTINGS BY DIXTON

			Name			
Band hall	✓	#1	McMullen Guide	50 x 60	7,500.00	3 000
Band Hall	X	2	Philisopher of the Hills	46 x 52	6,000.00	2000
Game Room	X	3	Start for the Hills (JFJHughes) at S.S.&.	34 x 42	4,000.00	1500
✓	✓	X 4	Romaldita (property NCS	25 x 30	3,600.00	1000
✓	✓	X 5	Last of the Buffalo	16 x 20	850.00	300
✓	✓	X 6	Taos Canyon in October	14 x 14	800.00	300
		✓ 7	Aspens and Grizzly	8 x 10	250.00	100
		✓ 8	Elk 31.21/181	8 x 10	250.00	100
		✓ 9	Green Trees and Deer	8 x 10	250.00	100
		✓ 10	Pattern of Fall	8 x 10	250.00	100
		✓ 11	Across Pueblo Canyon	5 x 8	125.00	50
		✓ 12	Along the River in Winter	6 x 8	125.00	50
		✓ 13	High in the Hills	5 x 8	125.00	50
		✓ 14	Tapestry of the Foothills 31.21/17	5 x 8	125.00	50
		X 15	In the Foothills	5 x 8	125.00	50
		X 16	Design of the Hills	5 x 8	125.00	50
		✓ 17	Sunset in the Mountains	5 x 8	125.00	50
		X 18-19	Two elk studies	@ 50.00	150.00 ea	100
		X 20-21	Two mule deer studies	275 ea	75.00 ea	55
		X 22-23	Two hound dog studies	@ 50.	150.00 ea	100.
		✓ 24.	The Renegades (Hughes or SS.&)		1,250.00	500

24

Page #1

✓ In Band Hall

*12
GERRIT DOU (LEIDEN 1613-1675)
A sleeping dog beside a terracotta jug, a basket, a pair of clogs
and a pile of kindling wood

signed and dated 'GDov. 1650' (GD linked, lower center)

oil on panel

6½ x 8½ in. (16.5 x 21.6 cm.)

Estimate: $2,000,000-3,000,000

PROVENANCE:
M. Pompe Van Meerdevoort, Leiden; sale, 19 May 1780
(800 florins to Cremer).
M. Th. Th. Cremer, Rotterdam; sale, 16 April 1816, lot 18
(900 florins to Josi).
M. Jurriaens, Amsterdam; sale, 28 August 1817, lot 11
(1,199 florins to Cranenburg).
Willem Diedrick Arnoud Maria, Baron van Brienen van de Grootelindt
(1815-1873), Chamberlain to the King of Holland (whose wax
collector's seal is on the reverse), The Hague; Le Roy, Paris, 8 May 1865,
lot 6 (22,000 francs).
Baroness von Rothschild, Frankfurt am Main.
with J. & S. Goldschmidt, Frankfurt am Main, from whom purchased by
Mrs. H. J. Stark on 7 December 1927.

LITERATURE:
J. Smith, *A Catalogue Raisonné*, etc., I, 1834, p. 20. no. 59, as dated
1664, 'It is impossible for painting to be carried to higher perfection
than that displayed in this exquisite little picture'.
J. Smith, Supplement to *A Catalogue Raisonné*, etc., I, 1908, p. 16,
no. 47, as signed and dated 1650, 'The skill of this ingenious painter has
given extraordinary interest and value to this humble subject'.
W. Martin, *Het Leven en de werken van G. Dou, beschouwd in verband
met het schildersleven van zijn tijd*, 1901, no. 361.
C. Hofstede de Groot, *A Catalogue Raisonné*, etc., I, 1908, p. 462,
no. 382, as signed and dated 1650, 'The dog is very delicately and
brilliantly painted...'
W. Sumowski, *Gemälde der Rembrandt Schüler*, Landau and Pfalz,
1983, I, p. 538, under no. 306.

fig. 1

Sales of Charitable Use Assets:

a Description	b How Acq	c Date Acquired	d Date Sold	e Gross Sales $	f Depr Allowed	g Cost/Basis plus expense of sale	h Gain(Loss) e plus f minus g
Sale of deaccessioned Europe. art	Estate Distr.	9/2/1965	5/20/2005	346,500.00	0.00	26,585.00	319,915.00
Sale of deaccessioned Europe. art	Estate Distr.	9/2/1965	6/30/2005	1,805,400.00	0.00	124,020.00	1,681,380.00
Sale of deaccessioned Europe. art	Estate Distr.	9/2/1965	7/10/2005	79,350.00	0.00	62,035.00	17,315.00
Sale of deaccessioned Europe. art	Estate Distr.	9/2/1965	8/26/2005	106,980.00	0.00	7,050.00	99,930.00
Sale of deaccessioned Europe. art	Estate Distr.	9/2/1965	8/26/2005	17,000.00	0.00	11,950.00	5,050.00
Sale of surplus 1969 Ford Econoline Van	Estate Distr.	12/13/1999	10/18/2005	500.00	0.00	0.00	500.00
Sale of deaccessioned Europe. art	Estate Distr.	9/2/1965	9/25/2005	5,330.00	0.00	1,900.00	3,430.00
Sale of deaccessioned Europe. art	Estate Distr.	9/2/1965	5/25/2005	106,990.00	0.00	0.00	106,990.00
Sale of deaccessioned Europe. art	Estate Distr.	9/2/1965	9/9/2005	7,050.00	0.00	1,475.00	5,575.00
Sale of deaccessioned Europe. art	Estate Distr.	9/2/1965	9/30/2005	3,500.00	0.00	1,800.00	1,700.00
Sale of deaccessioned Europe. art	Estate Distr.	9/2/1965	10/6/2005	6,000.00	0.00	75,000.00	-69,000.00
Sale of deaccessioned Europe. art	Estate Distr.	9/2/1965	10/06/05	1,350.00		1,100.00	250.00
				2,485,950.00		312,915.00	2,173,035.00

	e	f	g	h
Total Net Capital Gains (losses) from above Summary	309,998,301.38	0.00	292,529,092.22	17,469,209.16
Less: Sales of Charitable Use Assets	-2,485,950.00	0.00	-312,915.00	-2,173,035.00
Net Gains (losses) from non-charitable use assets	307,512,351.38	0.00	292,216,177.22	15,296,174.16

BARNARD AND BARNARD
ATTORNEYS AT LAW
GRANBY, COLORADO
TU: FFF 7 3363

JOHN B. BARNARD
DUANE L. BARNARD

June 1, 1960

Mr. H. J. Lutcher Stark
Orange, Texas

Attention: Mr. Clyde V. McKee, Jr.

Dear Mr. McKee:

I know it has been some time, but I have finally prepared the appropriate documents for probate of the Will of Frances A. Lutcher. I am enclosing herewith originals and copies of the necessary documents. I ask that you have Mr. Stark sign the petition for probate in two places indicated, before a notary public, returning the original to me. At the same time, return the original Order admitting the Will to probate. The carbon copies can be retained for your records.

After the signed petition and original order have been returned to me, I will cause them, together with the Will and Order probating the Will previously transmitted, to be filed with the County Court of Jackson County, Colorado, and obtain the entry of the Order. After it has been recorded, under the laws of Colorado, the ranch in Jackson County becomes, as a matter of record, the property of Mr. Stark. Of course, it must thereafter be established that the property in Jackson County was, in fact, the property of Mrs. Lutcher.* We are proceeding with those matters, and will report to you from time to time.

If there are any questions at all, Mr. McKee, please let me know.

Yours very truly,

Duane L. Barnard
for Barnard and Barnard

DLB:sc
enc.

* as mentioned in the Will.

THE PROVIDENT SAVINGS BANK AND TRUST COMPANY

MEMBER FEDERAL RESERVE SYSTEM

MEMBER FEDERAL DEPOSIT INSURANCE CORPORATION

HOME OFFICE: SEVENTH AND VINE STREETS

CINCINNATI, OHIO

(2)

May 8, 1946

Mr. H. L. Woodworth,
c/o H. J. Lutcher Stark,
Box 720,
Orange, Texas

Dear Sir:

Your letter of the 4th inst., has been received.

We note from the twenty first section of the will of Nita Hill Stark that all of the remainder of her estate is given to Homer Stark and William Stark upon certain terms and conditions.

From many papers which you have submitted, it would still seem that this stock should be transferred to the two sons or to their guardian if the two sons or either is under twenty-one years of age. It is also noted that the executor has the power under the will to sell any portion of the estate but if this is a sale, he certainly would not be entitled under the will to sell to himself.

If these points can be satisfactorily cleared up, the transfer will have our immediate attention.

Very truly yours,

H. Wehmer
Vice-Pres. &
Trust Officer

HSH/RH

346

	1-1-65 to 9-2-65	9-2-65 to 12-31-65	Total for 1965	Foundation Estimated Income 1966	Foundation Estimated Income 1967
Income					
Dividends	139,045.00	63,528.00	202,573.00	(1) 57,000.00	(2) 25,000.00
Lease Rentals	15,495.00	660.00	16,155.00	8,000.00	8,000.00
Salaries	50,400.00	None	50,400.00	None	None
Directors Fees	650.00	None	650.00	None	None
Oil & Gas Royalties	104,232.00	45,618.00	149,850.00	(3) 75,000.00	(3) 75,000.00
Rents	29,333.00	13,092.00	42,425.00	21,212.00	(4) 12,000.00
Oil Lease Bonuses	17,796.00	1,364.00	19,160.00	8,000.00	8,000.00
Timber Sales	34,807.00	32,052.00	66,859.00	13,625.00	None
Sale of Land	27,477.00	63,117.00	90,594.00	(5) None	(5) None
Farm and Ranch	(6,232.00)	16,863.00	10,631.00	(6) None	(6) None
Interest	30,186.00	12,865.00	43,051.00	(7) 8,000.00	(7) 8,000.00
Total Income	443,189.00	249,159.00	692,348.00	190,837.00	136,000.00
Expenses					
Attorneys and Legal	9,000.00	4,529.00	13,529.00	(1) 9,000.00	(1) 6,500.00
Accounting	5,156.00		5,156.00	8,000.00	5,000.00
Depreciation (2)					
Fence Repairs	3,452.00	1,667.00	5,119.00	2,500.00	2,500.00
General Expenses	1,619.00	1,479.00	3,098.00	1,500.00	1,500.00
Insurance	9,416.00	5,200.00	14,616.00	7,000.00	7,000.00
Office Expenses	8,445.00	4,423.00	12,868.00	7,000.00	7,000.00
Office Salaries	35,867.00	22,417.00	58,284.00	30,000.00	30,000.00
Social Security Tax	1,427.00	273.00	1,700.00	(3) 1,000.00	1,000.00
Advalorem Tax	2,790.00	159,400.00	162,190.00	(4) 79,400.00	70,900.00
Repairs and Upkeep	14,966.00	5,774.00	20,740.00	11,000.00	11,000.00
Roslyn Ranch	2,946.00	937.00	3,883.00	(5) 1,941.00	(5) 3,883.00
Bequest	1,200.00	600.00	1,800.00	(6) 1,800.00	(6) 1,800.00
Total Expenses	96,284.00	206,699.00	302,983.00	160,141.00	148,083.00
NET INCOME	346,905.00	42,460.00	389,365.00	30,696.00	(12,083.00)

FRANK MILLS

MEMORANDUM
OFFICE OF H. J. L. STARK
ORANGE, TEXAS

DATE February 21, 1957

TO office memo

FROM W. L. DeLane

SUBJECT AGREEMENTS between H. J. L. STARK and NELDA C. STARK partitioning the community funds acquired from the sale of Louisiana lands on June 29, 1956 to JOHN W. MECOM.

This file contains two agreements:

1) One dated July 9, 1956 partitioning the sum of $9,424,608.08 one-half to each HJLS and NCS, making the sum of $4,712,304.04 for each; and

2) One dated Feb. 12, 1957 partitioning the sum of $111,121.12 one-half to each HJLS and NCS, making the sum of $55,560.56 for each.

W. L. D.

IF THE DEVIL HAD A WIFE A TRUE TEXAS TALE

REPORT ON THE FRANCIS ANN LUTCHER ESTATE

Date SEPTEMBER 19 1988

	ITEM	DISPOSITION	GUARANTEE	COMMISSION	DUE & PAYABLE	COMMENTS
1	Tiffany necklace	SOLD & SETTLED	$40,000.			
2	Necklace Round Diam.	STILL OPEN SALE WORKING	30,000.			Expect to close any day
3	Pearl necklace	SOLD & SETTLED	7,500.			
4	Diamond bracelet	SOLD & SETTLED	17,500.			
5	Enamel Pendant	SOLD & SETTLED	500.			
6	Diamond pendant	STILL OPEN	10,000.			Working Have customer from Montana ?
7	Corsage Pin	SOLD & SETTLED	6,500.			
8	Pendant Watch	SOLD & SETTLED	300.			
9	Canary Diamond Sq.	SOLD & SETTLED	4,000.			
10	Alexandrite Ring	SOLD & SETTLED	30,000.			
11	Alexandrite brooch	SOLD FOR $130,000.	100,000.	$20,000.	CHECK ATTACHED $100,000.00	

Thank you
for your patience
Nelson Atha

349

Part VIII Information About Officers, Directors, Trustees, Foundation Managers, Highly Paid Employees, and Contractors

1 List all officers, directors, trustees, foundation managers and their compensation (see page 23 of the instructions):

(a) Name and address	(b) Title, and average hours per week devoted to position	(c) Compensation (If not paid, enter -0-)	(d) Contributions to employee benefit plans & deferred compensation	(e) Expense account, other allowances
Schedule Attached		565,385.33	89,017.92	0.00

2 Compensation of five highest-paid employees (other than those included on line 1 - see page 23 of the instructions). If none, enter "NONE."

(a) Name and address of each employee paid more than $50,000	(b) Title and average hours per week devoted to position	(c) Compensation	(d) Contributions to employee benefit plans & deferred compensation	(e) Expense account, other allowances
Sherrie Sheppard P O Box 909; Orange TX 77631-0909	Grants Admin. 40	145,407.54	52,437.67	0.00
James K Clark P O Box 2310; Orange TX 77631-2310	Theater Director 40	104,348.14	47,088.14	0.00
Kathleen Hardey P O Box 909; Orange TX 77631-909	HR Director 40	96,969.60	27,584.20	0.00
Michael Hoke P O Box 909; Orange TX 77631-0909	Shangri-La Dir. 40	92,551.94	29,674.23	0.00
Gary Outenreath P O Box 909, Orange TX 77631-0909	Horticulture-Dir. 40	81,370.12	24,940.86	0.00
Total number of other employees paid over $50,000			29	

Form 990-PF (2007)

350

NELDA C AND H. J LUTCHER STARK FOUNDATION 74-6047440
P.O. BOX 909
ORANGE, TEXAS 77631-0909
TWELVE MONTHS ENDING DECEMBER 31, 2007

FORM 990-PF, PART VIII, LINE 1

OFFICERS, DIRECTORS, TRUSTEES

(a) Name and Address	(b) Title	Hours/ Week	(C) Compensation	(d) Contributions to Benefit Plans	(e) Exp Acct/ Allowance
Laurence R David	Chairman	5	30,000.10	0 00	0 00
W. G Riedel, III	President/CEO	40	244.124.72	53.132 46	0 00
Ruby J Wimberley	Vice-Chairman	5	26,000.00	0 00	0 00
Roy S Wingate	Secretary	5	26,000.00	0 00	0.00
Deborah Hughes	Director	5	9,000 00	0.00	0.00
Clyde V McKee III	Treasurer/CFO	40	170,759.51	35,885.46	0.00
R Frederick Gregory, M D	Director	5	26,000.00	0.00	0 00
John Cash Smith	Director	5	26,000 00	0 00	0.00
Eunice R. Benckenstein	Trustee Emeritus	5	7,501 00	0.00	0.00

All persons listed above may be contacted at
P O Drawer 909, Orange, Texas 77631-0909

Total Compensation of Officers and Trustees			565,385.33	89,017 92	0.00

Part VIII, Line 1

351

Form 990-PF (2007)   NELDA C AND H J LUTCHER STARK FOUNDATION   74-6047440   Page 7

Part VIII Information About Officers, Directors, Trustees, Foundation Managers, Highly Paid Employees, and Contractors Continued

3 Five highest-paid independent contractors for professional services - (see page 23 of the instructions). If none, enter "NONE."

(a) Name and address of each person paid more than $50,000	(b) Type of service	(c) Compensation
Beck HSB Management GP Inc 1807 Ross Avenue Ste 500, Dallas, TX 75201-8006	General Contractor	6,550,135.19
Boyken International Inc 400 Northridge Rd Ste 1200, Atlanta, GA 30350-1826	Project Consultant	418,059.42
Jeffrey K Carbo ASLA 3600 Jackson Street, Ste 202; Alexandria LA 71303-3064	Landscape Architect	382,637.44
Hands On! Inc 689 Central Ave . Ste 200; St Petersburg, FL 33701-3665	Multi-media Display construction	272,363.00
Lake Flato 311 3rd Street, Ste 200; San Antonio, TX 78205-1930	Building Architect	257,067.46
Total number of others receiving over $50,000 for professional services		14

Part IX-A Summary of Direct Charitable Activities

List the foundation's four largest direct charitable activities during the tax year Include relevant statistical information such as the number of organizations and other beneficiaries served, conferences convened, research papers produced, etc

	Expenses
1 Stark Museum of Art - Schedule Attached (Includes capital expenditures)	3,459,780.37
2 W. H. Stark House - Schedule Attached (Includes capital expenditures)	1,037,863.97
3 Lutcher Theater - Schedule Attached (Includes capital expenditures)	2,078,905.65
4 Shangri-La Botanical Gardens and Nature Center - Schedule Attached (Includes capital expenditures)	16,752,091.57
5 Miriam Lutcher Stark Contest in Reading & Declamation - Schedule Attached	67,190.66

Mrs. H. J. Lutcher Stark
Orange, Texas
77630

March 29, 1972

Mr. John B. Scofield
Scofield, Bergstedt & Gerard
Attorneys at Law
P. O. Box 1136
Lake Charles, Louisiana 70601

Dear John:

You have raised two questions with regard to succesion proceedings in Louisiana and disposition of Louisiana properties.

The first question regards the legatee of the Louisiana property under the ancillary proceedings. By his will, Mr. Stark made a specific bequest to his wife of "an amount of property equal to the value of one-half of all separate property included in his gross estate for Federal estate tax purposes." The will further provided that in computing the value of this gift all values used would be those as finally determined for Federal estate tax purposes.

After having determined value of the various properties covered by the will and the total value of one-half of the separate property the executrix was authorized to satisfy this specific bequest by transferring to the beneficiary money or property equal to the value of one-half of the separate property. This Louisiana property is being transferred to Mrs. Stark in satisfaction of the specific bequest to her so I would assume that she will be the legatee under the Louisiana ancillary proceedings.

The second question regards handling of the problem of forced heirship under Louisiana law. The value of the Louisiana property belonging to Mr. Stark at the time of his death was determined to be $40,950.00. Mr. Stark had two sons by adoption. Each of these sons was bequeathed $1,000,000.00, and each of the sons has acknowledged payment of this amount in full.

If Mr. Stark had made no bequest to the two sons the most they would have been entitled to under the Louisiana law would be one-half of the value of his Louisiana estate, or $20,750.00 and as each of these sons was left a bequest far exceeding the value of property to which he would have been entitled under the Louisiana law we have been advised these two sons would not be successful in a suit to recover an interest in the property under consideration. In support of this contention we were referred to the following cases and law review comments:

1. Jarel vs. Moon's Succession, 190 So. 867
   Court of Appeal of La.
   (2nd Circuit) June 28, 1939.

2. Succession of Martin, 147 So. 2d 53.

3. Comment entitled "Computation of the Legitime when Estate of Deceased Consists of Assets in Several States", Volume X Louisiana Law Review, Page 525 (May, 1950).

If you are not in agreement with this conclusion we should discuss the question further.

Sincerely,

Clyde V. McKee, Jr.

CVMcK:lc